# Praise for

## *The Interplay of Psychology and Spirituality*

"This volume is a lovely introduction to some of the most important issues in transpersonal psychology. It brings a unique lens to view some of them, in particular the Enneagram and Jung's typology, and is an accessible approach to whoever wants to explore this area."

—BRANT CORTRIGHT, PhD, author of *Psychotherapy and Spirit, Integral Psychology* and *The Neurogenesis Diet and Lifestyle*

"Practicing psychotherapeutic training doesn't teach spiritual literacy. This readable volume fills that gap. It is, first, an intelligent guide to a series of the most advanced and rich theoretical frameworks for understanding the interplay of psychology and spirituality. And it applies those distinctions by guiding the reader through a far-reaching survey of the nature and varying expressions of spiritual experience, as well as their relationships to various neuroses and psychopathologies."

—TERRY PATTEN, author of *A New Republic of the Heart*, co-author *of Integral Life Practice*

"This book is written in an inclusive way that serves as an invitation to a dialogue: First within oneself about the nature of spirituality and one's own beliefs and practices. Second, to step back and see how such beliefs and practices are present in everyone at some level as part of the human existential condition. For the therapist, this book serves as an ice breaker for exploration about a client's experience of their spiritual strengths and any spiritual problems or crises."

—DAVID LUKOFF, PhD, Professor Emeritus of Psychology, Sofia University Founder, Spiritual Competency Resource Center

"Dr. Alexandra Hepburn has woven a beautiful tapestry that integrates the value of the Enneagram, an ancient key to unraveling the wounded ego and inspiring our integration of our highest virtues, along with very practical interventions that will serve all clinicians and clients alike. We must explore the depths in order to discover the heights and embody this wisdom into our everyday living."

—Diane Poole Heller, PhD, author of *Healing your Attachment Wounds; The Power of Attachment; Crash Course: A Self-Healing Guide to Auto Accident Trauma and Recovery,* creator of the DARe training programs for therapists (Dynamic Attachment Repatterning experience)

"*Interplay* is a gift that keeps on giving. Alexandra Hepburn has filled this book with treasure upon treasure, some you'll use now, some you'll come back for later. Her capacity for interweaving psychological and spiritual ways of seeing and being—for helping them play together—is remarkable. This is a work of wisdom."

—Russell Siler Jones, ThD, LPCS, author of *Spirit in Session: Working with Your Client's Spirituality (and Your Own) in Psychotherapy*

"Hepburn artistically and expertly interweaves spiritual development, self/other knowledge of the Enneagram, and spiritual intelligence. The result is both words and the melody of the beautiful dance between mental health and spirituality. This is a must-read for all psychotherapists interested in the spiritual journey, both their own and that of the clients they serve."

—Craig S. Cashwell, PhD, author, with J. Scott Young, of *Integrating Spirituality and Religion into Counseling: A Guide to Competent Practice*

"By wisely and skillfully deploying the Enneagram system of personality, perhaps the most powerful psycho-spiritual tool available today that addresses this integration, Hepburn clarifies the way these two approaches may be usefully combined and advances the ability of therapists everywhere to do deeper work with clients in a more effective way."

—Beatrice Chestnut, PhD, MA, author of *The Complete Enneagram: 27 Paths to Greater Self-Knowledge* and *The 9 Types of Leadership: Mastering the Art of People in the 21st-Century Workplace*

# The Interplay of Psychology and Spirituality

## A Resource for Counselors *and* Psychotherapists

Alexandra M. Hepburn

SHE WRITES PRESS

Published 2019
Printed in the United States of America
ISBN: 978-1-63152-650-3 pbk
ISBN: 978-1-63152-651-0 ebk
Library of Congress Control Number: 2019940673

For information, address:
She Writes Press
1569 Solano Ave #546
Berkeley, CA 94707

She Writes Press is a division of SparkPoint Studio, LLC.

Cover and interior design by Tabitha Lahr



Names and identifying characteristics have been changed to protect the privacy of certain individuals.

***Interplay:*** *The way in which two or more things have an effect on each other.*

—Oxford Living Dictionaries

***Interplay synonyms:*** *interaction, give-and-take, reciprocity, meshing.*

—Collinsdictionary.com/thesaurus

# Contents

# List of Figures

## Chapter One

# Setting the Stage

A woman in her mid-thirties has experienced her second miscarriage. She grieves these losses and wonders if God is punishing her for something. A retired man remembers that in his twenties he was searching for spiritual connection but forgot this over the years; he wants to reconnect with some kind of deeper meaning before his life runs out. After her children have grown and left home, a woman finds time to practice meditation and participate in spiritual retreats, but finds that old wounds and patterns keep clamoring for attention. A forty-year-old man is struggling to keep his marriage alive; his wife's religious faith has become increasingly important to her, but he does not share her devotion or church commitment. He agrees that this affects their connection as well as their approach to parenting, but is wary because of his experience growing up in a strict religious sect.

Not so long ago the responsibility of listening to and providing support and guidance for these personal stories of grief, loneliness, confusion, fear, or meaninglessness fell to religious leaders and spiritual teachers. Today this responsibility falls more and more often to counselors and psychotherapists. Perhaps those of us in the helping professions could use some of the wisdom offered by religious leaders, as well as some modern spiritual perspectives, in order to respond more fully to a wide range of human experience. I believe this is our invitation and our challenge.

When we try to help others (or find our own way), having an understanding of psychological dynamics is necessary and invaluable, but is not enough. If we overlook the territory that belongs to spirituality and religion, we miss essential possibilities, because this is where we may find an orientation to the deeper questions and a longing for something more. This is *not* to say that spirituality is relevant to everyone, but rather that we expand and enrich our capacity to help when we have some understanding of spiritual experience. In these pages I share some of the orienting perspectives that have emerged in my own life and work, in the hope that they will expand horizons and open possibilities for others.

I have come across the word *interplay* often in my reading over the years, and it has resonated so strongly that it has become a key theme in this book. The phrase "the *interplay* of psychology and spirituality" feels like an appealing invitation, unlike crisper terms like *interaction* and *intersection*. I am inviting the exploration of a process, a fluid interrelating that does not have fixed edges; *interweaving* is similar. If we can set a tone of openness and lightness, we can hopefully avoid becoming too attached to any one position or formula. Spirituality and psychology interplay in ways that are profoundly intricate, complex, and even mysterious. Bringing these two orientations together can be challenging for scientifically oriented professionals. Psychology has had, at best, an ambivalent attitude toward spirituality and religion, but the door is gradually opening, and we need an array of theories and practices to support us in working skillfully with our clients.

In the following chapters, you will encounter some broad theoretical frameworks that I have found particularly valuable, as well as useful guidelines for listening and responding to what clients bring to our conversations. I emphasize paying attention to individual, cultural, and developmental variations, and give special attention to concerns therapists may have about "what can go wrong" when we open the door to spirituality.

I also make use of a typology known as the Enneagram, which is an approach to the human psyche that began to gain attention in the 1970s.

One of the things I love about the Enneagram is that it offers both a rich perspective on personality types and an approach to spiritual growth. In other words, it is a psychospiritual system. Chapter 2 will provide more information on the Enneagram, and then we will follow nine fictional characters (based on the nine main patterns) throughout the ensuing chapters. The descriptions of these characters' experiences and hypothetical counseling processes will bring to life the perspectives that are offered.

Before sketching out the territory ahead in more detail, I would like to offer some personal background.

## My Story

The year is around 2011, and I am sitting with a group of students in a graduate course I am teaching for prospective counselors. The title of the course is "Introduction to Spirituality and Counseling." Since we are meeting for the first time, I ask them what has brought them to this class. Several students speak about their personal interest in spirituality. They have a cautious desire to include spirituality in their counseling work but have regarded this as dicey territory and wonder if it is best avoided. Then one student rather nervously speaks up: "I have no idea what this spirituality thing is. To be honest, it scares me, but I think I better know what it is about in case it walks into the room with a client." A second student follows with a similar confession.

These students hold a significant place in my memory. I had already begun to think about drawing together some of my ideas on this subject into written form, but it was these individuals who served as catalysts and inspirations. The unexpected gift was that by the end of the course, they both had discovered that indeed they had their particular ways of relating to "this thing called spirituality," even though one of them still described herself as an atheist. Their views did not match the religious frameworks they had grown up with, but they could relate to some sense of mystery in life, and recognized their own ways of finding peace and deeper meaning. There were other students who also played a role in inspiring this book. Some were deeply moved because spirituality did matter to them, and they finally glimpsed a possible place for this territory in their work. All these individuals—skeptics and enthusiasts—kindled my desire to share my perspective.

Let me acknowledge at the outset that my own personality pattern is inclined towards "seeing the big picture," and believing there is always more to learn. My doctoral dissertation was just over a thousand pages. The advice I received from faculty advisors was something like, "For heaven's sake, do something reasonable, because you will never get a faculty position with a thesis like that." I was in my early thirties and decided I had to do what had meaning for me, even if that meant I would need to return to teaching children with learning disabilities. I had almost dropped out of the program earlier because the traditional approach to psychology seemed so divorced from spirituality, which was becoming central in my life. But this program in interdisciplinary studies in human development allowed me enough room to explore meaningful questions. I did complete my degree and, looking back, have no regrets.

In my personal life, spirituality has been a central focus for many years. Although my parents had no particular religious inclinations (one was nominally Presbyterian, one Episcopalian), I remember at the age of seven finding refuge with Father and Mother God in our rose garden. (My father was a diplomat, and I grew up overseas; the rose garden was in Pretoria, South Africa.) In high school, I was drawn to Quaker work camps and Episcopalian communion services. In college, I found myself taking a course on Buddhism and Hinduism, which unexpectedly initiated a deeply meaningful thread throughout my life. Explorations of Christian mysticism unfolded in my thirties and forties, and I dipped into the waters of twentieth-century metaphysics. Over the years, my spiritual practices have included various forms of meditation and prayer.

After completing the doctoral program, I soon found myself drawn to hospice work. My parents had died when I was twenty-four, so the pull toward working with death and dying was no surprise. I volunteered at first, and later started a hospice program in central Arizona. Thus began a lifelong commitment to the arenas of death, dying, and grief. Looking back later, I discerned a spiritual journey that unfolded from head (academic study) to heart (hospice and grief work), and then to the body (through the birth of my son and the practice of massage therapy). Head, heart, and body have all contributed to my spiritual growth, and now feel integrated in a larger whole.

In my work with grieving clients, I found that spiritual dimensions often emerged spontaneously as they explored their feelings and perspectives around death and loss. I learned to listen more and more carefully and became increasingly aware of subtle cues and tentative openings. At times, these pointed to painful questions or confusions. In other contexts, they were hints of deeply meaningful experiences.

Spiritual or religious concerns may feel particularly relevant in the context of death, but I have also come to appreciate their presence in a wide variety of life circumstances and stories. Clients often drop hints to see if we, as counselors, are open to discussing these concerns. We miss vital opportunities when we miss these cues, and our lack of response suggests that our clients' deepest concerns are essentially irrelevant to the work we do together. My clients have continued to be my teachers and my inspiration.

Before we go further, let's address one of the first questions that typically surfaces for many people: What do we mean by spirituality and religion?

## Spirituality *and* Religion?

The two terms *spirituality* and *religion* can be confusing. While definitions of religion share some common themes, this is not true of spirituality. I've never run across two definitions that are the same. So the first challenge is to clarify what we mean when we use these words. In my courses, I would usually begin by placing the two words at the top of a whiteboard, asking students for associations and meanings for each. I encourage you to do this exercise yourself.

## Reflecting on Spirituality and religion

There are two parts to this reflection.

**1. On a (preferably large) piece of paper, put two headings at the top: "Religion" and "Spirituality."**

Spend a few minutes writing down all your associations and meanings under each heading. Be spontaneous and allow words to emerge. Don't try to be politically correct.

Do you notice a pattern in your associations or meanings? Any preferences? Biases from your history? Emotional overtones? Are the differences quite stark? As you keep generating associations, do you begin to find any overlap? It can be especially interesting to share this exercise with others in your personal or professional life and compare notes. Typically, there is an initial pattern of strong differentiation, and eventually, some fuzzier areas of convergence.

**2. For the second part of this reflection, begin with a new (again, preferably large) piece of paper and write the word *God* in a prominent place on the page.**

Now begin writing as many associated words as you can think of, all the possible permutations and variations. Take your time. You may be surprised at how many you come up with. (Focus here on an ultimate level, rather than on particular teachers that have appeared in different traditions.)

Some of the terms you find yourself using may be from different religions. Some may be masculine in flavor, some feminine, some neutral. Some may point to a distinct entity, separate from human beings (a dualistic view). Some words may point to one overarching Reality which embraces all that exists, including human beings (this is sometimes known as a nondual or not-two perspective).

Some you may feel an aversion to, and others you may feel drawn to. Just notice the variety and your reactions. This is not about narrowing the field or finding the right concept. Rather it is about realizing what a wide range of words and concepts human beings have found to point to something beyond their personal selves, something they relate to as sacred.

I offer the following words for reflection, if your list did not include them: Tao, the Beloved, the Mystery, Goddess, Creator, True Nature, Truth, the Ultimate, the Divine, Allah, Great Spirit, Brahman, Lord, Jehovah, the Light, Father, Mother, YHWH, Adonai, Ein Sof, Source, Being, the One. There are many more, in diverse languages.

In a broad sense, spirituality usually refers more to an inner perspective, personal and psychological, and religion to an outer one, institutional and sociological. The word *spirituality* comes from the Latin *spiritus* ("breath"), and its meaning has evolved since it first appeared in English around 1440 CE. Originally referring to "the body of spiritual or ecclesiastical persons," it came to refer to "things of the spirit" as opposed to material, bodily, or worldly matters. The term came into use in France in the seventeenth century, referring to a kind of prayerful piety with a mystical flavor.

There is no shortage of current definitions. Most are vague, sometimes emphasizing the indefinable nature of spirituality (comparing it to the fragrance of a rose, for instance). I think of spirituality as *a subjective orientation towards or valuing of the sacred*. What is felt to be sacred can vary widely: the sacred may be associated with a Supreme Being, an ultimate reality, the essence of our being, or simply what has the deepest value and meaning for us.

Although spirituality was at one time felt to be the living heart of religion, a distinction between the two terms has gradually come into being. Today, the word *religion* points more toward collective traditions and traditional forms, such as an organized system of beliefs, institutions, texts, worship, rules, rituals, authorities and holy figures—at least, this tends to be our modern, Western interpretation. Karen Armstrong, well-known author of numerous books on religion, tells us that this cluster of meanings has no corresponding term in other languages or even in early Christian writings. "The only faith tradition," she suggests, "that does fit the modern Western notion of religion as something codified and private is Protestant Christianity, which, like *religion* in this sense of the word, is also a product of the early modern period."[1] So even our common understanding of the word *religion* has a rather short history.

The Latin word *religare* had connotations of obligation and taboo. The word means "to bind together." Today, we tend to think of religion as more social or communal, while spirituality is seen as essentially personal and private, although it may also be shared in community. Spirituality may be expressed through religion, or without it. People who describe themselves as religious may or may not be spiritually inclined. While we can express the distinction in terms of an inside focus (spirituality) and an outside focus (religion), the two may be separate and distinct or blended and interwoven.

Are we talking about including both spirituality and religion in counseling work? The title of this volume refers only to spirituality, but I want to include the potential significance of religion in our clients' lives, particularly when their religious orientation is infused with subjective spiritual meaning.

Some people, of course, have no interest in either religion or spirituality. Secularism (indifference to or rejection of religion), rationalism (reliance on reason over faith), and materialism (the belief that matter is the fundamental reality) represent significant orientations in modern times. These aspects of the modern era, in turn, have contributed to the reactive rise of religious fundamentalism, which represents, at least in part, a call to return to the faith certainties and loyalties of earlier times. Fundamentalism across the religious spectrum emphasizes the strictly literal interpretation of scripture, and is intended to reinstate absolute faith and strengthen the unquestionable ideals associated with an undermined religious purity. (What we now call religious fundamentalism tends to be associated with the "religions of the book"—Christianity, Judaism, and Islam—and needs to be distinguished from religious extremism.[2])

Just as fundamentalism may be understood in part as a reaction to modernity, we can in turn observe popular reactions against fundamentalism's emphasis on form and doctrine. In response to the fundamentalist movement back to fixed answers and absolute frameworks for action, many with moderate religious perspectives continue to explore meaning in their current communities, beliefs, and practices. Spiritual seekers, on the other hand, often turn away from religious traditions and head off in the direction of freedom, wholeness, and personal experiences of the Divine. (We will look more closely at these trends in chapter 3.)

Some of my students who shied away from dealing with religion in counseling were not only struggling with their particular histories and feelings of ambivalence, but were also nervous about encountering clients with strong religious beliefs. It can be challenging to come face-to-face with convictions that differ from our own or with beliefs that we consider psychologically unhealthy. We will consider the risks of engaging directly with beliefs and explore alternative approaches in chapter 4.

With this basic foundation of understanding, let's move on to the essential principles that guide this work.

## Three Orienting Perspectives: Interplay, Connected Knowing, and Knowing from both Inside and Outside

Remembering the implications of the term *interplay*, let's approach our inquiry with a softly focused lens. We are not expecting rigid boundaries or crystal-clear definitions of the relationship between psychology and spirituality. On the contrary, we welcome a sense of dynamic interweaving, intermingling, and interflow. This may seem challenging or frustrating, especially if we are accustomed to more evidence-based, tangible information, but in this context, a more fluid orientation is invaluable.

*Interplay* is the first of three orienting perspectives that have guided my work. The word highlights the object of our attention: *what* we are exploring. The second guideline suggests *how* we need to make contact with the subject: through *connected knowing*. Finally, as a refinement of the *how*, I distinguish between *knowing from the inside* and *knowing from the outside*, both of which will play important roles. Let's elaborate on the two *how* principles.

Connected knowing stands in contrast to objective knowing from a distance. The French existential philosopher Gabriel Marcel was the source of this distinction when he contrasted "mystery" and "problem." As we focus on our work with clients, we are also engaging with questions about human existence in which we ourselves are intimately and inextricably involved. This is ultimately a mystery. Since we cannot stand apart from or ultimately be objective about this territory (as we can with a "problem"), we find ourselves engaging with it *from the inside*.[3] (It may be helpful to remember that even the paradigm of objectivity in science is often called into question these days, especially in physics.) This means that we need to appreciate possibilities, embrace questions, and hopefully become more comfortable with not knowing.

The third guideline expands the options, pointing to the need for both an *inside* and an *outside* perspective. What I mean by *inside* is the interior experience of oneself in relation to a sphere of ultimate meaning in life, to a Divine Other, a Sacred Reality. This subjective, inside point of view is essential if we are going to take these explorations seriously and meet our clients in authentic ways.

Here, the questions that matter have to do with themes such as:

- My life orientation. What beliefs, assumptions, and values guide my life? Am I sensing the guidance of, or navigating in relation to, this Other/Deeper Reality? Am I lost in my life, or feeling on course and at home? Am I growing, evolving, responding to a pull or call? Are there deep questions about meaning and purpose that repeatedly or intermittently draw my attention? What really matters? What is sacred, of ultimate worth?
- The quality of my relationship and response to this Other/Deeper Reality, as evidenced in feelings and actions. Am I feeling safe, loved, valued, or abandoned, betrayed, punished? Am I honoring, worshipping, obeying, remembering, paying attention to, loving, thanking this Other/Deeper Reality, or

am I turning my back, raging, cursing, pleading, or bargaining? How do I honor the sacred and orient my life around what is of ultimate concern?

- The tensions between the demands of my religious or spiritual loyalties and those of my "ordinary" life and self. How do I choose the right path? How do I deal with temptations and social pressures? How do I more fully embody my core beliefs and values in my relationships, work life, everyday interactions? How do I find my way through difficult internal experiences such as doubt and fear, and external challenges such as loss, death, relationship conflict, persecution? How do I avoid major pitfalls and find my way toward greater depth, love, wisdom? Am I able to be compassionate and forgiving toward myself when I make mistakes and lose my way, or does self-judgment win out?

These are the kinds of questions that many of us (counselors and clients alike) ponder, and sometimes share with others if we trust them. They are questions that inhabit our psyches, explicitly or implicitly, consciously or subconsciously. They may take the form of thoughts, but they are not purely cognitive explorations. They are more existential, likely to be accompanied by deep feelings and sensations. In our encounter with this territory, we may experience a felt sense of urgency or a weight in the body. This *matters*. We are not apt to risk inviting just anyone into this territory. It is sacred and close to the bone, and we guard its sanctity, intimacy, and ultimacy. No wonder clients are often very cautious about letting us into this domain.

On the other hand, when we approach the relationship between psychology and spirituality from the outside, we are in more public territory. With more distance comes more safety: we can look on as objective observers, analyze patterns and tendencies, and evaluate outcomes. We engage in what is recognized as more "scientific" inquiry. The outside point of view presents itself here, for instance, in the form of psychological theories or academic studies of religion.

Some people prefer to remain in the safe zone of the outside perspective, but the external viewpoint feels incomplete to me. I am committed to interweaving inside and outside perspectives; if we fail to keep both in mind, we may forget the deep mattering that is at stake. In this forgetting, we may miss the point of the whole undertaking.

We will honor the inner orientation of spirituality in chapter 4, for example, when exploring spirituality as a resource in times of pain and difficulty. It makes sense in that context to draw on the soulful language of human suffering. Because we are all confronted by experiences and questions that perplex, mystify, and move us in profound ways, I have also included frequent opportunities for personal reflection, invitations to pause and contemplate along the way. Lastly, as indicated earlier, I offer a set of hypothetical case studies which provide an opportunity to apply the learning to nine individuals, each with their own unfolding story. These characters (who are fictional composites and do not represent actual clients) will be introduced in the first chapter.

There is an additional lens that I have found valuable.

## A Spectrum of Connections

Therapists may find it useful to envision a *spectrum* of possible relationships between their psychological focus and spirituality/religion. At one end lies spirituality-as-resource, a concept which many counselors find more comfortable and easier to accept. (Chapter 4 is devoted to this topic.) At the other end of the spectrum lies the transformative potential of spirituality or religion. Here there may be gradual growth, but also the precipitous experience of feeling picked up or dropped down by the mysterious, shaken to the core, thrown into dark passages or encounters with dimensions of being that leave us radically altered. These turbulences, too, offer possibilities for expansion and deepening. (I address the theme of growth later, in connection with a discussion of psychospiritual development.)

Here is the spectrum I am suggesting:

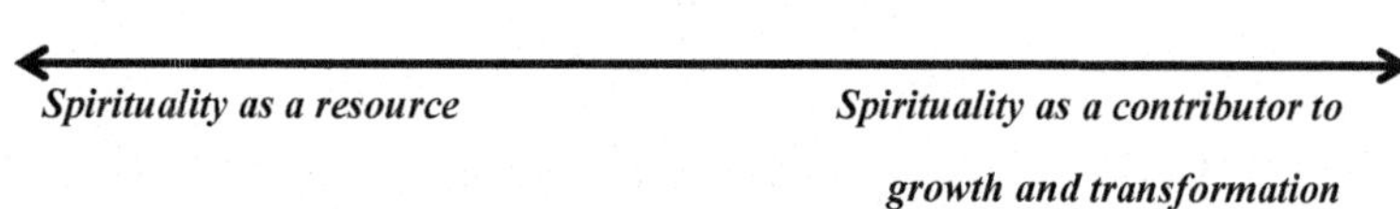


*Figure 1.1. Basic Spirituality-Psychology Spectrum*

Along this continuum, there are no clear lines of demarcation. Everything between resource and transformation is possible and meaningful, and much blurs and blends together. Finding our way through this territory can be demanding, from both the outside and the inside. We may encounter old assumptions and associations, new perspectives and mysteries. There are important individual and cultural variations, potential risks as well as gifts. What we *can* do is become familiar with various guide maps, develop a sense of the possible pathways and their intersections, and learn how to travel by feel (which I sometimes call "feeling our way by the Braille method"). Taking these steps can help us to deepen our capacity to meet our clients with grace, compassion, and skillfulness.

However, we also need to acknowledge another part of the spectrum:

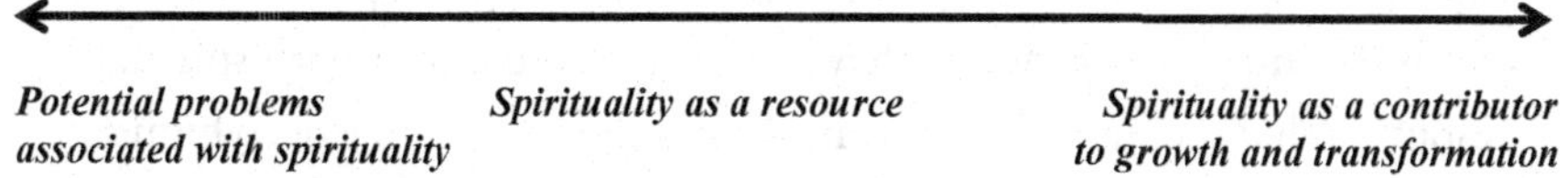


*Figure1.2 Expanded Spirituality-Psychology Spectrum*

While some professionals, like some of my students, might prefer to begin with the troublesome aspects of spirituality and religion, I intentionally leave that topic to the end. I have discovered that it is crucial to examine spirituality's gifts and contributions before turning our attention to potential problems. Chapter 9 is devoted to those psychospiritual challenges.

## What Lies Ahead

Chapter 2 sets the stage by introducing some key variations that profoundly shape our individual and collective relationship with life's religious and spiritual dimensions. The focus is on personal style (type) differences as they pertain to spirituality. I have chosen to concentrate on two of the most well-known: Jungian typology and the Enneagram. As indicated earlier, I have developed nine Enneagram-based characters through whose lenses we will view the topics we encounter over the course of the book. Chapter 2 also considers the relevance of gender and cultural styles to our topic. These are foundational "differences that make a difference," to quote anthropologist Gregory Bateson.

Chapter 3 steps back to offer a broad perspective on religion and spirituality in our world, highlighting the challenges we face as we open the door to including them in our work. This orientation also gives us the opportunity to reflect on why opening the door *matters* in our times. We will then take a closer look at the historical relationship between the discipline of psychology and the territory of religion and spirituality, and consider the softening of boundaries that is taking place now.

Chapter 4 brings us to the vital question of how religion and spirituality may serve as powerful therapeutic resources. Clients who are experiencing difficult and painful times can find support, comfort, strength, and guidance when they are invited to connect with spiritual resources that are significant for them. This lens points to a deep human experience, not the territory of conflicting beliefs but that of the heart's longing for help in enduring pain and finding meaning. The chapter closes with an exploration of spirituality and resilience. When we open to these possibilities, we become more sensitive to the healing potential of both spirituality and religion.

In chapter 5 we turn our attention to spirituality's potential role in fostering growth. Beginning with some examples of what it means to grow spiritually, we go on to explore the experience of the spiritual journey from an inside perspective. This focus on the journey brings us to the central role of metaphor: images and metaphors *abound* in portrayals of the spiritual path. In C. G. Jung's work we find particular emphasis on images and imagination, meaning-making, and the central role of the unconscious in the psyche. This is the path of depth and interiority. Of particular interest is the emphasis on the unconscious shadow: without attention to shadow work, the spiritual seeker is apt to go astray.

Chapter 6 shifts to an outside perspective on growth, moving from metaphors of the spiritual journey to maps of psychospiritual development. Development is not something we *experience* from inside (although we may certainly experience growth). Rather, we need to look through the theoretical lens of developmental psychology to understand and assess someone's development.[4] Why is this useful? When we understand development, we are better able to meet clients where they are and to choose appropriate approaches and methods that offer both support and challenge. Specific topics in this chapter include the work of professor of theology and human development James Fowler, some fundamental principles in developmental dynamics, and characterizations of the basic stages in human development. These stage depictions are drawn from transpersonal and integral theory, as well as from the work of Harvard psychologist Robert Kegan.

In chapter 7 we delve more deeply into psychological dimensions of some life experiences that have the potential to become either obstacles or openings to spiritual growth. (In chapter 4 we emphasized the other direction of influence, whereby spirituality can serve as both a resource and an opening to psychological growth.) We first differentiate four basic territories of human life, using the map of four quadrants created by integral philosopher Ken Wilber, and then focus on elements from these territories that may influence our psychospiritual lives. Major topics include attachment and early experience, trauma, depression, and grief. Our attention then turns to subpersonalities as potential contributors to growth, despite their possible origin in challenging circumstances. The chapter ends with an emphasis on direct somatic experience, which I see as an essential and often neglected aspect of psychospiritual work.

Chapter 8 ventures into realms and experiences of spirituality that lie beyond identification with the ego. Drawing on transpersonal and integral psychology, we explore some spiritual frameworks as well as contemporary research on transpersonal stages. As therapists, we need to have some understanding of the full range of human potential in order to appreciate the significance of psychospiritual work, whether or not we ever see clients with a stable base in a transpersonal stage.

This chapter also introduces nonordinary states of consciousness and explains the difference between states and stages. Many people report having temporary glimpses beyond ordinary reality, so these experiences may well show up in therapy, and we need to be skillful in our response to them. Other topics include a brief introduction to the emerging field of neurotheology and to a range of spiritual practices (sometimes called "technologies of the sacred") that might be meaningful in clients' lives. In closing, we consider the complex role of ego in personal and transpersonal life.

Finally, chapter 9 takes us into the territory of potential challenges and pitfalls arising from the interplay of psychology and spirituality. The chapter introduces transpersonal psychiatrist Stanislav Grof's work on spiritual emergencies, and includes suggestions for assisting those who are undergoing such an experience. We then turn our attention to complications that may arise in the context of spiritual practice, drawing on the work of the American Buddhist teacher, Jack Kornfield. We will also explore more common psychospiritual scenarios, such as those associated with an inflated or deflated ego (spiritual narcissism, spiritual bypassing, defensive and offensive spirituality, and religious extremism or authoritarianism). Finally, the chapter addresses ethical dilemmas in counseling and spirituality, and introduces some of the challenging diagnostic issues.

The closing pages, entitled "Afterimages: Roots and Wings," invite us to step back and reflect on this whole endeavor through a metaphoric lens.

My hope is that these ideas and reflections will lead to a deeper appreciation of the myriad ways in which spirituality and religion may *matter* in the lives of our clients, and potentially in our own. The discussion of therapeutic guidelines and practical suggestions offers a valuable foundation, both for new counselors and for those who have more experience but not much familiarity with this territory. For psychotherapists who are already comfortable with welcoming spiritual content, there may be new information and new questions to consider. Those whose work focuses directly on spirituality, such as spiritual directors, may find some of the psychological perspectives useful in their work. Finally, there is value here for readers who are primarily motivated to understand themselves and their own psychospiritual lives more fully. To them I extend an invitation to pause often, reflect, and play with whatever feels meaningful.

We are only beginning to explore some of the dimensions of this interplay. The possibilities for discovery are vast.

## Chapter Two

# Personal and Cultural Variations: Different Flavors of Spirituality

In contemporary conversations about religion or spirituality, you may have noticed that many people are very private about sharing their deepest convictions and experiences. Once they do share them, we often find that these convictions are firmly embedded in a particular perspective. A spiritual or religious orientation usually entails a particular worldview—an understanding of the world, of reality and how it all works—as well as a particular way of understanding oneself. I call this a *sense of self-and-world.*[1]

We all have a sense of self-and-world. Human beings are meaning-makers, and we have many ways of making meaning of life, only a few of which are cognitive and explicit. Our meaning-making is reflected in the way we carry our bodies, in our relationships, in our responses to events and experiences. But our spiritual and religious meaning-making is especially deep and broad. This is the territory of our ultimate concerns, so these interpretive lenses and commitments are not lightly held, not readily surrendered or changed. They are often felt as "the Truth."

When we encounter someone who holds a radically different spiritual or religious lens, we may well be at risk of misinterpreting, judging, or even engaging in outright conflict. Our work with clients clearly demands a more skillful approach to communication and interaction. While most human beings share some fundamental concerns and tendencies, we are *not* all the same. Our unexamined assumptions can be problematic, and we need a basic understanding of some of the deeper patterns that underlie our differences, the principal *sources* of variation. We will then be in a better position to listen to clients openly, appreciate the differences we encounter, and offer appropriate responses.

In this chapter we will identify a number of such sources, both individual and collective. We begin at the level of personality differences, introducing two psychological frameworks that also have spiritual implications. Then we will take a brief look at some patterns of gender and cultural variation, acknowledging (but not tackling directly) the sensitive territory of religious differences. Throughout this process, and explicitly at the conclusion of the chapter, I invite you to reflect on your own sense of self-and-world.

## Personal Style or Flavor

This source of variation is usually referred to as personality type. Some people are fascinated by typologies, but if you react negatively to the notion of being a "type," you are not alone. The word *type* suggests restriction to some people, giving them a feeling of being imprisoned in a rigid box. *Style* has a more fluid feel. *Flavor* is also an appealing option: it is nonthreatening, even playful, and encourages exploration. Both *style* and *flavor* invite us to approach personality differences with openness and curiosity, with a light touch.

### *Jungian Flavors (Styles)*

The idea that we each have our own individual way of being in the world is hardly new. Hindu and Buddhist thought made these kinds of distinctions centuries ago. In ancient Greek and Roman times, medicine used a system of four temperaments based on four humors in the body (choleric, sanguine, melancholic, and phlegmatic), and this perspective persisted until the emergence of modern medical research in the nineteenth century. Jerome Kagan's research on infant temperament is a contemporary form of this exploration.[2]

Today the psychological system that is most widely known is derived from the work of Carl Jung and associated with the assessment tool known as the Myers-Briggs Type Indicator (MBTI).[3] What follows is a basic introduction, which I hope will be enough to suggest the kinds of variations that can be relevant. We will then look at some of the potential implications for flavors of spirituality.

## INTROVERSION AND EXTRAVERSION

Jung, partly inspired by his understanding of Hinduism, elaborated a theoretical framework that begins with the distinction between introverted and extraverted attitudes. Introverts tend to withdraw their energy and attention from external objects and action, to defend themselves against demands from the outside world. Their focus is on the inner world, and they need alone time to recharge. Extraverts, on the other hand, are energized by action and have a positive relationship with objective happenings and conditions. Each of these orientations has its advantages, and each can be a liability when overdeveloped. Some introverted clients do feel misunderstood and marginalized in our largely extraverted culture, and appreciate recent publications that describe and value the Introvert experience.[4] Jung himself felt that strict Extraverts and Introverts are in the minority; most people are probably Ambiverts.

Complicating matters, Jung reminds us that these are *conscious* attitudes. We also have an *unconscious* attitude that is the opposite and compensates for our conscious orientation. For instance, a strongly extraverted person may have an introverted aspect that is unconscious; that is, she maintains an *unconscious* focus on her subjective needs and impulses. Similarly, the introvert, who is consciously interested in inner reflection, may develop an unconscious preoccupation with objective data.

## PERCEIVING AND JUDGING

Jung also proposes an important difference in our psychological functions of Perceiving (taking in information) and Judging (making decisions).

Perceiving is essentially irrational or non-rational, and has two variations. One leans towards Sensing, which focuses on perceptions of the actual, the literal, what *is*: the center of attention is direct concrete experience. Sensation-oriented types are interested in facts and how things work, as well as in bodily experiences. The Extraverted Sensation type is the quintessential realist, while the Introverted Sensation type is primarily influenced by the *subjective* sensations derived from the object. Such a person may, for instance, be a kind of realistic artist.

Some people prefer the other function of Perceiving, Intuition, which is oriented not so much to what *is*, but to what is *possible*, what may be imagined. An Intuitive type is not content with what is given but is always looking for new possibilities, whether in the world of external objects and situations (extraverted) or in the world of subjective images (introverted). Someone whose Intuitive function is dominant literally perceives a different reality than the Sensing-dominant individual.

In the rational realm of Judging, Thinking and Feeling are the two functions that have to do with how we make decisions. The Thinking function operates on the basis of true versus false, while the Feeling function *evaluates* in terms of meaning, value, importance, or desirability. (Note that *feeling* here does not mean the same as emotion.)

Let's take a quick look at some examples, beginning with the Thinking function. Someone with a strong *extraverted thinking* function emphasizes thinking that is focused on objective data and clear principles. The emphasis is on intellectual conclusions based on objective information, tending toward an impersonal perspective. An *introverted thinker*, on the other hand, begins with a subjective view and leads back to the subjective, raising questions, creating theories, considering insights, but not focusing a great deal on facts for their own sake.

An *extraverted feeling* type is likely to *appreciate* what is prized "out in the world," in terms of traditional values. Thinking is not the primary modality. *Introverted feeling* is extremely difficult to describe. In Jung's words, it "seldom appears on the surface" and is "continually seeking an image which has no existence in reality, but which it has seen in a kind of vision."[5]

## FOUR SPIRITUAL PATHS

What does all this have to do with spirituality? Unitarian Universalist minister Peter Richardson offers a thought-provoking discussion of this question in his book *Four Spiritualties*.[6] He lays out four distinct spiritual paths based on the four primary function pairs. The following overview suggests some significant style differences.

Let's begin with Intuitive Thinkers (NT). These individuals often gravitate toward what Richardson calls a Journey of Unity, characterized by four basic aspects:

- organizing principles operating throughout life and nature;
- truth that can be global, honest, and clear;
- social justice as the aim and context for personal involvement;
- clarity as the basis for spiritual enlightenment.

He offers examples from a variety of traditions and eras, including Albert Schweitzer, Islamic theologian al-Ghazali, and Trappist monk Thomas Merton. (Of course, we do not have to take his word for these classifications, but they are valuable suggestions.)

Richardson draws on the Hindu portrayal of four primary spiritual paths or *yogas*, suggesting that we each tend to follow one according to our natural inclination. The Journey of Unity is most closely aligned with *jnana yoga*, or the path of knowledge (reflecting the Thinking preference). The mind is used to inquire into its own nature and to realize the truth of the transcendent Self which is beyond thoughts and ego. Richardson points out that while NTs are a significant minority (about 12 percent of the population, according to him), spiritual literature is heavily weighted toward an NT orientation.

So what appeals to Introverted Thinkers in the context of spirituality? They usually want a place for solitude, retreat, and reflection. They often attempt to synthesize different faiths and pathways. They love and seek Truth, strive for comprehensive understanding, and pursue a just society. Again, it is important to remember that this search for a unifying Truth is not a detached intellectual pursuit; rather, it is a driving passion, a deep longing. NTs can also become one-sided, and part of their work is always to seek balance.

We can discern a contemporary example of the NT tendency in philosopher Ken Wilber. Listen to the passion for transcendent knowledge in the following words:

> Evolution in all forms has started to become conscious of itself. Evolution, as Spirit-in-action, is starting to awaken on a more collective scale. Kosmic evolution is now producing theories and performances of its own integral embrace. This Eros moves through you and me, urging us to include, to diversify, to honor, to enfold. The Love that moves the sun and other stars is moving theories such as this, and it will move many others, as Eros connects the previously unconnected, and pulls together the fragments of a world too weary to endure.[7]

Here is the vision of unity through an all-embracing theory that, we also notice, is not separate from Love, since Truth and Love are essentially seen as One.

The Journey of Devotion is the path likely to be followed by Sensing Feelers (SF). This approach to spirituality is personal, interactive, and highly experiential. Recall the Sensation-oriented focus on direct experience. Here this is joined with an emphasis on value and meaning. Important themes are pilgrimage, heroes and heroines, inspirational stories, subjective experience, service, simplicity, and a love of dance, music, and ancient rituals. This is the path of *bhakti yoga*, which approaches the Divine through an I–Thou relationship. Love, devotion, adoration, and loving service: Richardson suggests that these are the leanings of

Mohammed, Saint Francis of Assisi, and Hindu sage Ramakrishna, who was intoxicated with love and saw the Divine everywhere. A contemporary example is Mother Teresa, who was deeply devoted to Jesus: everything she did was an expression of her love for him. Most religious traditions include a devotional aspect which speaks deeply to SFs, and these devotees in turn cherish the grounded meaning of traditions and continuity.

Richardson describes the third path as the Journey of Works, favored by Sensing Thinkers (STs) for its practical commitment to duty and the orderly implementation of beliefs. He suggests that there are eight primary aspects of this journey, which may appear in different proportions:

- the foundation of law, covenant, order;
- a strong sense of right and righteousness;
- a sense of responsibility;
- clear-cut identity as essential for the spiritual life;
- work itself as life's aim and fulfillment;
- pragmatic realism;
- a favoring of administrative tasks;
- finally, a sense of justification.[8]

Richardson's examples of an ST orientation include the Protestant reformer Martin Luther, George Washington, Moses, and Confucius.

STs follow the path of *karma yoga*, which emphasizes disinterested action in service to one's responsibilities and duties. The ideal is involvement in the world with a selfless orientation. (Sensing Feelers also lean toward service, but with more emphasis on devotion.) The Bhagavad Gita is a beautiful expression of this way of being spiritual, as was the life of Mahatma Gandhi. Brother Lawrence, a Carmelite monk in the seventeenth century, practiced the presence of God while working in the kitchen. Every task, large and small, was carried out for God. Approached with care and discipline, his practical service became his selfless offering. While it can sometimes be challenging for those on the Journey of Works to see the validity of other paths, opening to different perspectives may offer a significant avenue of growth.

Finally there is the Journey of Harmony, the way of the Intuitive Feeler (NF). Richardson describes this path as emphasizing the quest for authentic selfhood, mystical harmony, an attitude of expectation, openness to healing and the role of dreams, social idealism, and a focus on relational processes.[9] Spiritual seeking is the nature of the journey, as there is always more to experience and discover. The quest itself is a deep calling. Mystical leanings may find fulfillment in nature, and visions of transcendent harmony reflect the NF spirit.

Unlike Intuitive Thinkers, NFs are not particularly concerned about whether all the diverse parts actually fit together in one grand Truth about reality. More important to them are harmonious blending and appreciation on a relational level. Richardson suggests that this spirit is particularly reflected in *raja yoga,* which embraces the other three yogic paths while developing its own NF-flavored forms of spiritual discipline leading toward spiritual liberation. Another example comes from the harmonizing of all the yogas in the Integral Yoga of Sri Aurobindo. Indian writer Rabindranath Tagore, a lyrical Bengali poet, gives us some beautiful NF-flavored imagery, celebrating the joyful dance of all creation and the mystery of all life. Taoist poetry often invites us to be like water, which is everywhere, yielding yet powerful. English poet William Blake points to the mystery of the infinite and eternal in the minute and fragile expressions of nature (a grain of sand, a flower). Many Native American teachings speak of this relational harmony among all living things.

Intuitive Feelers (NFs) sometimes react negatively to Sensing Thinkers' (STs) forms of religion and spirituality, which emphasize practical duties and orderly beliefs, as they may have been subjected to those kinds of pressures and judgments at home or in school. Anticipating the next chapter, I suggest that NFs and perhaps NTs are particularly likely to describe themselves as "spiritual but not religious" and as spiritual seekers.

Other writers might make different connections between Jungian typology and spiritual paths. And just as there are a lot of Ambiverts, there are probably many people who identify with two orientations. But these descriptions convey a sense of the possible variations.

## Enneagram Flavors (Styles)

Another significant approach to personality-style differences is the system known as the Enneagram. The word comes from the Greek word for *nine*, since the Enneagram is represented by a nine-pointed figure inside a circle. The symbol itself is ancient, but its introduction to the modern world is usually attributed to an intriguing spiritual teacher named George Gurdjieff, of Armenian and Greek descent, who was born around 1875. His use of the symbol focused on its representation of basic laws (the Law of Seven and the Law of Three) in the cosmos. A specifically *psychological* interpretation of the symbol comes to us through the work of two contemporary figures, Oscar Ichazo and Claudio Naranjo, both from South America.[10]

*Figure 2.1 The Enneagram. Courtesy of the Enneagram Institute. Copyright 2005, The Enneagram Institute. All Rights Reserved. Used with Permission.*

The Enneagram is often used as a personality system, but the spiritual dimension can be a primary focus. The underlying perspective is that we *have* personality patterns or fixations, but who we *are* is much more than our personality. Studying the Enneagram is a pathway to realizing that we have, each in our own way, fallen asleep to our essential nature. As we become aware of our patterns, and begin to *disidentify* from them, we may begin to wake up to our deeper Essence. The personality continues to function, but it becomes more and more transparent. I will return to this notion of disidentification a little later.

The difficult aspects of the Enneagram patterns often get a lot of attention, so much so that some authors offer a deliberate focus on a positive interpretation of the Enneagram.[11] However, just as with Jungian types, any pattern can have both gifts and limitations. The important thing to remember is that the nine Enneagram patterns are not really about *behavior.* They are more about what we *pay attention to,* and *what motivates us.* No one fits a pattern perfectly: there are subtleties, and our tendencies fluctuate to some degree. The premise is that while we may have aspects of all nine patterns, we each have one natural fixation or focus that obscures a particular aspect of spiritual Reality.

Let's begin with the division of the symbol into three sections. Points 8, 9, and 1 constitute the Gut or Instinctive Triad. Points 2, 3, and 4 make up the Feeling or Image Triad. Finally, points 5, 6, and 7 form the Thinking or Head Triad. We will look at each of these in turn.

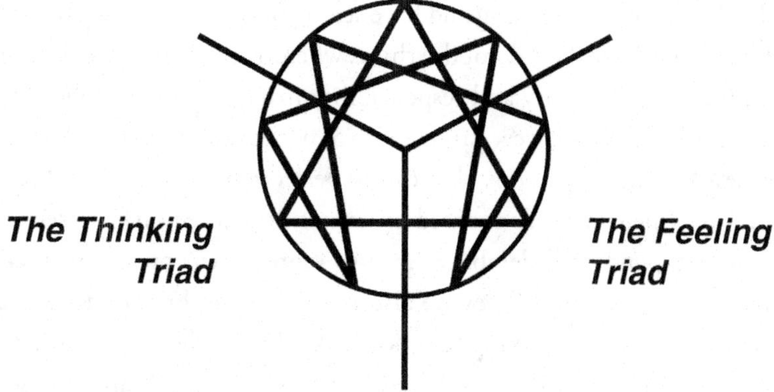


*Figure 2.2 The Enneagram Triads. Courtesy of the Enneagram Institute. Copyright 2005, The Enneagram Institute. All Rights Reserved. Used with Permission.*

## *The Instinctive Triad*

The Eight, Nine, and One patterns are concerned with "maintaining resistance to reality (creating boundaries for the self that are based on physical tensions)."[12] People who identify with these patterns tend to have distortions in their instincts, to be energetically focused in the body, and to have problems with anger or aggression in various ways. Sometimes they are called gut points, with the center point of the 9 paradoxically *out of touch* with the gut.

The Eight, known as the Asserter or Protector, has a strong, expansive presence, displaying what psychologist Karen Horney calls a "moving against" pattern of defense.[13] Not surprisingly, this aggressive pattern protects an inner vulnerability that can't be acknowledged. Eights know what they want and go after it, often with the sense that the rules don't apply to them. They like challenges and have the energy to pursue them. They can be generous and are often concerned with justice, coming to the defense of the underdog. Other types may find Eights to be intimidating or too intense and dominant. As you might expect, they tend to be extraverts, and are more likely to be Thinking types. At the very least, you would not be likely to find Eights drawn to a soft or Romantic flavor of spirituality.

The One, known as the Reformer or Perfectionist, expends a lot of energy maintaining his or her inner boundaries. Ones are concerned with what is right and wrong and have strong opinions about what they or others should or should not do: this is where anger or resentment can come into play. Integrity and responsibility matter greatly to Ones. At their healthiest, they have a strong sense of purpose and mission, and in their less healthy expressions, they can be perfectionistic and rigid. Their critical judgments may be focused on others; if focused on themselves, they may expend considerable energy to repress their own unwanted impulses and reactions. Ones are also more likely to be found among those with a strong Thinking function. Like Eights, they may gravitate toward spiritual paths that emphasize action, social justice, and reform, but they are more likely to appreciate religious systems with clear moral rules (which Eights might rebel against).

In the center of the instinctive triad, Nines put up both internal and external boundaries. Known as the Peacemaker or the Mediator, the Nine tends to avoid conflict at all cost, shielding against the world to try and keep anger and aggression out. At the same time, Nines cannot tolerate feeling their own anger or hostility, so they also guard themselves internally against such strong instinctive emotions. As a result, their way of expressing opposition is more likely to be through passive aggressiveness. Nines love peace and harmony, so it would not be surprising to find them on the Journey of Harmony in the style of Intuitive Feelers (NFs). While they belong to the body/instinct triad, they are typically out of touch with their bodies, just as they are out of touch with the instinctual energy of anger. Some Nines are oriented toward loving service in the external world, which might make them similar to Sensing Feelers (SFs). They often have difficulty initiating and sustaining action, so are more likely to be found on spiritual paths where they can follow rather than lead, as long as the rules are not too rigid.

## *The Feeling Triad*

This group includes Twos, Threes, and Fours. Here the heart is the center of identity, although the center point, 3, can appear to be disconnected from heart feelings, just as the center point of the Nine is often disconnected from gut anger in the Instinctive Triad. Those in the Feeling Triad are most concerned with their relationships, wanting above all to be loved and valued by others (as they may not have been in childhood). Because they place a lot of importance on the image that others have of them, they are sometimes called image points as well as feeling or heart points.

Known as the Giver or Helper, the Two's particular strategy is to focus on meeting the needs of others in order to get love. In the process of moving *toward* others (a Karen Horney category), the Two loses touch with what he or she is actually feeling or needing. Twos may take pride in how well they take care of others' needs, but are also likely to be resentful when they feel unappreciated. They generally avoid feeling vulnerable themselves. Although women frequently identify as Twos, the deeper dynamic has to be distinguished from female cultural conditioning. Twos are strong in the Feeling function category, and are often drawn to a spiritual path that involves connectedness and service.

The Four is known as the Individualist or the Romantic (sometimes the Tragic-Romantic). Here the energy and focus are more inward: a Four is concerned with maintaining a self-image as someone whose value and significance lies in his or her uniqueness and depth. Fours are particularly sensitive to the feeling dimension of life. Drawn to fantasies and stories that support this self-image, they sometimes dwell on the wounds and suffering of the past. They may describe themselves as feeling at home with melancholy. Not surprisingly, they often feel lonely and abandoned. Many Fours are oriented toward beauty, and may be creative in unique ways; at the very least, a Four's spiritual path is likely to shy away from the commonplace. They may, for instance, have a Romantic reverence for nature, which offers a deeply felt sense of connection and belonging. Fours often resonate with the Intuitive Feeler orientation.

In the center of the Feeling Triad is the Three, the Performer or Achiever. As we noted, Threes tend to be out of touch with their feelings. Image, however, remains very important to them. They tend to focus outward, seeking positive feedback from others, usually for what they *do* and accomplish. They may also adjust the image they present to others in order to gain approval. Internally, they focus on sustaining a consistent self-image and story about themselves. This ideal image emphasizes confidence and efficiency, competence and achievement. When they seem impatient with feelings, it is because they get in the way of the task. Not surprisingly, encountering authentic emotional pain challenges them in profound ways; if they can move beyond denial and masking, they can discover depths they had no idea existed. Threes are more likely to be extraverted, and favor the Thinking function over Feeling. While they seem more likely to be Sensing-oriented, they are also found in the Intuitive category. Spiritual paths that are action-oriented, practical, and orderly would be common.

## *The Thinking Triad*

Finally, in the Thinking or Head Triad, we find the Five, Six, and Seven. The dominant feeling here is fear or anxiety focused on the future. While we all have busy minds, people with these Enneagram patterns have a strong tendency to overthink.

Fives, known as Observers or Investigators, find safety in their minds as they seek knowledge and mastery in some domain. They try to remain detached, at some distance from the energy of life, which can feel like "too much." Just as the energy of the Eight moves *against*, and the Two moves *toward*, the Five typically moves *away*. Fives minimize their own needs and try to avoid excessive needs or demands from others. They also tend to view the resources of energy, time, and space through the lens of scarcity, so they try to withdraw and protect these resources as much as possible. They are at home in the realm of thought, so not surprisingly, much less comfortable in the territory of strong feelings. On the other hand, Fives can also have considerable depth, like Fours. They are likely to be Intuitive Thinkers(NTs), and to favor spiritual paths that value those qualities.

A very different energy characterizes Sevens, known as Enthusiasts or Epicures. Rather than retreating from life, they approach it enthusiastically and actively. They are optimistic, curious, and hungry for new experiences and adventures. They dislike feeling constrained, bored, or limited, and their busy minds gravitate toward a grand mental vision of the future where something better always awaits. In this respect they definitely belong in the Thinking Triad, even though they are usually more extraverted than Fives. What they are afraid of is not likely to be obvious: they are avoiding pain, grief, anxiety in the inner world, so their drive is to keep escaping into outer activity. Sevens may find it challenging to stay with any one spiritual path and pursue it in depth, so they may well be among those who are enticed by the multiple possibilities offered by contemporary spiritual paths. When they are able to slow down and remain open to the present, their gift is the ability to embrace the spiritual in the material world, to be in touch with joy, awe, and wonder.

In the center of the Thinking Triad is the Six, the Loyalist or Loyal Skeptic, possibly the most complex point in the Enneagram. Here attention and energy are directed both inward and outward. When Sixes experience anxiety, they jump into action in order to avoid potential catastrophes, but then they become overwhelmed and retreat inside. Lacking a firm sense of inner guidance, they have difficulty trusting their own judgment and making decisions. On the other hand, they often develop an ambivalent relationship with anyone they lean on for support and guidance because trusting authority is also risky. The loyalty of the Six grows out of the desire to hold on to connections—to be abandoned is to be unsafe. In general, a Six tends to be plagued by doubts and uncertainties.

There are two kinds of responses to this doubt and fear. The *phobic* Six is clearly in touch with the fear, while the *counterphobic* Six responds to anxiety and vigilance by plunging headlong into potential threats and dangers. A classic example is Evel Knievel, who displayed a daredevil approach in jumping his motorcycle over tremendous obstacles. Whether he is actually a counterphobic Six or not, the spirit with which he throws himself into dangerous situations is characteristic of this pattern..

## *Instinctual Subtypes*

Another dimension of complexity in the Six arises from the differences among its three subtypes. This introduces an additional source of variation which reflects an appreciation of nuances. For each Enneagram pattern, there are three instinctual subtypes representing three basic instincts that motivate human behavior: the self-preservation, relational or sexual, and social subtypes. This source of variation gives us twenty-seven distinct patterns.

*Self-preservation* points to a focus on physical safety and comfort. The *relational* or *sexual* instinct reflects a preoccupation with one-to-one or intimate relationships. Finally, the *social* instinct has more to do with one's place in the group and the desire to be liked, approved of, and needed by others. Each of these instincts is represented in each of the nine patterns.[14]

As an example, a Self-Preservation Six is often characterized by *warmth*. Fear is focused on insecurity and the need for protection in order to survive, so the motivation is to seek out friendships and alliances with people perceived as strong and trustworthy. The warm friendliness of Self-Preservation Sixes helps them approach and connect with these potential protectors in order to find the security they need. They may appear heart-centered, but on the inside, they are still driven by mental doubts and questions.

In contrast, the Sexual Six (associated with strength/beauty) is often counterphobic, moving energetically against threat and danger as a way of overcoming fear. The emphasis is on being strong, physically attractive, assertive, and even intimidating; Sexual Sixes value a mate who has similar qualities.

Social Sixes find safety in allies and authority figures, as well as in relying on reason and rules. This is known as the Duty subtype. They find rationality and ideology to be reassuring and are most comfortable with a certain degree of structure. Both phobic and counterphobic tendencies may be found in this group. These three patterns all share common characteristics of the Six archetype, but with distinctly different emphases.

## *Wings*

The points on either side of a number can also add nuances to the underlying pattern. These are known as *wings*, and we are often influenced by one wing more than the other. For instance, a Three with a strong Four wing may be drawn to a spiritual approach that has more feeling and depth to it, even though the Three pattern continues to flavor the experience. Likewise, an Eight with a strong Nine wing may have a softer side, and a Five with a strong Six wing may be more head oriented than a Five with a Four wing.

## *Pathways to Growth*

There are numerous pathways to growth in the Enneagram system. The most obvious is that we can experience movement along the lines which connect the points. When you look at the diagram, you can see that each number has lines connecting it to two other numbers. Some schools of Enneagram thought maintain that moving along one line is moving in the direction of integration, while the other is the direction of disintegration. Others maintain that we can move in either direction depending on circumstances, and that we can move to the healthy or unhealthy version of the point in question. Point 8, for example, has lines connecting to both 2 and 5. An Eight who feels supported and is able to let go of defenses may be able to soften and open to the vulnerable heart of the Two. When encountering more challenge and pressure than feels tolerable, the Eight may pull back into the Five pattern, retreating in order to buy time, build strength, and decide on the next move.

Each Enneagram flavor also has a particular *passion*, which suggests a growth path toward the corresponding *virtue*. Passions are the ego-based emotional states that dominate our lives. For instance, the passion for Six is fear, and the virtue is courage. For Two, the passion is pride, and the virtue is humility.

At an even deeper level, each type is also particularly connected to one or more Holy Ideas, which are views of Ultimate Reality or True Nature free from the distortions of personality. This pathway to growth involves committed psychospiritual work in order to lift the veils which obscure our experience of the Holy Idea to which we are most attuned. The Holy Idea for point 9 is Holy Love, which allows those with a Nine pattern to realize that Reality is ultimately loving and that they are embraced in that love. For point 5, Holy Omniscience describes the direct understanding of the ultimate oneness of Reality, which heals the illusion of separation to which the Five is particularly susceptible.

Let me reiterate that Enneagram patterns can have both positive and challenging aspects. One way of highlighting this is through a developmental system that includes a range of healthy, average, and unhealthy manifestations of each point's characteristics.[15] This scheme can also be helpful in suggesting the direction for growth toward healthier versions of one's pattern.

If this feels too complicated at the moment, I encourage you to be patient: appreciation of this lens grows with study and practice.

## *My Pattern Is Not Who I Am*

When we approach the Enneagram from a spiritual perspective rather than simply as a personality system, the purpose is to recognize our pattern or fixation so that we can loosen our identification with it. *Disidentification* is a term that is often used in transpersonal and integral psychology, and it plays a prominent role in the Diamond Approach (a spiritual school that features the Enneagram). What does it mean? Simply put, if you are becoming less identified with a particular pattern, you are less likely to be caught up in it and more able to observe it. With growing awareness, you may even develop the capacity *not* to act it out. The personality pattern is something you *have* rather than something you *are*.

This process of disidentifying from the conditioned personal self allows us to open to the deeper recognition that our true identity is beyond the personal, deeper and vaster than ever imagined. As I pointed out earlier, disidentification from our fixation is described as ultimately bringing us into contact with the Essence of our Being, also referred to as True Nature, or Being itself. The premise is that in the course of growing up and living, we have fallen asleep to the deeper truth of what we are. The invitation is to awaken to our essential nature, which is always present no matter how much it has become obscured from awareness.[16]

## *Jung's Typology and the Enneagram*

How can we understand the relationship between these two approaches to personality differences? Here is one possible comparison. The Jungian typology emphasizes moving toward wholeness through balancing opposite tendencies (wholeness as symbolized by the archetype of the Self and the image of a mandala, both of which will be discussed in chapter 5). Wholeness rather than perfection is the aspiration. The Enneagram, on the other hand, focuses more on transformation through a process of uncovering, seeing through the veils or layers of personality to reconnect with the deep essence of soul or Being.

## *The Nine Enneagram Characters*

It is time to introduce the nine characters who will be featured as hypothetical clients in the rest of the book. To repeat an earlier statement, these characters are fictional composites based on numerous people I have known (including clients). As we get to know them through the different lenses in the chapters to come, my goal is to bring to life the perspectives we are exploring, and to illustrate the rich possibilities for attuning counseling approaches to different flavors.

On a practical note, some clients are interested in exploring the Enneagram for themselves. While there are numerous online tests, I have found it wise not to put a lot of faith in them. There are some good introductory books that clients can read in order to find the patterns that feel familiar; inner recognition rather than external labeling is important.[17] Then a shared exploration can follow. If clients are not interested, I still find it valuable to try and discern their underlying flavor so that I can tailor my approach to meet their particular needs.

The three Triads (Instinctive, Feeling, and Thinking) will help organize this introduction. Again, the focus is not on behavior but rather on underlying patterns of what motivates these characters and where their attention is apt to go. As we follow them through the chapters ahead, I will be emphasizing general tendencies rather than the more subtle details of instinctive types, wings, and pathways to growth.

### INSTINCTIVE TRIAD: EIGHT, NINE, ONE

### Eight, the Challenger or Asserter: Rob

Rob is forty-three, Jewish, married with two preteen daughters, and in a self-described midlife crisis. There's an intense energy in him, as if he is tightly wound. His communication style is direct, and he wants people to be straightforward and honest with him in turn. Sometimes people find him confrontational. His father was highly critical, controlling, and abusive, and not surprisingly, Rob acknowledges carrying a lot of anger toward him. Rob describes himself as craving strong experiences: in the past he has abused alcohol and "done drugs." He was in Alcoholics Anonymous for a while and found it valuable. Currently, he is dissatisfied with his life and is searching for more meaningful relationships and work. He readily recognizes the Eight pattern in himself.

### Nine, the Peacemaker or Mediator: Devin

Devin is a sixty-nine-year-old African American woman who has been on a long and meandering spiritual journey, beginning with ACOA (Adult Children of Alcoholics) groups in her twenties. She has been married and divorced twice and has a thirty-five-year-old married daughter as well as a grandson. Devin describes herself as a seeker and a peacemaker, and identifies with the Enneagram Nine pattern. She is drawn to a variety of different paths and acknowledges that she has difficulty knowing what she really wants and pursuing it. Her tendency is to get distracted with trivial things and to lose her focus. Devin also finds it challenging to be in the minority in many of the spiritual contexts she seeks out, since these are heavily attended by white women. At this point in her life she wants to unearth the inner obstacles to focusing and choosing, with the goal of going deeper on a single path.

### One, the Reformer or Perfectionist: Charles

Charles is a fifty-seven-year-old Caucasian man whose wife died of cancer a year ago. He is profoundly lonely and questioning his lifelong Christian faith; his wife was the one who maintained social and church (Episcopalian) connections. His relationship with his three young-adult children is somewhat distant and superficial. He describes himself as someone who cares a lot about right and wrong, and says his faith has provided him with guidelines for moral behavior. He has focused a lot on supporting his family and "being a good person." Now, he sometimes finds himself wondering if God is punishing him by taking his wife from him so early because he wasn't good enough. My impression is that his home base is probably the Enneagram One pattern. In grief counseling for the loss of his wife, he is also acutely aware of the loss of his faith. He is questioning whether there is really a *right* way to live or even a right way to do this grief work, and he is beginning to allow some difficult feelings to surface.

## FEELING TRIAD: TWO, THREE, FOUR

### Two, the Helper or Giver: Sienna

Sienna is thirty-four years old, with a supportive husband and two children, six and eight years old. Taking care of her family is very important to her. She was raised by her Caucasian mother, whom she describes as a hippie, and by her loving grandmother. Sienna was never told anything about her father except that he was African American, and she proudly identifies as biracial. In her midtwenties she found her way to a Christian Bible Church, and speaks warmly about her love for this secure community and her joy in helping out and being appreciated. Despite the caution about not assuming that women are Twos, Sienna seems to fit best in this Enneagram pattern. Being generous and helpful is deeply important to her. She acknowledges that she is proud of the way she can anticipate and meet the needs of others, although it takes her a while to realize that what she longs for is to be loved in return. But recently her church community discovered that the pastor was having an affair. All the sacrifices she has made for him and his congregation have, she feels, amounted to nothing. This betrayal has impacted her deeply: he was her "rock," her church family has been shattered, and she is floundering in a mix of strong feelings.

### Three, the Achiever or Performer: Linn

A successful single businesswoman and an Asian American, Linn is an achiever who resonates with the Enneagram Three pattern. She is the daughter of immigrant parents from Korea, for whom academic and business achievement was a priority. At age forty-three, she enjoys focusing on work and presenting an image of competence and efficiency. Her leadership role has great significance for her. While she is not particularly comfortable with feelings, she finds herself seeking counseling for the first time in the wake of a major car accident. The accident itself was traumatic, but even more challenging for her is the accompanying near-death experience, which is playing havoc with her sense of who she is and what is real in the world. Her world has turned upside down.

### Four, the Individualist or Romantic: Janice

Janice is forty-one years old, Caucasian, and two years out from a divorce. She has two children who see their father on a regular basis, and she is back in school in order to create a new career. She has always been emotionally sensitive, and felt lonely growing up in her more practical and intellectually oriented family. Her two siblings teased her, and her parents were often impatient. The message was: Why can't you be different? The nurturing and connection that she longed for never seemed to be available. Early in her life, she wondered what was wrong with her, and over the years, she has felt waves of overwhelming shame and self-doubt. These were times of depression. After a brief exploration of the Enneagram, she readily identifies as a Four. Now working through this major life transition, she wants to find her way through the grief over her marriage and the challenges of creating a new life and identity for herself.

## THINKING TRIAD: FIVE, SIX, SEVEN

### Five, the Observer or Investigator: Kyle

Kyle is a young man of twenty-two who identifies as bisexual and is trying to find his way in the world. He is the only child of a Caucasian father and an East Indian mother. His parents divorced when he was about eleven, and his mother is paying for his counseling. They are well educated and are, in his words, "liberals." He is in a transitional space, taking a break from formal education, working basic jobs, and considering college options. Quiet, sensitive, and introverted, he takes refuge in his intellect. As a child, he often found himself more comfortable in the company of adults than with others his age, and he has always felt different. Being knowledgeable is a source of satisfaction, but at the same time it separates him from peers who resent his display of knowledge. He approaches spirituality as a philosophical inquiry, drawing on many conversations with his parents about Eastern and Western perspectives. Like many Fives, Kyle tends to hide in his mind. Knowledge is his refuge, but he also wants meaningful social connection, which is challenging for him to find. His natural curiosity draws him to explore the Enneagram, and he immediately relates to the Five.

## Six, the Loyalist or Loyal Skeptic: Gabriela

At fifty-two, Gabriela is in the midst of a major life transition. Identifying herself as Latina, she is married with two grown children and has returned to school to follow a dream of becoming a social worker. Torn between her Mexican family's Catholic roots and her current exposure to new ideas and people, she is struggling with doubts, questions, and conflicting loyalties. When she is introduced to the Enneagram, she immediately recognizes herself as a Six, the Loyal Skeptic. She talks with both enthusiasm and skepticism about what she is learning in her graduate program and her new school-related women's group, which is introducing her to some unfamiliar and challenging spiritual perspectives. A lot of new ideas are coming her way, and she feels confused about how much to trust the authority of church and family versus that of her new peer group and educational institution. She experiences anxiety in the midst of all this questioning, and is looking for direction.

### Seven, Enthusiast or Epicure: Marissa

Marissa is a young woman of twenty-eight who has been diagnosed with melanoma. She describes herself as having a spirited love of freedom, novelty, and positive feelings, and she loves to imagine possibilities. These tendencies suggest an Enneagram Seven pattern. But this carefree optimism has been severely challenged by her potentially life-threatening illness. She tries to be upbeat but feels frightened and alone, and is not finding much help in her traditional Christian upbringing. As she receives support and validation in counseling, she gradually opens to exploring not only her fear but also her experience in her body, including the melanoma and the treatment process. She begins sharing more with her family, and begins to hear about her Native American roots as her grandmother remembers and shares traditional stories about healing.

Once again, I offer a cautionary word about types and patterns. Because some people strongly reject these kinds of systems as too rigid or confining, I cannot say this often enough: these are generalizations. While we may find them useful for various purposes, they have limits. Human minds find it useful to detect patterns since they simplify the amount of information we have to deal with, but no individual is fully explained by a type analysis. When we use typologies to help us understand and even anticipate possibilities, we do so with the understanding that people are more complex than can be explained by any single lens. An individual with a particular Myers-Briggs or Enneagram pattern may, for a variety of reasons, gravitate to a surprising spiritual or religious path that appears uncharacteristic of the pattern. When we use typologies to criticize or attack others, to reduce them to a formula, or to excuse our own behavior, we have fallen into a dangerous trap. This is why I appreciate the word *flavors*. We can notice and appreciate different flavors without judgment or rigidity. With this caveat in mind, let us move into challenging territory of gender and cultural patterns.

# Gender and Cultural Styles

Once we shift our focus from *individual* style variations to the possibility of *group* patterns, some readers may find doubts and concerns surfacing even more intensely. This is partly because we often have powerful group identifications, and also because many of us are rightfully wary of dangerous stereotypes. Perhaps we can minimize some of the controversy by focusing on the implications for spirituality, but we need to tread carefully.

## *Masculine and Feminine*

One way to talk about group differences is to distinguish between two styles that are often associated with masculine and feminine. Of course, not all men fit the masculine pattern, and not all women fit the feminine pattern; historical and cultural influences are also involved. If we avoid masculine/feminine language, we may acknowledge related distinctions such as rational/analytic versus emotional/synthetic, and autonomous versus relational. In spirituality we often come across a third distinction: transcendence-oriented versus immanence-oriented styles.

*Transcendence*, sometimes associated with a masculine preference, refers to a sense of the Divine that lies primarily beyond the material, physical universe, reachable only through practices that overcome physical and mental limitations (such as meditation, prayer, or ecstatic experiences). An *immanent* perspective is sometimes viewed as more feminine, experiencing the Divine as fully present and accessible in the material world, in the body, and in nature. (There is also a third perspective known as *panentheism*, which views the Divine as both within physical reality and beyond it, "in it" but not "of it.")

What does contemporary research have to say about actual masculine-feminine differences? It has been well documented that the corpus callosum (that part of the brain that connects the two hemispheres) is somewhat thicker in the average female than in the average male. There is additional brain research indicating that women on the average show more physical symmetry between the left and right hemispheres than men, and this symmetry shows up in fetuses as early as twenty weeks old. The implication is that "women tend to process information in a more holistic, bilateral manner, and men in a more focused, uni-hemispheric manner."[18] There are also differences between the substructures of the hypothalamus of average male and female brains, which have implications for the endocrine (hormonal) systems.

Some well-documented findings correlate with these neuroanatomical differences. For instance, females are stronger in verbal aptitude and emotional recognition, while males are stronger in visuospatial abilities. Hormonal differences may be involved in the contrast between the female tendency toward more nurturing and relational behaviors and the male tendency toward more active and physically aggressive behaviors. Women (across diverse cultures) are quite consistently found to be more likely to seek and receive social support during stressful times, to "tend-and-befriend" rather than fight or flee.

The difference may be viewed as a contrast between *agency* and *communion*, in the words of Ken Wilber. If we acknowledge two basic human drives, the drive to assert oneself as an individual and the drive to connect with others, then men are more commonly associated with the former (agency) and women with the latter (communion).[19] This generalization is well represented in feminist theory, particularly the work of the Stone Center at Wellesley College, which maintains that the appropriate unit for psychological consideration of women is not the separate self but the self-in-relation.[20]

In the context of spirituality, this suggests that males tend to emphasize the cognitive, transcendent dimensions of spirituality, while females orient more towards the emotional and immanent aspects. Another way of expressing this is that more men prefer spiritual perspectives that focus on penetrating through the illusion of physical reality to the spiritual reality behind or deeper than the material world; this movement is associated with the experience of freedom. More women seem to be oriented toward paths that emphasize embodiment, relationships, nature, and earth-based practices; embracing this reality with love and compassion is associated with a sense of fullness.[21] Wilber describes these two spiritual tendencies, using Greek terms, as the movements of Eros and Agape. Eros turns the attention upward, in an evolutionary, vertically ascending movement beyond form: "Eros reaches up, as it were, and assaults the heavens," while Agape focuses downward and cherishes the deep meaning and beauty in the world of form, embracing the earth.[22] Both men and women grow and evolve, of course. This view simply suggests that they are given to facing, valuing, or placing their attention, in different directions. Agape and Eros: compassion and wisdom, roots and wings.[23]

These are clearly broad generalizations with many individual exceptions. Rather than thinking in gender categories, which overlook many nuances of difference, we may approach this as an archetypal difference, going beyond the framework of research and theory to a deeper polarity reminiscent of yin and yang.

*Figure 2.3 Yin Yang Symbol*

Whatever one's gender identification, if any, one might find oneself leaning toward one or the other of these poles, or embracing both (as in panentheism).

In the research arena, actual male-female differences are relatively small.[24] Over 90 percent of human beings have a mix of both masculine and feminine attributes. Yet we are inclined to focus attention on the exemplars at the two extremes, just as we do with Introverts and Extraverts. This reflects a human tendency to "hold 'prototypes' or central examples as a way to organize information." In other words, we unconsciously compare the extremes, a tendency which "obscures the vast majority of men and women who are not archetypally much of anything."[25]

## *Cultural Differences*

Consideration of cultural differences in relation to religion now receives heavy emphasis in the literature on counseling and psychotherapy. The ADDRESSING model of multiculturalism, which is widely used, specifically includes religion and spirituality as a central aspect of culturally responsive counseling. (The framework title is an acronym for Age and generational influences, Developmental or other Disabilities, Religion and spirituality, Ethnic and racial identity, Socioeconomic status, Sexual orientation, Indigenous heritage, National origin, and Gender.)[26]

In an attempt to be helpful to counselors, some counseling publications describe the religious beliefs and practices associated with the major ethnic and cultural groups in the United States. This literature emphasizes group variations rather than typologies, but we may also think of these as *deep flavors*. We need to bear in mind that these generalizations can, of course, be overly simplistic and compartmentalizing. Complexity is increased by the differences in national origin even within a broad ethnic group, as well as by the generational factor: Is the client a first generation immigrant, 1.5 generation (arriving as a child or young adolescent), or second generation?

With these cautions in mind, let's briefly consider some broad cultural categories.[27] For many African Americans, spirituality and identity are experienced as inseparable. Religion and spirituality are strengths associated with resilience and survival of both slavery and present struggles. In particular, the Black Church provides a place of communal worship that offers meaning, opportunities for full expression, and a refuge from harsh realities, in addition to social support for adolescents and aging parents. But deeper than that, psychological pain often finds expression in spiritual terms, and answers are sought in deeper faith. Traditionally, the African American focus is on a personal God who, through his son, Jesus, heals, guides, and comforts believers. In worship, the congregation often engages in shared expressions of faith, gratitude, and love, involving music, emotions, senses, and the whole body.

It is particularly difficult to discuss Latinxs as a single category, since there is such diversity in national origin and identity. There are important differences among those who come from Mexico, Puerto Rico, and Cuba, as well as other Central and South American countries. But there are some shared values, such as the importance of family and the respect for authority. In the realm of spirituality and religion, Roman Catholicism is of widespread importance but not the only framework of belief and practice. Protestant denominations, Jehovah's Witnesses, Pentecostals, and various Evangelical groups are represented, as is Judaism. Latinxs may also rely on folk practices and magical beliefs that are part of their shared heritage.

Let's take a closer look at some of the health and illness beliefs of these immigrant families and how those are embedded in spiritual frameworks.[28] The mental health field recognizes the existence of culture-bound "syndromes." These kinds of difficulties exist within the context of a cultural belief system, and often have to do with the assumption of supernatural causes and treatment. Some examples include *mal de ojo* ("evil eye"), *susto* or *expanto* ("fright"), and *empacho* ("indigestion"), each of which is explained with reference to spiritual forces, strong emotions or social relationships, or a strong power possessed by certain people. In these contexts, consultation with indigenous healers (witches, *curanderos*, spiritualists) may be the first recourse.

Of particular interest is the exploration of locus of control and coping styles. Latinxs tend to attribute the cause of suffering or emotional problems (and the relief of suffering) to external sources, referred to as God, fate, or destiny. (They are not alone: consider the Muslim phrase, "Allah willing.") This is not the preferred style of most Anglo Americans, who see this as an example of fatalism that reflects a kind of victim mentality, a problematic belief that life is beyond our control. But this perspective may serve as a valuable resource, particularly for low-income families (introducing the additional variation of social class): it makes sense that fatalism would be more common among those who experience their lives as under the control of powerful people and forces. Accepting conditions that are beyond one's control may be a healthy response. Consider as a comparison current mindfulness-based approaches to psychotherapy that emphasize the value of "being present with what is."

Integral psychotherapist Mark Forman explores this dimension of difference in terms of a typology:

> Western cultures tend to emphasize an instrumental and assertive style of control, where the person actively seeks to change an internal or external situation. . . . A passive style of control, more common in Eastern cultures, emphasizes acceptance and yielding to those things one can't control; in modern Western parlance, this would be called "letting go" or "letting be."[29]

Each approach may have a potential positive or negative effect, depending on circumstances. Too much or too little sense of control can both turn out to be problematic.

It is also impossible to generalize about Asian Americans, whose countries of origin include Japan, Korea, China, the Philippines, Vietnam, Laos, Cambodia, India, Indonesia, Malaysia, and the Pacific Islands. There are diverse religious backgrounds, such as Confucianism, Buddhism, Hinduism, and Taoism, but also a variety of indigenous healing practices and beliefs in spiritual realms. And due to missionary history, many Asian immigrants embrace some form of Christianity.

Here is a good opportunity to introduce another typological difference with a cultural dimension: individualism versus collectivism. For instance, in Naikan and Morita therapies, drawn from collectivist Japanese culture, the "emphasis would shift from helping the client learn to meet his or her own needs, to helping the client learn to meet the needs of others more accurately and empathically."[30] The latter is viewed as a healthier approach to life.

In the context of this typology, all cultures display a delicate balance or tension between individualist and collectivist orientations, with each culture tending to emphasize one over the other. Mainstream America clearly leans toward individualism, but many cultural groups within the United States are more collectively oriented and experience this conflict in numerous aspects of their lives.

Because of the American emphasis on independence, problems can arise for Western therapists when they fall into the trap of equating collectivism with conformity and enmeshment, and therefore assess this orientation as less healthy. In a similar vein, the Western system of psychological diagnosis includes "dependent personality disorder." Relationally oriented feminist theorists, on the other hand, argue that there should be an "independent personality disorder"! Individualism and collectivism are two different styles, and one is not superior to the other.[31]

These are some of the prominent issues that fall under the heading of personal and cultural styles, highlighting the variety of flavors that are relevant to understanding how human beings differ in their sense of self-and-world. If we want to approach spirituality with an appreciation for variation, this has been a good place to start. What is missing from this account, however, is the territory of *religious* diversity, which needs much deeper elaboration. We will briefly consider this in the next chapter.

In the following chapters the thread of personal differences will be interwoven with "Reflecting on Enneagram Style Variations" sections, since more attention is given to multicultural diversity in the counseling field. But cultural (and religious) differences are still likely to be in play. When personal reflections are invited, I hope that you will consider all relevant sources of variation.

## Reflecting on Personal Style/Flavor

Take some time to consider any reactions you had in response to this chapter. What pushed your buttons? What was overwhelming or confusing? What intrigued you? See if you can make room for whatever thoughts and feelings may be present, and also pay attention to body sensations—tension in the gut or shoulders, contraction in the hands, general discomfort, or excitement. Bringing these into awareness is an important step.

I also invite you to explore your own style and flavor. What do you connect with in terms of the Jungian or Enneagram types? Is there any resonance for you with the descriptions or the associated spiritual leanings? If you are intrigued enough to explore further, you might want to look at the readings suggested in this chapter's notes.

Then consider your responses to the gender/archetypal differences as well as any of the recognized cultural differences. Do you identify with any of these patterns? You may find yourself rejecting any attempts at categorizing, preferring to consider yourself and others as purely individual. I suggest that that, too, is a kind of flavor.

From some spiritual or religious perspectives, such variations may not be very important. If you are connected to a particular tradition or path, explore whether that path has a point of view on this subject.

# Chapter Three

# The Broader Context of Religion and Spirituality in Today's World

Why does this exploration matter? Why now? From an inside perspective, there may be many possible answers. You may find that you want to learn more for professional reasons: you may be in a counselor education program, or want to feel more confident in working with these issues in an existing counseling practice. You may also be curious on a personal level, wanting to make sense of your own experiences and impulses.

From an outside perspective, some of the answers have to do with the prominent roles religion and spirituality play in our world and the emerging direction of professional psychology. You may be curious about the field's attitude toward religion and spirituality: there are forces and trends that are bringing psychospiritual questions into focus. We will now take a look at some themes in this larger outside context.

At the end of the chapter, we will return to an inside perspective, listening to the imagined words of our nine Enneagram characters about the relevance of religion and/or spirituality in their lives.

## Religion and Spirituality in our World

We live in a time when religion features prominently in national and world affairs. While contemporary polls indicate that interest in religion (defined traditionally in terms of church attendance) has declined significantly in Western Europe, this is not the case for its immigrant populations. In Central and Eastern Europe more people are embracing religion as a form of national belonging. For information about religion in public life, the Public Religion Research Institute and the Pew Research Center are good sources. I will use some Pew research in what follows.

A 2017 Pew report on global religious demographics, based on 2015 data, states:

> Christians were the largest religious group in the world in 2015, making up nearly a third (31%) of Earth's 7.3 billion people. Muslims were second, with 1.8 billion people, or 24% of the global population, followed by religious "nones" (16%), Hindus (15%) and Buddhists (7%). Adherents of folk religions, Jews and members of other religions make up smaller shares of the world's people.
>
> Between 2015 and 2060, the world's population is expected to increase by 32%, to 9.6 billion. Over that same period, the number of Muslims—the major religious group with the youngest population and the highest fertility—is projected to increase by 70%. The number of Christians is projected to rise by 34%, slightly faster than the global population overall yet far more slowly than Muslims.
>
> As a result, according to Pew Research Center projections, by 2060, the count of Muslims (3.0 billion, or 31% of the population) will near the Christian count (3.1 billion, or 32%).
>
> Except for Muslims and Christians, all major world religions are projected to make up a smaller percentage of the global population in 2060 than they did in 2015. While

> Hindus, Jews and adherents of folk religions are expected to grow in absolute numbers in the coming decades, none of these groups will keep pace with global population growth.
>
> Worldwide, the number of Hindus is projected to rise by 27%. . . Jews, the smallest religious group for which separate projections were made, are expected to grow by 15%, from 14.3 million in 2015 to 16.4 million worldwide in 2060. And adherents of various folk religions—including African traditional religions, Chinese folk religions, Native American religions and Australian aboriginal religions, among others—are projected to increase by 5%, from 418 million to 441 million.[1]

These numbers give us a snapshot of the role of religion in our world. We need to supplement this by recognizing the dynamic and painful flow of immigrants and refugees whose movements are triggered by religious conflicts and persecution.

## *The Religious Landscape in the United States*

In a 2015 report titled "America's Changing Religious Landscape," the Pew Center reports that the percentage of the population that identifies as Christian is declining, particularly among younger adults.[2] While there are still more people who identify as Christian in America than in any other country, and a majority of Americans (about seven out of ten) identify as Christian, overall there is a decline among Protestants and Catholics. Both the mainline Protestant tradition and the Catholic tradition show a drop, while the Evangelical tradition shows a slight increase or at least stability. At the same time, there are more racially and ethnically diverse people within the Christian segment of the population, and the historically Black Protestant tradition remains largely unchanged. The percentage of Americans who identify with non-Christian faiths has risen slightly, especially among Muslims and Hindus.

The impact of immigration on the American religious landscape is beautifully explored by Harvard University's Diana Eck in her 2001 book *A*

*New Religious America: How a Christian Country Has Become the World's Most Religiously Diverse Nation.* The information in the book is drawn from a body of Harvard research entitled the Pluralism Project, initiated in 1991.[3] While the research may be somewhat dated, the portrayal of religious multiplicity is not. With vivid stories and portrayals, Eck describes this unfolding landscape with chapters on American Hindus, Buddhists, and Muslims. She highlights the distinction between religious *diversity*, which is a neutral term describing the existence of differences, and religious *pluralism*, which is an achievement rather than a fact, actively engaging diversity towards positive goals. Recently we have seen the appearance of more interfaith endeavors that emphasize this pluralistic undertaking in the context of the contemporary religious conflicts in America and the world.[4]

Eck's call for religious pluralism and spiritual dialogue is especially valuable in the context of the current backlash against immigrants and non-Christians. Intensifying immigration to America (initiated by the 1965 Immigration Act), as well as to Europe, has been accompanied by growing resentment of the newcomers. Particularly in the United States, even though church attendance is declining, the identification of "American" with "Christian" (and white) is a substantial force in public conversation. Some Christian Americans strongly believe that America was founded as a Christian country.[5] (Many Americans do not realize that Congress only added "under God" to the Pledge of Allegiance in 1954, at Eisenhower's urging.[6])

As counselors we need to consider multicultural perspectives, but also to understand some of the essential differences within American Protestant Christianity. One of these distinctions is between Evangelicals and fundamentalists. The Evangelical movement itself spans a broad range, but some of the primary characteristics include an emphasis on being "born again," on spreading the word (proselytizing), and on living a pious Christian life. There have been various attempts among Evangelicals to insulate themselves from the negative influence of secular life. Fundamentalism, as I noted in chapter 1, focuses on Biblical literalism and orthodoxy, including a particular view of history that highlights the expectation of the second coming of Christ. For a valuable discussion of

Evangelicalism, fundamentalism, and Pentecostalism, I recommend the discussion offered by Harvard University's Pluralism Project, mentioned in the previous section.[7]

There is another important group to recognize. The 2015 Pew report highlights a growing number of people who identify as unaffiliated, particularly among the younger generation (millennials). In addition, more baby boomers and Generation Xers, and even older adults, report a growing disinterest in organized religion.[8] What do we know about the religiously unaffiliated?

## *Spiritual but not Religious*

The 2015 Pew Center report tells us that about a third of older millennials (those in their late twenties and early thirties) claim to have no religion, a figure up considerably from a 2007 survey. What is concealed by these statistics is *additional* information about the growing number of people who, when asked about religious affiliation, report "none."

These respondents may include atheists, meaning they do not believe in God or gods, and agnostics, meaning they don't know whether there is a God and are noncommittal on the matter. A more recent Pew survey (December 2017) focuses on what Americans mean when they say they do or do not believe in God.

> Seven-in-ten religiously unaffiliated adults believe in a higher power of some kind, including 17% who say they believe in God as described in the Bible and 53% who believe in some other form of higher power or spiritual force in the universe. . . . None of the survey respondents who describe themselves as atheists believe in God as described in the Bible. About one-in-five, however, do believe in some other kind of higher power or spiritual force in the universe (18%). . . . None of the survey respondents who describe themselves as atheists believe in God as described in the Bible. About one-in-five, however, do believe in some other kind of higher power or spiritual force in the universe (18%).[9]

A great deal depends on what questions are asked and how they are phrased: the picture is more complex than it appears on the surface.

We learn some details from surveys that go beyond the "none" category to include the more informative "spiritual but not religious" option, which applies to a growing segment of the American population. A 2012 Pew report suggests that while these respondents are skeptical about religious organizations, they still have a meaningful spiritual orientation. The information that follows gives us a more nuanced picture, despite drawing from an older survey.

> A new survey by the Pew Research Center's Forum on Religion & Public Life, conducted jointly with the PBS television program Religion & Ethics News Weekly, finds that many of the country's 46 million unaffiliated adults are religious or spiritual in some way. Two-thirds of them say they believe in God (68%). More than half say they often feel a deep connection with nature and the earth (58%), while more than a third classify themselves as "spiritual" but not "religious" (37%), and one-in-five (21%) say they pray every day.[10]

Australian scholar David Tacey offers an intriguing perspective on this phenomenon: "In stable times, spirituality is the personal and lived experience of the revealed mystery celebrated in religious services, prayers, liturgies, and sacraments."[11] However, in times of change, volatility, and disruption, spiritual energy seeks its own spontaneous expression, and there is a widening split between spirituality and religion.

Here I want to offer a practical note for therapists: if an intake form asks for "religious affiliation," without providing other options, important information may be overlooked. "None" may be a valid response, but does not leave the door open for "spiritual but not religious."

Those who identify as spiritual but not religious are moving away from the traditional emphasis on doctrine, rules, and authority, but are also exploring a wide range of options. They are often characterized as "seekers," and are both praised and criticized for these inclinations.[12] Their degree of commitment to the search varies considerably. Some seekers are seriously dedicated to a process of learning and deepening. They may draw on more than one tradition, or none, but are usually invested in a disciplined approach involving daily practice. Whatever their particular framework of meaning, they consciously seek to surrender personal ego and experience a deeper Truth or Reality. Sometimes this path is described as interspiritual.[13]

Other self-identified seekers are more motivated by novel discoveries, by an ongoing exposure to new paths and practices that promise to enhance the seekers' current lives. This orientation has come under criticism for remaining superficial, offering comfort and satisfaction to the ego rather than focusing on substantial transformation. Wade Clark Roof, a religion professor, describes some baby boomers as content to shop around in the "spiritual marketplace."[14]

Sociologist of religion Robert Wuthnow offers a framework that suggests there are two essential orientations. One is a *spirituality of dwelling*, which emphasizes familiar themes such as belonging, security, stability, and responsibility. The predominant images are those of temple, priest, and king. The other is a *spirituality of seeking*, which leans toward the search for home and community, growth and exploration, negotiation. Here we find images of tabernacle, prophets, journey, and pilgrimage. Each has its gifts and limitations. The conflict between these two orientations characterizes much of the current discord around religion and spirituality in America.[15]

## Reflecting on "Velcro" Issues and Button-Pushers

Let's shift to an inside view for a moment, in order to unearth prejudices and biases. First, explore these questions on your own, and then, ideally, with one or more colleagues or friends. Be as honest as you can.

- What words, phrases, or images (related to religion or spirituality) "hook" you? Evoke a negative gut reaction in you—an aversion or pulling away, a literal tightening in your gut? What uncomfortable pictures form in your mind? What religious gestures make you cringe or make your heart race? Are there any parts of what you read so far in this chapter that you find inviting or reassuring?

- What religion-related news items arouse instinctive negative reactions in you? Positive reactions?
- What thoughts, judgments, or strong opinions are triggered? Take time to notice their impact as well as their content.
- What experiences in your past make you vulnerable to these triggers? Reflect on any history that may be relevant.
- If you give yourself some space to notice these reactions, are you able to step back a bit? Take a few slow deep breaths. Notice the tensions in your body. Keep breathing. Are you aware of any personal experiences behind your responses?
- What can you carry forward from this exploration? It is crucial to be clear about our biases and limitations, and important to make use of supervision or consultation to explore and work with our triggers.

## *"Mapping" Religions and Spiritual Perspectives*

For those who are drawn to religion/spirituality, there are many paths and many different frameworks of meaning and practice. I cannot do justice here to such a vast and complex territory, but find that establishing a context of basic information can be helpful. Here is a simplified contemporary "map" with pertinent vocabulary.

### WESTERN RELIGIONS

The three main religions that fall into this category—Judaism, Christianity, and Islam—are also known as the Abrahamic traditions, since they share a common Semitic root and trace their ancestry to the figure of Abraham. Although we may describe them as Western, their common geographic roots are actually Middle Eastern. They are monotheistic religions and mostly text based or scripture oriented. Christianity and Islam are focused on specific texts, beliefs, and doctrines, while Judaism takes a more pragmatic interest in guidelines for living, action, duty, responsibility, and community.

## EASTERN RELIGIONS

This category includes Hinduism, Buddhism, Jainism, and Sikhism. There are many forms of Buddhism, ranging from Tibetan Buddhism to Zen. Despite their common origin, these paths differ in meaningful ways. In China, Buddhism is joined by the ancient paths of Confucianism and Taoism. These are not monotheistic traditions, but vary widely in their beliefs, practices, and traditions.

The newer religion of Baha'i (founded in 1863) draws from both Western and Eastern traditions.

## INDIGENOUS RELIGIONS

This category includes a broad range of ancient traditions, many of which have found their way into the modern world. They are the religions of the First Peoples, typically orally transmitted, animistic, and oriented toward nature (the earth) and ritual. They are found everywhere on the planet: Africa, Asia, the Americas, Oceania (South Pacific), and in Europe (where they persist largely as mythologies). Pagan or neo-pagan religions and neo-shamanic paths are contemporary revivals of some of these ancient traditions. We find deep respect for Native Traditions in some North American spiritual groups, although some Native Americans feel that their teachings have been coopted by non-natives.

## OTHER VARIATIONS

Many religions have an *exoteric* version (for the general public) and an *esoteric* version (for those who have progressed to an inner circle with a more advanced level of knowledge.) Alchemy, a major inspiration for

Jung, is a Western esoteric system; others include occultism, Rosicrucianism, and Gnosticism.

The Western traditions also have mystical versions, such as Sufism (Islam), Kabbalah (Judaism), and mystical Christianity (Catholicism). These paths are pursued by some who describe themselves as spiritual but not religious. We may think of mysticism as the path of seeking communion or union with Ultimate Reality, the Divine, spiritual truth, or God. The emphasis is on direct experience, intuition, or insight. Mysticism is often associated with esotericism, but they are not identical. For instance, magical traditions are typically considered esoteric but not mystical. The notion of mysticism can be redundant in the Eastern religions, but there are some branches (such as Advaita Vedanta in Hinduism, and Dzogchen in Buddhism) that may be considered more mystical than others. There is also a host of new religious movements, smaller groups founded since 1850; these take a wide variety of forms in all parts of the world.[16]

Contemporary spiritual paths that are becoming increasingly familiar to many through the media and personal acquaintance include American forms of Buddhism and mindfulness practice, the recovery movement, and approaches that are rooted in nature (for example, Native American, neo-Pagan). Less widely recognized is the emerging interest in nondual paths influenced by Eastern traditions and brought to popular attention by Eckhart Tolle, in particular. The Diamond Approach is a contemporary spiritual approach informed by contemporary psychology and psychotherapy. A label that is widely used, but with very little agreement as to its precise meaning, is "New Age." Broadly speaking, New Age movements are Western, contemporary, eclectic, alternative, and based on direct experience. They often overlap with interest in holistic health and alternative approaches to healing.[17]

Whether as counselors and therapists or as citizens and seekers, we are likely to encounter people for whom religion or spirituality has deep meaning, and their beliefs and practices vary widely. To use the language of Stephen Prothero, a professor of religion at Boston University, we need to develop *religious literacy*, but also, I suggest, *spiritual literacy*.[18]

Given the current picture we are discussing, there are ample reasons to educate ourselves.

We have now established two important frameworks. First, we have briefly considered the place of religion and spirituality in the contemporary world and in the United States. The second framework is a basic map of religious and spiritual traditions. Let's turn our attention to a third outside view: the relationship between the discipline of psychology and the domains of religion and spirituality.

## Psychology's Relationship to Religion and Spirituality

Bringing psychological and spiritual concerns together in substantive ways is no easy feat, since the discipline of psychology has historically not taken religion or spirituality seriously or has been highly suspicious of this territory.

### *Historical View: Separation*

The gulf between the field of psychology and religion dates back to the beginnings of the former in the late nineteenth century. The challenge for the emerging social sciences (sociology, anthropology, psychology) was to establish their respectability by following the path of the physical sciences. The latter had achieved noteworthy successes since the sixteenth and seventeenth centuries by firmly discarding the medieval reliance on the opinions of religious authorities (the Catholic Church) and on metaphysical analysis. The foundation of real knowledge, both philosophers and scientists maintained, was the crucial combination of empirical (sensory) observation and reason. Being modern, educated, and scientifically oriented meant being committed both to rationality and to the evidence of the senses.

This commitment (articulated in the philosophy of logical positivism) was understood to be the basis for the scientific study not only of the physical world, but also of the human mind and human behavior. Here, too, freedom from religious constraints was viewed as essential for progress. A firm differentiation had to be maintained between the young discipline of psychology and the "soft," murky territories of religion and spirituality. There was much to be learned about the human mind and behavior, but religion and spirituality, while recognized as traditional human concerns, were at best irrelevant to the science of psychology—and threatening at worst.

## *Trends toward Integration*

As recently as the 1960s, all signs in Western culture seemed to point toward the conclusion that God was dead. The discipline of psychology was free to pursue its scientific questions and concerns. But over the years there have been countermovements toward the meaningful integration of spirituality and psychology.

An early bridge was created by American philosopher and psychologist William James in his work *The Varieties of Religious Experience*, published in 1902. Carl Jung, who died in 1961, was also a pioneer in this regard, and Jungian psychology continues to be a prominent pathway to exploring this interplay. James Hillman, Thomas Moore, and Robert Sardello have taken his work in powerful new directions. Robert Assagioli, who died in 1974, was another pioneer who differentiated a lower unconscious from a higher unconscious. He saw the latter as the source of material from realms *beyond* the personal psyche. Assagioli's work is most fully reflected in the therapeutic approach known as *psychosynthesis*.

Transpersonal psychology developed out of humanistic psychology in the late 1960s and early 1970s, and has continued to represent a commitment to integrating the best of Western psychology with the wisdom of the world's spiritual traditions. The transpersonal school, however, remains marginal within the field of American psychology, finding wider embrace in the international arena. The most recent outgrowth of this movement has been integral psychology, originally conceived in the mid-1990s by Ken Wilber, but now being further developed by other theorists and practitioners. I find Jungian, transpersonal, and integral perspectives helpful and thought provoking, and incorporate them in this volume.

We now see evidence that, in general, the dividing walls are thinning, apart from the existence of specific theoretical orientations. One sign of this opening is the growing number of publications on the topic by the American Psychological Association and the American Counseling Association, beginning around 2000. Both organizations also took a significant step by adding "competencies for addressing spiritual and religious issues" to their list of professional competencies. These include understanding of diverse cultures and worldviews, and of human and spiritual development, self-awareness, communication skills, and relevant skills in assessment, diagnosis, and treatment.[19] In 2013, the American Psychological Association published a valuable resource in the form of the two-volume *APA Handbook of Psychology, Religion, and Spirituality*, which should be in every graduate psychology program library.[20]

There has also been a burgeoning interest in Buddhist perspectives in professional therapeutic circles as well as in the world of spiritual seekers and practitioners. Mindfulness practice has emerged as a major focus in both, along with compassion practice, although sometimes with a focus that is more practical than spiritual.[21]

But despite the evidence that religion and spirituality continue to figure prominently in American lives, when therapists are advised to consider their clients' religious orientations, this is often placed under the heading of *multicultural diversity*. This is an important perspective, but I feel it misses deeper dimensions of meaning.

Another force is also at work. Psychology has expanded into the general population, which displays a growing awareness of the psychological dimensions of life. A relatively large number of Americans are "psychologized." They use psychological language, buy self-help books, and think about themselves and their lives in psychological terms. *They are also exploring the potential connections between psychology and spirituality for themselves*.[22] It is difficult to say how widespread this is, but chances are that this is a modern trend that will continue to expand. Whether it proves healthy or valuable is another question. There are critics who point out the dangers of self-absorbed narcissism in this preoccupation with psychological issues.[23]

Numerous educational efforts in the popular domain reach out to both professionals and the larger public. In 2017, an online Psychotherapy and Spirituality Summit was sponsored by Sounds True, a multimedia publishing company dedicated to the "dissemination of spiritual wisdom." Thirty presenters from different backgrounds explored the "emerging synthesis" of Western psychotherapy and spiritual practice.[24] The summit featured such well-known teachers as Jack Kornfield (Buddhist), Bill Plotkin (eco-psychologist and depth psychologist), Stan Grof (transpersonal psychologist), Pat Ogden (embodied relational mindfulness), John Welwood (psychotherapist), and Mariana Caplan (yoga teacher and psychotherapist).

Research suggests that there is still a considerable gap between the orientation of psychologists and counselors and that of their clients, with many more clients than therapists reporting an interest in religion and spirituality.[25] Where does this leave the client searching for a therapist who is not only open to this territory but also knowledgeable and skilled?

Clients search for insights and help in the rapidly growing internet market, such as the summit I just described. They consult the spiritual marketplace, read books, and go to workshops and retreats. The names of these teachers and writers may be familiar. They come from a variety of traditions and perspectives: Carolyn Myss, Pema Chödrön, James Hollis, Thomas Moore, Joan Borysenko, Clarissa Pinkola Estes, Marianne Williamson, Deepak Chopra, Tara Brach, Jack Kornfield, and Eckhart Tolle, to name a few.

Will the profession keep expanding its capacity to respond more effectively to the needs and interests of these clients? If we want to understand more of the human experience, we have come far enough in our commitment to empirical science that we can now soften the boundaries. A psychology that can open to aspects of human life that are *beyond* the rational (not the same as *irrational*) will be a richer discipline.

## *What Might Clients Bring to Therapy?*

Clients may bring a wide range of religious or spiritual orientations to therapy. Our initial challenge is to pay attention, follow subtle hints, express interest and curiosity, and remain open and receptive to whatever presents itself. We need to learn as much as possible about how these matters might interface with clients' lives so that we don't miss potential opportunities for both healing and growth.

Some clients are staunch followers of the religion in which they were raised. Some are lukewarm toward that religious background but have not explored options for deepening or searching elsewhere. Others have discarded their religion of origin (whether traditional or alternative) and are either completely disinterested or wary-but-curious about exploring other options. We may meet clients who have no grounding in a particular tradition but are consciously looking for relief, meaning, and guidance, often motivated by their own pain. I have found, for instance, that losing a loved one to death often sparks a search: "I know there must be something more." A client who learns mindfulness practice as a way to relieve anxiety may unexpectedly discover that the practice opens the door to something larger. Some, as previously noted, are drawn by widely available online resources and by books and workshops that promise relief from suffering or new horizons to explore. A few clients may be seriously committed to a spiritual path but find themselves encountering psychological challenges along the way. If they are intent on meeting these challenges rather than doing a spiritual bypass (see chapter 9), they seek out therapy as a vital part of their work.

If there is no interest—or outright rejection—that is fine. In situations where it is unclear, I have learned to listen deeply for subtle clues that point the way to hidden longings, intuitions, or wounding. When we remain alert to hints that show up in dreams or in somatic experiences, we may be surprised by what emerges. It is important that we then feel enough confidence to "follow the bread crumbs" and explore further. Having some basic frameworks of understanding can help us discern the subtle interplay of psychology and spirituality, to support clients and also challenge them when appropriate.

## Reflecting on Enneagram Style Variations

Let's hear from the nine characters who were introduced in the previous chapter. I offer words that are representative but not necessarily what a client might say in therapy. Spirituality or religion might enter the conversation much more subtly, sometimes as a tentative feeler to see if the therapist is paying attention and cares enough to ask more. But what follows might be the characters' overall perspectives and their relationship to the information presented in this chapter. If the Enneagram is new to you, I suggest you go back and look at these characters' basic descriptions before proceeding.

**Rob (Eight, Challenger):** I'm not really looking for anything magical here. I just know there has to be something more. I want some kind of real connection, and I'm not feeling that in my life right now. Maybe that's partly my fault, but there has to be something worth going after and committing to. I'm kind of bored with my life, it feels flat. I don't connect with Judaism any more, and even when I was growing up, it was mostly about tradition and history. I have no interest in believing in a new God, or any particular doctrine. Something practical and down-to-earth would be good. Of course, I do like the highs I get with pot and stuff. I kind of miss that, but I know I can get addicted and am not going there. I have a good Jewish buddy who's really into Buddhism and meditation right now. Seems to be a thing these days. Maybe I'll check that out.

**Devin (Nine, Peacemaker):** It feels like I've been on the spiritual path forever. I was always looking for peace, and love, and harmony, which isn't surprising since they were mostly missing in my own family. As an African American, I don't see much of those qualities in the world around me either. I liked my ACOA group when I was younger. We all shared on a deep level and were tuned into spiritual questions. I've checked out a lot of paths since then: some New Age stuff, and Eastern religions. I learned Transcendental Meditation and read about near-death experiences and Tibetan Buddhist monks. I did meditation and yoga retreats. I guess I was the classic spiritual seeker. I *loved* exploring. But I still don't have a focus, and I'm getting older. I really want to work with a therapist who is comfortable with all of this, knows some of the territory, and isn't going to judge me. But I also need someone who actually *is* a therapist and can help me deal with some of the personal stuff that may be in the way. It's all connected.

**Charles (One, Perfectionist):** When my wife died, I lost everything. She was my best friend. She was my connection to the church. Somehow when I lost her, I lost the connection with my faith. I don't feel like going to church anymore, or even praying. I guess maybe I'm angry at God, and I wonder if he's angry at me. I thought I was a good Christian, followed the commandments, was a contributing member of my church, but I'm not sure if it was enough. The Episcopalian church has felt like a good mix of ritual and sermons and service and learning. But now here I am all alone, my wife gone, and kids that don't connect with me much. I honestly don't know what I believe anymore. But I'm afraid to do nothing, afraid that God will be angry at me. I'm scared to walk out of the church, like that would make me a worthless person. This is all I know. Seems like a poor reason to stay, but that's how it is right now. I know everyone says I need grief counseling, and I think I do, but I hope this can be part of it.

**Sienna (Two, Giver):** I've put so much energy and love into my church. It's been like family, maybe the family I wish I had growing up. I really looked up to my pastor and did everything I could to help and support him. My mother was way too liberal and flaky, all over the place, into woo-woo stuff. I wanted something solid and real, where people could worship together and support each other. Some place where being a good, loving person would be appreciated. My mom used to tell me I was too *nice* to people. Isn't that what we're *supposed* to be? Merciful and kind? And then Pastor B. acted like all our giving didn't really mean anything to him. I know this happens sometimes—but not in *my* church home! Maybe I need to talk to some other Christians and see how they deal with this. I need some help from someone who won't make fun of my faith but can make space for all my feelings and questions. I want to have something valuable to teach my kids.

**Linn (Three, Achiever):** I've never been into religion. My parents brought over their mix of Christianity and Buddhism and folk superstitions, and they hung on to them even more because immigrating was so traumatic for them. None of it ever made sense to me. So I guess I made them happy in other ways, mostly by being successful. The American dream, right? But now this weird thing happens and it makes no sense to me. Am I crazy? I can't tell anyone. I've been so focused on recovering physically from the accident, I haven't really had much time to think about my bizarre experience, but I need to talk to someone who can help me figure it out. Not someone who will preach religion, please. Just someone who knows what I'm talking about, who can see how scared I am, and who can either tell me it was just a brain thing or something other people have gone through and made sense of. Does it mean anything?

**Janice (Four, Romantic):** I follow my own path. I guess I always have. It's not religious, has no belief system or rules. I just feel there is a purpose to life, a meaning, but I need to go deep inside to explore what it is for me. I do believe there are other dimensions and realities, but I'm not really a New Age person. I don't want to follow anyone else. I want to listen to my own inner voice and my dreams and let them guide me. I'm tired of feeling different. "Too sensitive" was my label growing up, and it was painful. I've been depressed a lot and even felt ashamed of that. But I guess I have to face that I *am* different in some ways, and try to make peace with who I am. I really need to feel connected to a therapist who can understand and appreciate me, and support me through all this change and searching.

**Kyle (Five, Observer):** I don't really feel comfortable talking about that deeper stuff. It's very private. I'm not religious myself, though I find it pretty interesting and have read a lot. It's just too rigid for me, like you have to believe what you're told to believe. I want to think for myself. I had good talks with my parents growing up, even after their divorce. I know about some Eastern religions from my mom, and my dad always liked the sixties stuff, even though he missed it. So he talked about peace and meditation and yoga. I just kind of watch what other people do and think it all over. Most of my friends are not really into spiritual stuff, though one guy says he's a Christian and did the whole born-again thing. He's kind of fallen off, I think. But—and this is private—I do have these experiences sometimes that I don't share with anyone. Like touching some place that's *more real* than this one. When I'm alone and quiet. Hard to describe, but wow. Still got lots of Big questions, with a capital *B*.

**Gabriela (Six, Loyal Skeptic):** It's all so confusing. I kind of wish I was still back in my safe little world, with my parents and husband and kids. My community. But I had to go after this dream. I wanted to learn how to really be useful to other people, and I needed to go back to school to do that. Now I'm praying to God and Jesus and Mother Mary to help me find my way. So many new ideas and questions. Some days I just want someone to tell me what to believe. But I can't go back, and that's hard for my family. I still go to church but I'm full of doubts, and they can tell it's not the same. I feel like I'm disrespecting them, and my husband just tells me I'm making life too complicated. I don't know where this will all end up, and I want to be a good example for my kids, but I have to keep going. I need some place to sort this out, with someone who won't make fun of me for feeling confused, and definitely someone who won't think having doubts is a sin.

**Marissa (Seven, Enthusiast):** Wow. This is all so crazy. I was just living my life, having a good time. My parents weren't super happy with me because I wasn't really interested in going to church any more. They were kind of worried, but I was fine! Then cancer shows up. It turned my world upside down. I need help dealing with it, obviously, but I want someone who gets what it's like to be scared of dying, and to feel really different from all my friends. I'm having so many intense feelings I just don't want. And I keep wondering: Why? What's going on? My parents just tell me to pray, but it's not that simple. Something's missing, and I have to be free to check out every possible thing. I have so much more life to live and things to experience! How can I make it through and not just give up because it's all a meaningless game? Will I ever feel happy again?

## What Our Times Are Asking of Us

We have now considered some of the landmarks that can guide us as we make our way in this psychospiritual territory. The historical big picture, the times in which we live, may also feel relevant to some readers. While humanity has endured many major upheavals, and life on the planet has survived earlier catastrophic events, what if we now have a significant opportunity to shift our trajectory and make choices that have profound consequences? This endeavor to change our global course requires the contribution of many perspectives and skill sets—from the physical and biological sciences, the political and economic disciplines, the psychological and social fields of study, *and* the arenas of religion and spirituality.

The more we understand about religion and spirituality and their interplay with psychology, the better prepared we will be to respond creatively to the needs of our clients and of the world.

Psychologist Kenneth Pargament points out that spirituality is, for many, a source of support and guidance in times of stress. He makes a wider claim as well:

> There is a deeper dimension to our problems. Illness, accident, interpersonal conflicts, divorce, layoffs, and death are more than "significant life events." They raise profound and disturbing questions about our place and purpose in the world, they point to the limits of our powers, and they underscore our finitude. These are, as theologian Paul Tillich (1952) put it, matters of "ultimate anxiety": the anxiety of fate and death, the anxiety of emptiness and meaninglessness, and the anxiety of guilt and condemnation. These deep questions seem to call for a spiritual response.[26]

James Fowler uses the term "ultimate concern."[27] The times in which we live feel like ones of ultimate concern—times when we are asked to draw on all of our psychospiritual resources in order to bear, and help clients bear, the fears, the grief and despair, the anger and confusion. Embracing the interplay of psychology and spirituality may also help us create healthier options. Is it possible that our understanding and skills could contribute to the growth and transformation that are needed?

## Reflecting on Purpose: Why Does This Exploration Matter?

Take a few minutes to reflect on what has brought you to this inquiry, whether it's part of an educational program, a professional learning agenda, or a personal search for understanding. Whatever your motivation—curiosity, deep interest, passionate desire—give this question some time to take root in you. What matters enough to keep you reading?

Is it primarily an intellectual curiosity? Or is there some feeling or emotion behind it? Imagine pursuing the exploration fully, and then give yourself some time to imagine giving it up completely. Do you notice any feelings or sensation in your body when you contemplate either option?

Take note of any memories that may emerge in this process, or imagined outcomes. Pay attention to whether your focus is primarily personal, professional, global, or all of the above. There might be some anxiety about *not* knowing enough: What are the imagined consequences of that? What might be exciting about pursuing this subject?

In the next chapter we move in a more intimate direction, from this larger context to the deep and familiar territory of human suffering. How may spirituality and religion offer resources for clients who are struggling and in pain?

## Chapter Four

# Spirituality as a Resource

At some point during our lives we are all likely to suffer, struggle, or feel lost and alone. We often say, "We are only human." Implying what—that we're limited? Fallible? Weak? Imperfect? In contrast with what—God/Goddess? A higher power? Some Divine and perfect Being or Reality? When we experience losses and crises of all kinds (death, divorce, illness, injury, abandonment, abuse, midlife crisis, job loss, loss of faith) in the context of our only-humanness, we often instinctively cry out for help, support, courage, and guidance. In times of great stress, grief, or fear, even "non-believers" may turn to a higher power. It is clear that religion and spirituality serve as a resource for many, whether or not they belong to a specific religious tradition or follow a particular spiritual path.

Acknowledging and exploring this experience is important in terms of understanding our role in the helping professions. This chapter focuses on the basic question: How can spirituality serve as a helpful resource? The perspective will mostly be an inside view (of subjective experience), but we will start out with an outside look at some research efforts.

## Research Directions

There is a substantial body of research that confirms the value of religion in our lives. One of the prominent figures in this field is Harold Koenig, director of Duke University's Center for Spirituality, Theology, and Health. He is a highly regarded psychiatrist who has devoted his professional career to exploring how spiritual and religious involvement can affect both physical and mental health.

As a researcher, his first challenge is defining the object of study. Here is his definition of religion: "Religion may be defined as a system of beliefs and practices observed by a community, supported by rituals that acknowledge, worship, communicate with, or approach the Sacred, the Divine, God (in Western cultures), or Ultimate Truth, Reality, or nirvana (in Eastern cultures)."[1] He adds that religion usually involves a set of scriptures or teachings and a moral code of conduct.

Spirituality, he recognizes, involves broad connections with meaning, purpose, inner peace and comfort, feelings of wonder, awe, and love. He urges health professionals to be as broad and inclusive as possible in their definition of spirituality so that they can meet the needs of their patients. But these aspects of spirituality are too vague for the purpose of research, so Koenig proposes that *in the context of research*, spirituality needs to be defined as having some connection to religion, whether traditional or nontraditional (such as astrology, witchcraft, and indigenous traditions). This stipulation is pivotal to his work.

In general, Koenig's research suggests that greater religious involvement is related to better mental health, which also directly impacts physical health. Here are some glimpses of his findings:

- Everything else being equal, religious people experience higher levels of well-being, happiness, and life satisfaction.
- Many people turn to religion for comfort and meaning when they encounter difficult circumstances, especially those involving loss, change, illness, or trauma.

- Research indicates that religious people, everything else being equal, experience fewer consequences of uncontrolled stress, including less depression, less anxiety, lower rates of suicide, and lower likelihood of drug or alcohol addiction.

Involvement in faith communities plays a crucial role, which is consistent with what we know about the positive effects of social support when in crisis.

As valuable as these indicators are, much of the research has been conducted with Christian populations in Western countries, although this is changing. In addition, the scope of the research is limited since clear and measurable definitions of spirituality are challenging to produce. So we have the research-backed injunction to take religious resources into serious consideration, but we are also left not knowing much from formal research about the role of broadly defined spirituality in getting us through difficult times.

## The Landscape of Suffering

The term *suffering* can be problematic for some people. While the literature of most religions addresses the place of suffering in human life, the attitude toward that suffering varies. Traditions often explore the causes as well as ways of enduring or alleviating suffering and finding higher meaning through the suffering. On the other hand, you may have heard the saying: "Pain is inevitable, but suffering is optional" (sometimes cited as a Buddhist proverb, but also attributed to Japanese author Haruki Murakami.[2]) The premise is that pain is more physical, while suffering involves mental pain that we create or increase through our thoughts, beliefs, and stories about ourselves and what is happening. Suffering is especially likely when we reject and go to war with our pain. This more psychological dimension is highlighted when the Buddhist word *dukkha*, often translated as "suffering," is translated instead as "dissatisfaction."

When our minds are dissatisfied with or fighting against the pain that comes our way, we fall into suffering.

While this second point of view has gained considerable traction in spiritual and some professional counseling circles, it can be challenging for some people who feel that it carries a subtle form of judgment. Because many people do relate to the compassionate implications of the term *suffering*, I choose to use it here. In its root sense, after all, to suffer simply means to bear from below, or to undergo. If you are more comfortable with a phrase like "emotional pain," feel free to substitute that language.

## *The Longing for Comfort, Strength, and Guidance*

When we suffer, what do we seek that spirituality and religion might offer? Some evocative words come to mind: comfort, consolation, solace, reassurance, soothing, strength, courage, guidance, hope. Drawing on Jewish and Christian tradition, here are the words from psalm 23: "Yea, though I walk through the valley of the shadow of death, I will fear no evil: for thou art with me; thy rod and thy staff they comfort me." (23:4 KJB) And from psalm 18: "The Lord is my rock, and my fortress, and my deliverer." (18:2 KJB) Some people may turn to religious figures (Jesus, Mohammed, Bodhisattvas, Krishna, Hestia, guardian angels) as well as to havens of natural beauty, wise guides, or teachers (a guru, an imam, a rabbi, a grandmother). It can be helpful to have a relationship with a tradition which offers compassion for us in our suffering: the Sufi tradition, for example, encourages us to embrace the ten thousand sorrows as well as the ten thousand joys.[3] We plead, we pray, we surrender, we bow our heads, prostrate ourselves, are brought to our knees. Even if we have never connected with any figure or force in this way before, we may find ourselves going down this road for the first time. We may feel led to new or old sources of comfort such as music, painting, a book, a special friend, a place in nature. Sometimes the strength or inspiration or comfort comes out of the blue, unsought, unbidden, and we find ourselves in gratitude.

## *Darkness*

Suffering often feels like darkness. This brings to mind the image of the "dark night of the soul." In its original usage by Saint John of the Cross, a sixteenth-century Spanish mystic, the phrase referred to a particular aspect of the spiritual journey toward union with God: the individual loses the gift of God's presence and blessings, and undergoes a purification in which detachment from everything is demanded. But the phrase is often used these days to refer to any kind of difficult time or spiritual crisis (and in this wide application, unfortunately, is sometimes trivialized). We may experience the dark as frightening, and fear it will never lift.

## *Feeling Lost and Alone*

In the darkness, there is often a sense of absence: no light to see by, but also no presence, company, or guidance. The experience of darkness can coincide with feeling lost and alone. Sometimes there is a feeling of floating alone in the vast darkness of space, as some clients have described it to me. The loss of God's presence, or of any presence larger than our own, can feel devastating, like the deepest abandonment. Muslims may find solace in praying with the angels. In Mary Stevenson's poem "Footprints in the Sand," the poet laments to the Lord that she has been walking all alone, but learns that the reason she sees one set of footprints only is that the Lord has been carrying her.[4] Strength and presence are also reflected in the image of clinging to the Rock of the Divine: "Rock of Ages / cleft for me / let me hide myself in Thee." Here we have a palpable sense of solid and unwavering support. We find refuge. Any experience of feeling accompanied, held, carried, or supported may be welcome.

We can help clients look for and notice these kinds of resources, and need to validate and explore them when they appear spontaneously. I have often heard clients speak (once they know they won't be seen as crazy) of feeling a loved one nearby, hearing a whisper, or sensing clear guidance toward some path of action. Clients, in the midst of suffering, have found this kind of support through the felt presence of a protective wolf figure from childhood, the bodhisattva of compassion (Kuan Yin), an ancestor, or an angel. This kind of sacred experience is held closely, only to be shared in a safe space with someone who can be trusted to receive and honor it.

Related to the experience of aloneness is the sense of feeling lost. Dante expresses this in his famous words (variously translated) from the opening to the *Divine Comedy*: "In the middle of the journey of our life I came to myself in a dark wood, where the direct way was lost." The way forward is hidden, obscure. Where to turn? In these moments we cannot *think* our way through by the light of what we already know. With some clients who express a desperate desire to get out of a painful place, I may suggest that the way out is the way through, but this can be an overwhelming thought unless it is clearly accompanied by the commitment to accompany them along the way. The familiar words of "Amazing Grace" express it this way: "I once was lost but now am found." Here the longing is described from the perspective of coming home, bringing together the deep gratitude for the experience of being found by Another with the relief of no longer being lost.

## *Shame and Worthlessness*

Childhood sometimes leaves an imprint of *shame*, a debilitating legacy that undermines one's sense of being fundamentally "OK." Shame plays a huge role in the context of spirituality, reflecting a deep experience of not being, in one's essence, lovable or worthy. This is the ultimate denial of one's soul, spiritual essence, relationship to God, or participation in the Divine Ground of Being. In the grip of shame, the relational dimension of life is both the source of pain and the potential path to healing and self-compassion.

It is intriguing to note the perspective of the Dalai Lama and other Tibetan teachers:

> [They] have spoken of their great surprise and shock at discovering just how much self-hatred Westerners carry around inside them. Such an intense degree of self-blame is not found in traditional Buddhist cultures, where there is an understanding

> that the heart-mind, also known as buddha-nature, is unconditionally open, compassionate, and wholesome.[5]

The roots of our Western vulnerability to shame are unclear. Perhaps it has something to do with Western individualism, as contrasted with more collective, communal cultures. Whatever the source, feeling unlovable or worthless at the core is a profound source of suffering. Human love and kindness can gradually penetrate this dark hole of self-judgment, but sometimes help comes through an essential spiritual experience. Such openings vary in focus: having inherent value as a child of God, being a vital participant in the mystery of life, an inseparable part of the One Reality, a valued member of a healthy religious community. Whatever the framework of meaning, a taste like this can initiate a healing process. Identification with a worthless self begins to open to something inexpressible: intimate Presence, unconditional Love.

## *Liminal Space*

The experience of feeling lost is also an aspect of being in *liminal space*. This phrase comes from the work of anthropologist Arnold van Gennep, who describes rites of passage that are found in many cultures.[6] These initiations involve a transition from one social group (e.g. children) to another (adults), usually in three phases: *separation* from the old group/identity, *liminality* (the in-between space), and *incorporation* into the new group/identity. The rites-of-passage model is valuable in helping clients frame their experience when they feel in-between worlds and identities, lost, at sea, directionless, confused, and afraid. (It is helpful to draw a simple sketch of the three phases, emphasizing the experience of empty liminal space in the middle.)

The word *liminal* comes from the Latin word *limen*, meaning "threshold." When we are in liminal space, we are literally on a threshold between two worlds or realities. The experience is typically one of disorientation and fear. The old reality no longer holds, and the new is invisible, unreal. Indeed, it may be helpful just to hear that there *is* a new one ahead, that it will emerge in time. Even learning that this is an ancient and well-known experience can alleviate some anxiety and desperation.

This perspective is relevant for several of our Enneagram characters, including Charles, Janice, and Marissa, all of whom are in transition. A striking example is also evident in clients who leave their religion of origin and find themselves in liminal space between communities and meaning systems. This is particularly devastating for those whose religion of origin has strong boundaries in terms of membership, beliefs, and practices, such as Jehovah's Witnesses. Those who choose to leave this path are dis-fellowshipped and shunned by family and community, potentially losing access to health care and employment. They typically experience a loss of identity, home, and relationships, living without a sense of solid ground until new ground slowly emerges.

Despite this deep experience of loss, liminal space may also be a potential opening to a transformation in consciousness. We are *between* the established roles and realities of the past and a future reality that we cannot yet see. The hidden key in the traditional experience of liminality is, however, that there were guides—initiated elders, for instance, who held the space and served as way-showers. As therapists we can play this role, in however modest a form, *if* we are aware and prepared.[7]

## *Embodied Experiences of Suffering*

In the territory of suffering, I am often reminded of what Donald Winnicott, English pediatrician and psychoanalyst, describes as the "primitive agonies" of the young infant who experiences a breakdown in the mother-infant bond:

- going to pieces
- falling forever
- having no orientation
- complete isolation

These are primal fears associated with the absence of a secure base. Clients may experience feelings like these in the midst of their suffering, not simply as thoughts but in their *bodies*. No wonder they are not "coping well." If we have had our own taste of this kind of suffering, we know the territory intimately. If not, we can at least try to imagine what it might be like. Later we will turn our attention to the particular needs of clients who have experienced trauma, but for now we can simply recognize the existence of these primal fears. At times only turning to Something Beyond, Something Larger, can begin to offer what is so desperately longed for, whether that comes in the form of direct experience, faith, practices, or intuitively reaching beyond ourselves.

This is not to minimize the significance of the therapeutic relationship: the space offered by a fully present, compassionate other is crucial. But spiritual resources have their own depth and power. When we welcome them in our therapy practice, their value to clients may even be strengthened by the shared relational field in which they are held.

What can spirituality offer clients in terms of practices that can sustain, soothe, and offer comfort?

## Where We May Turn

Before we consider more traditional practices that can be helpful, I want to highlight some experiences that many people seek to sustain themselves through times of suffering. Prominent among these is time in nature: walking in woods or by water, sitting under a tree, contemplating a sunset, listening to birds. These are often mentioned as sources of help. What do they offer? A feeling of peace, a sense of being part of something larger and ongoing, a belonging, an unexpected opening to beauty, a resonance with *life*. These experiences have a spiritual flavor, and are often acknowledged as such. For many of those who identify as "spiritual but not religious," nature is their church, temple, mosque or synagogue.

Some find refuge in listening to music. Whatever its style, music has the power to surround us with something beyond words, to soothe the heart, and sometimes literally to bring the body and the breath into a harmonious rhythm.[8] Others turn to creative expression of various kinds: drawing or painting, singing, movement or dance, playing an instrument. In the process of creating and expressing there can be a kind of release, a solace, an opening into relationship with something larger. A possibility emerges of seeing or feeling something in a new way. Dreams may also be a vital source of comfort, strength, and guidance. As we attend to the images, explore themes, and experience being "visited" by imaginal figures, we may open to a deeper Reality or Presence and feel listened to, cared for. (The imaginal realm will be a focus in the next chapter.)

Some clients may already have some kind of altar space in their homes, either featuring a traditional religious figure or created along more personal lines: a candle, a photo of a loved one who has died, or a flower. They may simply call it their special place. Asking if a client has such a place can open up a deeper conversation about spiritual or religious resources. If this place memorializes someone who has been lost, there may be some comfort in lighting a candle and sitting in this dedicated space, where the person feels the permission to remember, to cry, to have an inner conversation, write, or listen to special music. We may even suggest to some clients that they create such a space to invite, honor, and hold their grief. (When grief is too overwhelming, sitting in this kind of contained space for a limited period of time can actually offer boundaries for the flood of feelings.) If the altar is dedicated to a religious figure, we can respectfully ask about its meaning and importance, listening for mention of comfort, strength, or guidance. One of my clients talked about how angry she was at this holy figure because of the suffering she had been experiencing, but still she came and sat at her little altar to share her heart and open herself to some possibility of grace.

We turn our attention now to spiritual practices as a resource.

## *Prayer*

For those who align themselves with a religious tradition, this territory is probably familiar. For the spiritual but not religious, or for those counselors who have negative associations with a religion of origin, exploring this domain may feel challenging. But this is a well-worn pathway in human experience and deserves attention. If our clients tell us that they pray, we would do well to approach respectfully and ask if they would be willing to share with us *how* they pray.

We first need to appreciate the different kinds of prayer as well as their different systems of classification.[9] While many prayers are addressed to a personal God or holy figure (including angels, guides, ancestors), reflecting an I-Thou relationship, others may go out to the Universe, the Mystery, the Infinite. One of my clients simply calls it The Big. Most familiar, especially in the context of crisis or suffering, is *petitionary prayer*, in which we ask for a particular outcome for ourselves or others (*intercessory prayer*). *Ritual* or *liturgical prayer* refers to prayers that are prescribed, familiar parts of religious texts or rituals. Their familiarity may be part of the comfort that they offer. *Contemplative prayer* is more receptive, opening to the Divine presence, waiting and listening. There is a contemporary revival of a practice that originates in the Catholic tradition, *Lectio Divina*. This involves reading a passage of scripture (or an alternative), meditating or reflecting on its meaning, praying as a form of dialoguing with God, and finally, sitting in silent contemplation. *Invocatory prayer*—repeating the Divine name, for instance—may help by centering our attention and calming our agitated minds and bodies. This is similar to the recitation of a mantra in Hinduism. *Colloquial* or *spontaneous prayer* is a conversation with God or one's Higher Power. Finally, *prayers of adoration and praise* may be less common in the context of suffering, but can be soothingly familiar if they are a client's form of regular practice.

One young client had been given a complex, life-threatening diagnosis. In her early twenties and a recently converted Mormon, she described her prayer life as a powerful source of strength. While some people had told her that she must not be praying hard enough or she would be healed, she clearly affirmed her view that not all prayer leads to healing. "Things also happen to make you grow. I believe every life has a plan. I like having that strength. I pray to endure it. I get comfort from prayer." This was a powerful, spontaneous expression of the power of prayer as a resource.

Prayer may emerge from *trust* that something larger than ourselves is present or available, a "felt sense of being held by a benevolent presence or field that is greater than the little me."[10] But for many who feel lost and alone in their suffering, prayer is not so much a matter of trust as a *reaching for faith*, in relation to a new or once-familiar belief in *something*. At the edges of such reaching is the perspective suggested by Trappist monk Thomas Merton in a widely quoted observation: "Prayer and love are really learned in the hour when prayer becomes impossible and the heart turns to stone."[11] Sometimes no words can be found. Even reaching out seems out of reach. How comforting it can feel to clients to hear this message, to consider that even *this* frozen aloneness may be part of an unfolding journey. They glimpse the possibility of believing that they are essentially in good company. How moving it can be to realize that while crisis or loss can propel us into the dreaded experience of nothingness or groundlessness, we may at some unknown point emerge, unexpectedly, with the gift of trust and felt presence.

For those who are uncomfortable with the theistic or dualistic implications of prayer, there are alternative perspectives. Even if, for example, I do not believe in a separate transcendent Being, when I am suffering I may well *feel* alone, separate, lost, small. Prayer may then be experienced as a spontaneous movement of yearning and also of self-compassion, opening to the pain that is present in the moment rather than attempting to tough it out in a cold, impersonal universe. We might approach prayer "as a bridge that is accessible to us in our seeming condition of distance, confusion and longing. It provides a sense of direction, a *towardness*, a flowing, a promise of reconnection."[12] The atheist or agnostic who is shocked by his own impulse to pray in the face of devastating loss, for instance, may find this perspective helpful. The counselor can normalize the movement *toward* a source of strength and comfort as natural. The longing for support and connection is human. These impulses do not have to originate in belief or in a dualistic view of reality.

## THE GOD-IMAGE

Carl Jung's concept of the God-Image can serve as a rich source of insight for therapists. Jung suggests that all we can know of God is our own psychic image of God. All that we can interact with is our own experienced images; whatever the Reality might be, it is beyond our comprehension. So from a psychological perspective it is useful to understand the nature of someone's God-Image, which often seems to reproduce early object relations with a caregiver.

For instance, an idealized image—God as "all good"—may take the form of the grand Old Man or the perfect Heavenly Mother. The difficulty here is that this all-positive image is often inadequate to address human pain and suffering, and the client's response is likely to be confusion, disillusionment, or anger. If the expectation is that God is always fair, then how *unfair* life's trials can feel. Someone who had a punitive parent may relate to an omnipotent Policeman God who bullies him into being good but has no compassion. Either way, totally positive or punitive, such a one-sided image is likely to prove too limited and small. If we expect limitless comfort with nothing asked of us, or if we experience a God who only makes demands and punishes us for being imperfect, our image of God still remains bound within an early developmental pattern. Such a God-Image, rooted in childhood, may be inadequate to respond to the fullness of life, either its sorrows or its gifts.[13]

The coping strategies that we developed early in life may shape our prayers during times of suffering. We may plead for help from, or helplessly defer to, an All-Powerful Being. (I distinguish between *deferring* and *surrender*, which can have a deeper meaning.) We may fear a judgmental God who belittles our prayers and pleas as spiritually weak, thus leaving us mired in guilt and shame. We may feel conflicted about praying because long ago we learned the survival strategy of self-direction and independence: "I'll do it myself." We may be angry at a Supreme Being who appears vengeful and unjust. So if a client talks about praying, it is important for us to explore with them *how* they pray.

### THE PLACE OF PRAYER IN THERAPY

Some of the literature on spirituality and counseling raises a more controversial question: Should we *pray with* our clients? Unless we clearly share the client's spiritual framework, this is a delicate issue. When asked by one client if I would pray with her, I responded that I would be honored to be present as she prayed. I closed my eyes and offered my silence as I witnessed her prayer, and that seemed to work well for her. Inviting the client to take the lead is usually wise. Some therapists might feel more comfortable *praying for* their clients in some form that is meaningful for them (the therapists), outside of sessions.[14]

### Reflecting on Personal Reactions to Spiritual/Religious Resources

If your experience of your religion of origin was challenging or painful, you may have strong reactions to some of these ideas about how spirituality or religion can serve as a resource. I encourage you to bring as much compassionate awareness as possible to your bodily responses, emotions, and thoughts. What in particular leads to an experience of contraction and pushes your buttons? Which resources, if any, feel most problematic to you? The more you can bring awareness to these experiences and be honest about them (to yourself, perhaps to someone else), the less power they will have to determine your subsequent choices and actions.

## *Meditation*

Meditation has gained recent recognition in psychotherapy, particularly in the form of mindfulness. There are different approaches to meditation, and different purposes for it. In some contexts, of course, people practice meditation for spiritual growth and deepening. Here I will focus primarily on the ways in which meditation may be helpful as a spiritual resource for those who are suffering.[15]

## CONCENTRATION PRACTICES

One form of meditation practice emphasizes concentration: repeatedly bringing the attention back to a single point of focus. The mind is in the habit of wandering all over the place—"monkey mind" is the common phrase. In that wandering we keep returning to thoughts about our suffering, thereby adding more layers, and in the contemporary language of neuroscience, solidifying the associated neural pathways. We get more and more lost in our pain. Practicing the art of returning the attention to a visual focus such as a candle flame, to a word or mantra, or to the sensation of the breath, can provide some relief and even some peace.

We have to realize that it is the nature of the mind to wander and that the practice actually consists of bringing attention back to the focus over and over again. Trouble arises when we react with horror to the realization that we are not in control of our thoughts, and we begin to judge ourselves for "failing" at the task of concentration. Meditation teachers repeatedly remind us that the key is simply to refocus attention without judgment, with compassion. I like the image of a toddler who repeatedly wanders off on the playground. Our task is simply, kindly, to go and take the wanderer by the hand and bring him or her back, over and over. For some clients, staying out of the clutches of the superego or judging mind is a significant challenge in itself.

The effects of meditation often include a temporary calming of the mind and quieting of the body. If we practice enough, we can develop a habit of returning to the practice in small ways throughout the day, whenever we find ourselves "lost" in our suffering. Is this a spiritual resource? Yes, if it is held in the context of returning to a deeper source of strength, comfort, and peace. It all depends on the way we approach the practice. The experience of quieting may even allow us to open to a sense of something greater than ourselves. On the other hand, a concentration practice may also be undertaken in a purely secular context, simply as a useful tool for quieting the brain and body.

## AWARENESS PRACTICES

The same applies to what is often called awareness meditation, which may serve a spiritual or purely pragmatic purpose (stress management). This practice usually begins with a focusing of attention on a single object such as the breath. Then the invitation is to open up, like opening a camera lens wide, and allowing whatever is there to be present in awareness, without holding on or pushing anything away. Teachers may suggest initial images to help the meditator get the feel for open awareness: imagine watching clouds (thoughts) float across an open sky or leaves floating down a river. Awareness simply notices, without grabbing at anything or trying to get rid of it. There is simply a flow: being present with what is.

Perhaps the most well-known approach to this type of meditation is mindfulness-based stress reduction (MBSR). Originated by Jon Kabat-Zinn in the 1970s to help patients at Massachusetts General Hospital, MBSR has now been welcomed into the world of counseling. The format is usually an eight-week program with trained facilitators. There are also books and online programs available for teaching the skills of mindfulness meditation, including both concentration and awareness approaches.

Meditators find that this experience offers both some distance from the sources of suffering and also a taste of freedom from *identification* with these sources. "I am not my thoughts or emotions or stories." This concept of disidentification, which we discussed briefly in relation to the Enneagram, plays a particularly important role in psychospiritual growth. Whether we dialogue with various parts of the self, work with dreams, generate new narratives, or practice mindfulness, we often find that some ability to disidentify from our conditioned definition of self opens the way for new experiences and perspectives.

Just as prayer may reflect less than ideal relational and coping patterns from a psychological perspective, meditation too may turn out to be problematic. For instance, this ability to simply notice or disidentify may serve a defensive pattern of detachment. If we use meditation to disengage, to avoid any and all pain or discomfort, we are walling ourselves off from the vulnerability and natural fullness of being human. This is known as *spiritual bypassing*. I am distinguishing here between a dry, aloof kind of detachment and a gentle, compassionate nonattachment, an ability to be present with whatever is arising in experience without getting so caught up in the story/drama of "me."

While meditation can lead to defensive distancing, it can also produce reactivation. Counselors need to know that intensive meditation can have a disturbing impact, especially on clients with a trauma history. The deep internal focus can unearth buried material and trigger somatic memories. (We will return to the subject of problematic psychospiritual experiences in chapter 9.)

## MEDITATION AND THE BRAIN

Research on this topic has mushroomed in recent years. Developing some familiarity with this outside perspective may be useful for psychotherapists, as well as for more skeptical clients. One of the best-known sources is the work of Rick Hanson, whose book *Buddha's Brain: The Practical Neuroscience of Happiness, Love, and Wisdom* interweaves research information with practices and exercises.[16] The concept of neuroplasticity suggests that we can rewire our brains through meditation practice, so that well-worn pathways toward negative states can be replaced with new pathways toward more positive ones. At the heart of this approach is the principle, now widely acknowledged, that neurons that fire together, wire together. The implication is that meditation practice can, over time, not only serve as a temporary resource but also shift our ongoing experience.

In their book *Altered Traits: Science Reveals How Meditation Changes Your Mind, Brain, and Body*, Daniel Goleman and Richard Davidson introduce a valuable distinction between the deep path and the wide path in meditation.[17] The deep path follows the focus of the spiritual/religious traditions in working toward a profound transformation and awakening. The wide path forgoes the spiritual motivation in favor of helping a larger number of people cope with destructive emotions and difficult thoughts. The effects of meditation include enhanced capacity for attention, more consistent access to internal quiet, greater ability to regulate emotional states, and reduction in the experience of physical pain. There are also studies suggesting that particular practices, such as those focused on loving kindness and compassion, actually do enhance those capacities over time.

**DEEPER DIMENSIONS OF MEDITATION**

In its emphasis on the immediate pragmatic effects of meditation, therapy sometimes overlooks the deeper dimensions that may emerge if we keep going. This is the deep path. As we allow the flow of content, we may find ourselves not just liberated from identifying with the content itself but also beginning to realize that what is always present is the Awareness itself, sometimes described as the Ground of Being or the Divine Mystery. The Awareness is the "I" that is limitless, spacious, transparent, and at the same time not separate from the content that arises. This can be directly, intimately known, although it is beyond words. Such a perspective goes beyond the resources of comfort, strength, and guidance, and will be explored further in chapter 8.

## *Practices with a Specific Healing Focus*

Some practices are specifically designed to help with difficult emotions (fear and anger, for instance) and with cravings. Roger Walsh, a transpersonal psychiatrist, has created a useful resource that draws from a wide range of spiritual traditions.[18]

For instance, Walsh suggests that we may be suffering because we have an underlying craving. Working with its root attachments can be a powerful remedy: paying close attention to the sensation of craving itself, reflecting on the costs of craving, and recognizing underlying thoughts and beliefs (for example, "I must have *x* in order to be happy."). These are not appropriate for loss and grief, but might be useful for attachment to physical pleasures. In terms of difficult emotions, he recommends some gentle approaches: facing and exploring the actual experience of fear, for example; or recognizing the costs of anger, communicating about the anger, and recalling our own mistakes. Walsh also introduces higher octaves of practice, such as finding your soul's desire and cultivating love and gratitude. We see a gradual movement from a resource emphasis to growth-oriented practices.

## *Devotional Practices*

Other meditation practices, less well known in the mainstream but part of many religious and spiritual traditions (particularly theistic traditions), are more devotional in nature. Transpersonal psychologist Brant Cortright describes these approaches as soul paths as opposed to spirit paths, in which deep connection with a Personal Divine is the focus. Meditating on the heart or on the Beloved may be wordless, and may involve chanting, dance, or contemplation of an image. Any of these can bring comfort and a sense of presence to those who are feeling lost and alone in their suffering.[19] While awareness practices emphasize quieting or observing the activity of the mind, devotional practices highlight opening the heart and soul to the deeply intimate love of the Divine. These practices are less widely accepted in the context of secular therapy.

Clearly, when a client says that he or she meditates, this can mean a wide variety of things. Just as with prayer, counselors need to understand more about the client's particular approach. It's also helpful to ask about frequency of practice, length of a typical meditation period, and experiences that may arise during or after meditation.

We have so far considered spirituality as a resource in terms of the search for comfort, sustenance, and strength. Consideration of rituals and acts of forgiveness begins to point us in a slightly different direction, toward the search for meaning.

## *The Power of Ritual*

Almost any action that has a sacred intention may serve as a resource when we are suffering. Rituals are particularly important because they often have a symbolic dimension that moves us out of the ordinary realm, touching on the mysterious and the transcendent. I am referring to forms of enactment that have the power to comfort, strengthen, and heal. Some rituals are familiar cultural, religious, or family practices. Whether we are speaking of traditional mourning rituals, rituals of worship, or holiday rituals, these may offer a sense of relatedness, containment, and remembrance (reminding us of what is of abiding value and importance, for instance). When working with clients who are searching for spiritual support, it is important to explore the presence of such traditions in their lives.

On the other hand, this kind of established ritual may no longer hold meaning for some. They may find it empty or restrictive, and chafe at its boundaries. In this case, more personal, nontraditional rituals may be worth exploring. Bear in mind that for some people the word *ritual* has negative connotations, and we need to watch for that. We can talk instead about ceremonies or simply symbolic actions.

A ritual that has personal significance may be spontaneously created and enacted, or designed in collaboration with a therapist. In either case, it is important to reflect on the purpose of the ritual. Is the client feeling a need to call for higher help, or to reaffirm belonging to a larger community (sometimes one that is beyond the physical)? Is there a longing to enact the experience of feeling lost and searching for "home"? Does the client want to acknowledge an ending of some kind in her life, to allow herself to remember and honor someone or something of deep value? Once the intention is clarified, then attention can turn to possible symbolic actions and objects. While words may be spoken during a ritual, these symbolic dimensions are what give ritual its unique power in our lives.

Symbols offer outward expression of an inner reality, typically involving a "nonverbal, bodily experience of meaning."[20] The choice of objects and actions depends on the intention: clients may want to include objects that symbolize what they have loved and/or lost, or a spiritual source of comfort and sustenance, or a change they are undergoing.

Symbolic actions are often connected to elements in nature. Fire and burning, or simply using a candle, can symbolize letting go or a transformative process. The theme of releasing may be expressed with water: setting objects in water to float away, or throwing objects (such as rocks) into water to sink to the bottom, out of sight. Earth may lend itself to burying (endings) or planting (sowing seeds of hope, continuation, or beginning). Air allows us to let something go in the wind, or connects us with higher realities through rising smoke. (Please note that releasing balloons, however, is an environmental hazard.)

Other symbolic actions include cutting, breaking or ripping, sewing or binding together, gathering together what was separated, and physical gestures (raising one's hands, touching the heart, holding hands, kneeling or lying down). As I mentioned, there may be a desire to symbolize the experience of feeling lost and alone, or reaching out to an unknown source of strength. Pictures and artwork may play a role. Dreams may be enacted. The possibilities are wide open, and intuition often serves well.

Sometimes the symbolism emerges in unexpected ways. One of my clients, a middle-aged man, was struggling with his father's death. The relationship had been complicated: the father was highly critical and demanding, and my client was ambivalent about his death. After we worked through a lot of his mixed feelings, he decided he wanted to do some kind of ritual. Together we came up with the idea of burying some of his father's small belongings in a special place in his backyard, with the intention of laying something to rest and making peace with the reality of the relationship. I supported him in designing the ritual, which he planned for the end of the week. When I saw him the following week, he had a powerful story to tell. He buried the objects on Friday. When Sunday came along, he changed his mind and decided he wanted to keep his father's watch, so in a ceremonial spirit, he dug up the belongings and retrieved the watch. Only afterward did he realize that the Friday of the burial was Good Friday and the Sunday of "resurrecting" the watch was Easter Sunday. For him, the impact of this synchronistic timing added an unanticipated depth to the ritual.

Traditionally, rituals have been performed in community. It can be powerful to invite a community (or even one co-participant) to witness and honor the experience, to "hold space" together. But sometimes there is a strong desire to enact a ritual alone. If a client feels a strong need for a solo ritual, even after we have explored the positive aspects of sharing with a witness, then the therapist may serve as a kind of witness when the client returns to describe his or her experience.

This worked well for a client whose significant other had died. She was not accepted in his family, so was not included in his funeral. Since he was buried in a neighboring state, and she was searching for closure, we agreed that this was important enough for her to travel to his grave. Together we designed a ritual that included the opportunity for intimate communication with him, recognizing their spiritual connection and the depth of the meaning that their relationship had for her. An essential part of the ritual involved taking a tape recorder so that I could be indirectly present as a witness. When she returned from her trip, she played the tape for me, and we were able to experience and reflect on the ritual together.

## *Forgiveness as a Resource*

There are other forms of action that may serve as resources as well. I am thinking particularly of forgiveness, which is a complex subject that receives considerable attention in contemporary books on spirituality and counseling. An act of true forgiveness may indeed bring comfort and a sense of peace. At the same time, I am wary of religious pressure to forgive, since a peremptory rush to forgiveness may be an attempt to avoid feeling pain. If clients can explore the experience of hurt first, then the healing move toward forgiveness may come from a more grounded place.[21]

There is also the profound challenge and gift of *self*-forgiveness. When plagued by guilt, clients often benefit from some reality testing to explore whether the guilt is in any way warranted. If there is some real culpability, then exploration of religious or spiritual resources can prove invaluable. Confession may offer some comfort to Catholics, for instance, but in other contexts as well, actions of confession and atonement may open up pathways to the crucial sense of being forgiven by the Divine or Higher Power.

This is powerful and evocative territory. Let's pause to consider how some of these resources might be relevant for our Enneagram characters.

## Reflecting on Enneagram Style Variations

Have any of the experiences described thus far in this chapter resonated for you? If so, take some time to feel into the specifics of your own process. If you have connected with one or two of the Enneagram patterns at this point, take a few moments to consider how your relationship to suffering might be related to your Enneagram perspective.

Let's consider suffering through the lens of the Enneagram Four pattern (the Individualist or Romantic) and the Seven (the Enthusiast or Epicure), as contrasting types. The Four, as part of the Feeling Triad, is often familiar with feelings of melancholy and abandonment. Some Fours feel relatively at home in these darker places and want to be met in those depths. But Fours may also find themselves drowning and losing hope of surfacing again. These descriptions are a good fit for Janice, our Four. She feels she has been alone and misunderstood a lot in her life, and relates deeply to the experience of feeling lost and unsupported. She needs to feel the solid presence of her therapist beside her.

While she is not drawn to a particular religious tradition as a source of comfort, metaphors and images have a lot of meaning for her. They speak to the deepest part of her, which she calls her soul or spirit. We listen together for the images that emerge spontaneously, taking time to explore them. Dreams can be a valuable source of images and stories.

One image that holds meaning for Janice is that of crossing a vast desert alone, in despair, searching for direction. As we periodically revisit her experience of this image, a sense of a presence gradually emerges. She begins to experience this as a guiding female figure, a wise older woman, and over time this being becomes a potent source of comfort and strength for her. Finding a resource like this is often important with Fours because they can fall into a trap of romanticizing their own suffering and may need encouragement to focus on possibilities in the present.

The Seven, on the other hand, is part of the Thinking Triad, and is typically uncomfortable in the deep waters of feeling or suffering. Sevens prefer to be upbeat and positive. They love having new possibilities to explore. The dark is both frightening and limiting, so they often try to minimize or disconnect from their pain. When escape from suffering is not forthcoming, Sevens need a great deal of gentle support and may find an introduction to spiritual resources helpful.

Our Seven, Marissa, has tried to minimize the impact of her cancer and to maintain an almost cavalier attitude of detachment. But simply staying mentally positive hasn't worked. She has been brought to her knees by the cancer experience, and finds this frightening and unfamiliar territory. The first step is to help her acknowledge that she is masking her fear, and then to offer some information about the natural emotional process she is experiencing. As she begins to acknowledge the deeper feelings that are present, we can work to strengthen her inner and outer resources.

Spirituality becomes meaningful as she begins to share more authentically with her family, and unexpectedly, her grandmother in turn shares more of her own Native American roots. Marissa is eventually able to appreciate the quiet of the Five (a connecting line for the Seven), which helps her to open to the solace and strength she finds in nature, in the simplicity of natural forces, rhythms, and creatures. Instead of seeing her body as the enemy of freedom, she slowly opens to feeling her larger energetic connection with the sacred mystery of the natural world. She is surprised to find herself learning to pray and to perform traditional Native American rituals within the context of this belonging.

What about some of the other characters? As an Eight, Rob is not likely to speak in terms of suffering; he is more likely to use terms like frustration and restlessness. Well into his counseling process, he is able to get in touch with a young and vulnerable part of himself (along the line to the Two) that he has been protecting for years. His challenge is to soften his defenses and open to this hidden need, but he is not interested in comfort or support as such. What does turn out to have meaning for him is meditation. As he begins to explore Buddhism and mindfulness practice, he likes the initial challenge of learning concentration and later learns to sit in open awareness. The more he is able to notice the thoughts and feelings that capture his attention, the more he can allow himself to be present with the vulnerability of his young self. He also begins to recognize the existence of a space that is still, quiet, and unaffected by the commotion. Although he complains about the slow pace of his learning and about his lack of control in this process, he gradually begins to have more access to clarity.

Since Devin (Nine) has such a broad background of spiritual experiences, she has numerous resources and practices to draw from when she feels especially lost or in need of guidance. Still, in her most painful moments, she feels empty, without a core. Nines often fall asleep to their own deepest needs and desires. When Devin is invited to remember moments of feeling more grounded, she is able to recall experiences of strength and focus while sitting with a spiritual teacher or in deep meditation. It is easy to forget these resources in the midst of suffering, so therapists play a valuable role when they inquire into possibilities or offer reminders. When Devin laments that she used to feel more of a foundation, a helpful response is: "When did you have an experience like that? Can you share that with me?" Then she is invited to feel this in her body and allow it to expand and deepen. For Nines it is often especially important to invite attention into the belly and lower torso. The anger that they avoid also holds the energy they need, so we want to open the door to gut anger and "fire in the belly." Such fire can also come from spiritual resources: it is not necessary to focus only on peaceful experiences.

With Charles (One), we need to make ample space for his grief as we look for spiritual resources. At first these are difficult to find, because they were originally connected with his wife or the church. But eventually he recalls quiet moments looking at a stained-glass window or reading a psalm. When he contemplates these memories, he is inspired to seek out these kinds of experiences again and, in these contexts, finds himself feeling more at peace with God. The weight of judgment, God's or his own, sometimes melts away. He even recalls a dream, after his wife's death, in which he felt a mysterious presence. At the time he interpreted this as Jesus. Now he is not so sure of that interpretation, but is able to revisit the experience to help him feel less alone.

Sienna (Two) wants very much to draw on her faith to help her through the painful experience with her pastor and church. She remembers favorite hymns: "Amazing Grace," "Be Thou my Vision," "His Eye is on the Sparrow." When she softly hums or sings them in our sessions, she opens her heart and feels "held up." Special moments come to mind: a deeply moving connection with her Bible study group, the births of her children, a strong feeling of being watched over by a guardian angel in the midst of prayer. These are precious and sustaining to her.

Linn (Three) can only think of one memory she would describe as a spiritual experience. She remembers sitting as a young child in front of her parents' Buddhist shrine. On one occasion she felt an unfamiliar but immense feeling of peace that lasted for several minutes. She never told anyone about it. Her near-death experience evoked a similar feeling at one point, but she is so conflicted and confused about the meaning of this experience that it is not until some time has passed that she can allow herself to revisit some of what she felt.

For twenty-two year old Kyle (Five), resourcing in this way does not feel relevant for quite a while. He certainly has had some strong experiences that he considers spiritual, or at least mysterious, but he guards them closely. They may serve as internal resources for him when he feels especially lonely. But some time passes in his counseling process before he allows his intellectual identity to soften enough to share his social and emotional vulnerabilities. At that point there is the possibility of inviting him to share some of his private experience. We explore cautiously, wary of possible spiritual bypassing when we move in this direction, but open to the resourcing potential of a deeper sense of identity and a larger view of reality.

Finally, let's consider Gabriela (Six). In the context of her major life transition and anxiety, resources are very much needed. While relaxation, grounding in her breath and body, and a practical approach to mindfulness are all helpful, she encounters more of a challenge when she looks for religious sources of comfort, strength, and guidance. She is experiencing a conflicted relationship with her Catholic background, so it is essential to listen carefully for cues about what has meaning for her. At the same time, encouraging her to talk about her experience in her new women's group unearths some new images that appeal to her.

We feel our way slowly. She continues to sense a meaningful connection with the Blessed Virgin as a comforting mother figure. She is surprised that she still finds Communion to be a soothing experience: she loves the familiar ritual, especially the sense of being fed by the Holy One. "I can feel loved even though I have doubts." Her women's group has exposed her to new spiritual lenses and themes. For instance, being a spiritual seeker is an ancient path and is permissible. It is all right *not to know.* She finds it reassuring that there is even a mystical medieval text called *The Cloud of Unknowing.* The existence of such a religious tradition offers both permission and encouragement to make peace with not knowing (which is particularly challenging for a Six). Practices begin to take on more meaning than creeds and offer new resource experiences: she can simply practice the presence of God.

For all these characters, and for many of our clients, the search for meaning is also an essential aspect of their healing journey.

## The Search for Meaning

The experience of devastating loss or crisis can propel people into a wasteland of meaninglessness. These are times when nothing seems to make sense, and there seems to be no point in anything. Our reasons for getting up in the morning, for living itself, all feel shattered and empty. We may be unaware of the fundamental, life-sustaining assumptions that make up our worldview until we find ourselves trying to keep going without them. We take them for granted until they are gone.

There is a cognitive aspect to this experience: "The assumptive world concept refers to the assumptions or beliefs that ground, secure, or orient people, that give a sense of reality, meaning, or purpose to life."[22] On the other hand, we miss the depth of the experience of meaninglessness if we only focus on the mental aspect of cognition and belief. On a phenomenological level, our lives tend to unfold within a *felt sense* of identity and meaning: Who am I? What is my life about? What is real? What really matters?

We may encounter this loss of meaning in clients who are grieving the death of someone they love, and in clients who can no longer participate in an activity they love because of physical injury or illness. Retirement for someone who has been fully invested in his or her work may precipitate the loss of meaning that we label *depression*. Individual and collective trauma often precipitates loss of meaning as well.

Human beings are meaning-making creatures: most people seem to need meaning in order to live. Austrian psychiatrist and Holocaust survivor Viktor Frankl compellingly describes how even the most precarious experience of meaningfulness can keep people alive in the hell of a concentration camp.[23] Without meaning, we fall into despair, or into a mechanical existence, or we die. In the wake of loss or trauma, we can feel the shattering of the assumptive world immediately, but there are so many other survival issues pressing for attention that the search for meaning is more likely to emerge later in the healing process. Then we may recognize that, in addition to the loss or trauma that we consciously recognized, we have also experienced a spiritual crisis or a loss of faith that was not evident at first.

What might this search for meaning look like? This varies widely. Cultural and personality patterns play a prominent role. Some people may engage in intense introspection and need to spend considerable time alone, reflecting on their lives and experiences. Some read hungrily for possible guidance, or devour internet sources. Some talk with friends, relatives, strangers, therapists, fellow seekers, raising deeply existential questions about human purpose, a larger plan, the nature of reality, the point of it all. If they use religious or spiritual language, then the focus may be on God or a Higher Power: How could God let this happen? What does God want from me? What could possibly make any spiritual sense of this? Is there some bigger picture I can't see or understand? A religious community or teacher may offer guidance.

Again, the individual's God-Image often comes into play. In the Old Testament, Job starts out with the assumption that God is "fair" and sustains order and justice in the world—a common assumption and a potential source of suffering. Eventually he comes to accept that he is unable to comprehend the mind of his Creator. His search for meaning brings him to his knees before the Mystery.

Regardless of the presence of religious language and stories, this search for meaning is essentially spiritual in nature. Here are the words of James Fowler:

> Our real worship, our true devotion directs itself toward the objects of our ultimate concern. That ultimate concern may center finally in our own ego or its extensions—work, prestige and recognition, power and influence, wealth. One's ultimate concern may be invested in family, university, nation, or church. Love, sex and a loved partner might be the passionate center of one's ultimate concern. Ultimate concern is a much more powerful matter than claimed belief in a creed or a set of doctrinal propositions. Faith as a state of being ultimately concerned may or may not find its expression in institutional or cultic religious forms. Faith so understood is a very serious business. It involves how we make our life wagers. It shapes the ways we invest our deepest loves and our most costly loyalties.[24]

Some may not agree with such a broad definition, preferring to maintain the connection between spirituality and a transcendent or ultimate reality, whether defined theistically or not. I am suggesting that we maintain a spacious perspective as we support clients in their search for meaning: what is of ultimate concern to human beings is life-giving or life-enriching, and when they have lost touch with this kind of faith, they often fail to thrive.

## *Potential Concerns about Clients' Choices*

The search for meaning sometimes leads clients into territories that we may not feel is sacred or even healthy. We need to explore these together, accompanying clients in their search as much as we can. In the process we may find ourselves inclined to challenge their choices, as we do in other therapeutic contexts. If we sense deeply that the meaning toward which they are gravitating is too shallow to serve them well—if their gods are too small (insufficient to help them cope with the complexities of life) or offer false promises (such as alcohol or drugs)—it is important to consider those limitations with them.[25] We can raise questions and invite exploration.

## *The Wisdom of* Not *Challenging Religious Beliefs*

Raising questions is one thing, but directly challenging religious or spiritual beliefs is rarely productive. Here is the advice of psychotherapists James and Melissa Griffith:

> In therapy, it may be more risky to inquire about a person's religious beliefs than about his or her metaphors or stories of spiritual experience, unless a solid sense of trust and safety has been already established in the relationship.[26]

Commitment to religious beliefs is often deeply rooted and not open to casual questioning: these may be profound *convictions*, not simply provisional assumptions. A religious belief is not simply an idea, but is rooted in specific physical states that may be described as "emotional postures." The Griffiths describe the latter in terms of perceptual, cognitive, and motor systems of the brain that create a state of focused attention and readiness for action. There are two major categories: emotional postures of tranquility, and emotional postures of mobilization.

A healthy spiritual life, the Griffiths suggest, grows out of emotional postures of tranquility, nurturing such qualities as reverence, peace, compassion, and inner reflection. The beliefs that underlie this kind of emotional posture are typically *assumptions*. In contrast, *convictions* are empowering and passionate, sometimes engendering positive emotional postures of mobilization: Gandhi, Martin Luther King, Jr., and Mother Teresa were moved by such convictions. But if rigidly held, convictions tolerate no argument or obstacle. The resulting mobilization can be destructive, as we see all too often in our contemporary world.

## *Alternative Ways of Suggesting New Possibilities*

Attempting to challenge or argue with a client's religious or spiritual convictions is not usually a wise path. It may be more helpful to focus on the stories and metaphors within which these beliefs are embedded. The Griffiths suggest a rich array of therapeutic possibilities that revolve around meaning-making in a narrative tradition, giving attention to metaphor, stories of spiritual experience, and imagined conversations with God.

As we listen carefully, we may hear spiritual comfort or distress described in terms such as these: "I felt as if I were wrapped in a warm quilt of light." "It was like being left to swim alone in a vast ocean with no land in sight." "I was thrown into a pit of darkness by some force with no mercy." These are worlds of experience that convey meaning or meaninglessness.

In response, we may wonder with the first client: "What does it feel like to be wrapped in this warm quilt? Is it always available for you? If you feel the need to move, can you take it with you, or are there times when you want to put it aside? What kinds of experiences evoke this feeling? What is the source of this light?"

In the metaphor of the ocean, questions such as these may open the door: "How long does it feel like you have been swimming like this? How do you keep going?" The image suggests that the client feels abandoned, perhaps by Spirit or the Divine: "You felt you were left alone and helpless . . . was there some kind of Presence with you before this?" There may well be a story associated with this metaphor, and if so, we need to hear it. We may learn that it is recent, associated with a particular loss or crisis, and we can ask about a possible connection with the sacred before this time. On the other hand, the client may reveal that this is an old story of loneliness and struggle, going back to family of origin. Then we may be able to make space for the pain and offer compassion. Eventually we may elicit an alternative story by searching for some unnoticed element or asking about unconsidered possibilities.

Some metaphors are simple and clear, while others have multiple dimensions. With the client who felt she was swimming without land in sight, after our initial exploration I continued to check in with her over multiple sessions. "How is the swimming today?" A day came when she connected with the experience and exclaimed with surprise, "Oh! I see some land off in the distance!" Then we had a new experience, a new metaphor, and a new possibility of meaning. "What is it that offers the possibility of ground, of rest? Is it there even when you can't see it?" The spiritual dimensions of this may or may not be explicit, but the themes of ground and of refuge have rich possibilities. At some point I shared Langston Hughes's poem "Island," in which he asks, in the simplest of words, for the "wave of sorrow" not to drown him, but to take him to the island that lies somewhere ahead. She felt less alone, and sensed some exhaustion draining from her body.[27]

For the client in darkness, questions like these might arise: "What was happening before you were thrown in? Do you have some image of this merciless force? Have you experienced it before? What does it want from you?" What a helpless, despairing feeling it is, to be thrown into a dark pit by a force with no mercy. Is this a God-Image that is vindictive? A manifestation of shame or unworthiness with a long history? Where does it originate, how is it experienced in the body, and how does it operate in the client's life? What does it say about the client's relationship to meaning?

Naturally, the initial response needs to be compassionate and supportive. Eventually, the therapist may suggest some alternative possibilities, but always needs to be ready to face outright rejection. In the Griffiths' words, "Fortunately, where there is one metaphor, there are many. There are always multiple metaphors for God, spirit, and sacred experience."[28] It may, for instance, be possible for the client to imagine a conversation with the merciless force, or to create a larger story within which this terrifying event occurs. Eventually we might encourage exploration to see if there is some passage out of the pit or if help might appear. Whatever the avenue of approach, the attribution of "no mercy" to the force can even be brought into question as an interpretation, and the meaning of being in the deep dark may be opened up to surprising new possibilities. "What if you were never actually alone in this ordeal, and the pit turned out to be more like a cocoon that offered rest, perhaps even the possibility of a deep shift?"

### *Ethical Concerns*

The idea of challenging a client's sense of the sacred may make some therapists uncomfortable. While the counseling role often involves challenge as well as support, in the context of our professional commitment to multiculturalism and to religious/spiritual diversity, are we in danger of imposing our own biases in such a situation? Absolutely. And that must indeed remain a serious ethical concern. At the same time, our work is never value-neutral, and we are often assessing the relative health and appropriateness of our clients' choices and actions. We tread cautiously here, but we are inevitably faced with ethical dilemmas and confronted with choices. (See chapter 9 for more discussion of ethical issues.)

### *Pathways to Meaning*

In the search for meaning, what are some of the possible outcomes? Clients may find themselves reaffirming their original values and beliefs. Despite the challenges, the meanings which once made life livable are sustained. Alternatively, they may lose whatever sources of meaning they had and find themselves unable to replace them despite prolonged searching. They may redefine or modify the original assumptions that grounded and oriented them, then emerge with more resilience and depth—or head down a path of constriction with qualities of bitterness or cynicism, for instance, or coping strategies that limit possibilities, such as addiction.

## Resilience

The focus on spirituality as a resource brings us to the subject of resilience. A major aspect of resilience has to do with the ability to find meaning in the most challenging situations, and it turns out that such meaning frequently has a spiritual flavor. Attention to this topic, and to the related subject of posttraumatic growth, is increasing in the professional literature. There is an emerging body of research into the factors that contribute to resilience in the wake of trauma. Resilience is the ability to adapt to or rebound from stress, crisis, or adversity. In other words, someone who displays resilience, rather than collapsing or developing lasting psychological problems, eventually manages to find a healthy way through the crisis. When we describe someone as resilient, we often mean that they are able to "bounce back" from trials and tragedies, which suggests "returning to where one started." But resilience can also involve a capacity to grow in significant new directions.

A healthy spirituality (sometimes described as faith) can help people to make peace with life as it is, and to emerge from adversity strengthened and more resourceful. Many people also report a profound spiritual experience, sudden or gradual, that dramatically alters their lives in the wake of a loss. The outcome may be a new sense of trust in a larger purpose, a reordering of life's priorities, a changed sense of self, and a deeper sense of connection to and compassion for others. The heart may feel as if it is breaking to pieces, but it can also break open. This outcome is not sought out. It unfolds; it simply presents itself. The response is often something like this: "I would give it all back in a minute to have *x* back in my life, but I just find myself more open to life, more loving, more at peace with everything."

I have heard some clients talk about growing *through the pain* into a better person with a larger perspective and an acceptance of life's ups and downs. They sometimes speak of devastation as a vehicle for gifts of grace: more gratitude and appreciation of life, more love and open-heartedness, a sense of "coming home." The self may be experienced as stronger, wiser, more reflective, less conformist, less fearful—not as a result of positive thinking, but as an expression of a substantial shift in identity and worldview.

We may hear a new life narrative, a "re-storying" of the events. For instance, "I" may no longer be at the center of the life narrative, which becomes larger and less personal. The individual is able to sense the unbroken in the midst of the experience of brokenness. Resilience and growth often come from surrender and from a willingness to confront the mystery and obscurity of the "dark night." The deeper meaning that emerges may even offer *less comfort*, not necessarily reducing psychological distress but rather enlarging the context in which the suffering is held. This may be described as a re-visioning of the sacred, a reimagining of the Divine, a transforming of the God-Image. Somehow human life takes its place within a deeper, vaster Reality, which may be felt to be in the hands of a personal Deity or saturated with the Holy in some mysterious way. This is a radical spiritual journey.[29]

It is crucial to remember that this kind of resilience does not emerge for everyone, and if it does manifest, it is usually after a considerable passage of time. We can encourage clients to build on their spiritual resources and inner strengths, but we cannot control the process. As we gain a deeper understanding of the roots and foundations that make it possible for resilience to emerge, we may be inspired to remain open to the work of the sacred in clients' lives.

## Closing Thoughts

We have wandered through some of the painful territory of human life. We have highlighted ways in which religion and spirituality can offer experiences of comfort, strength, presence, and guidance, and also play a crucial role in the search for meaning and the development of resilience. Some therapists may welcome these insights. Others may be more skeptical. Hopefully, those with no particular interest in spirituality (or with negative associations) may be able to appreciate the potential value of including this dimension in their work.

Our attention now turns to the complex territory of psychospiritual growth and development.

## Chapter Five

# Journeys Unfolding: Meaning, Wholeness, and Depth

Drawing on spiritual and religious resources can help people endure what Hamlet calls "the slings and arrows of outrageous fortune." When we are aware of the possibilities and can make skillful use of such resources, we are better able to help clients bear their suffering and live through painful experiences. But life's spiritual dimensions also have the potential to contribute significantly to human growth and transformation. We have glimpsed this aspect when we described resilience as the potential to *emerge from pain and trauma with new capacities and perspectives*.

What do we mean by human growth and development? We are now entering territory inhabited by different theoretical perspectives and challenging questions. What counts as growth? Is growth the same as development? What is transformation? And the essential question: How are psychological and spiritual growth and development related? Approaching such questions as mysteries rather than as purely objective problems, we can draw on a variety of lenses.

## Growth: Psychological and Spiritual

Let's start with some general notions about psychological growth and development. Well-known psychological theories include Freud's psychosexual stages and Erikson's stages of psychosocial development. Let's add to this list Jean Piaget's theory of cognitive development, Lawrence Kohlberg's and Carol Gilligan's theories of moral development, and Abraham Maslow's hierarchy of needs. Some of these theories focus on childhood and adolescence; some include the entire lifespan. Some are broad in scope, while others emphasize specific aspects such as cognitive and moral capacities. Levinson's seasons of life theory lays out an age-related description of how adult life typically unfolds, and Vaillant's research highlights adult life tasks. There are also approaches to adult development that argue against any kinds of generalizations about the post-adolescent life course, and maintain that sociocultural context and life events are of paramount importance. Clearly, there are multiple lenses available.

If we set aside formal theories, what do we usually mean when we say someone has grown? It depends heavily on sociocultural context. For example, concern with individual growth may not be particularly relevant in more collectively oriented cultures. But we may relate psychological growth to capacities such as the following:

- understanding oneself better, more deeply (self-awareness)
- becoming capable of more complex thinking (seeing two or more sides of an issue)
- gaining more degrees of freedom from being triggered by old wounds and childhood experiences (tolerance of painful emotions, resilience, perspective)
- developing more ability to see things from other people's perspectives (and acting on this ability)
- increasing one's capacity for both autonomy (pursuing independent goals) and relatedness (connecting with others)

This list is only suggestive, but perhaps it will stimulate some reflection. If we now turn our attention to what we mean by *spiritual growth*, we encounter similar challenges. The focus clearly varies in different spiritual and religious contexts, but again, we may be able to identify some common themes. Spiritual growth suggests the following possibilities:

- becoming more loving, compassionate, and generous (toward others and also oneself);
- trusting more in God/Goddess/the Infinite/the Mystery (implying less anxiety, less focus on being in control);
- developing a wider sense of identity (broadening beyond "me, myself, and mine");
- focusing more on present moment experience (less on past and future);
- experiencing more inner peace and gratitude (freedom from attachments).

What are some contemporary variations on these themes? Related to the theme of gratitude is a tradition of positive thinking that flows out of the New Thought movement that emerged in the United States in the nineteenth century. Spiritual growth from this perspective involves learning to think more positively about life, thereby creating more health, happiness, and success.[1]

Related to positive thinking and gratitude, another contemporary path proposes the law of attraction ("like attracts like").[2] From this perspective, spiritual growth might be interpreted as the capacity to create the reality we desire through thoughts and visualization. The deeper intent is to align with the creativity of the Divine, thereby becoming a co-creator with God through the God-given power of the mind.

The emphasis on trust may be interpreted as surrendering more deeply to the will of God. Sometimes growth toward more complete obedience is interpreted in relation to a living religious leader who is believed to represent God. Alternatively, the growth of trust can be more inwardly focused, suggesting a deepening orientation to inner guidance (the soul or Higher

Self). Commitment to developing these deeper kinds of discernment may be associated with a growing capacity to live out the life for which we are each destined, to embody our wholeness and fulfill our potential, to express our gifts and serve life in the highest and fullest way possible.

Yet another direction emerges from the cultivation of awareness or consciousness, widening the psychospiritual lens beyond a preoccupation with the personal self, and awakening the capacity to be aware of what is being experienced, to be present with what is, as an observer or witness. The premise here is that the Infinite *is* this Awareness or Consciousness (which cannot be described or understood, but is also imbued with love and compassion). This orientation is typically associated with the search for Absolute Truth or Reality. Similarly, those of a mystical bent are likely to characterize spiritual growth in terms of the deepening capacity to experience communion or union with the Divine Beloved.[3]

When we compare these psychological and spiritual interpretations of what it means to grow, we can recognize some arenas of overlap as well as some differences in emphasis. In terms of overlap, for instance, there is an overall movement beyond the viewpoint of a separate "me." As for differences, the spiritual version reaches into territories that extend beyond the purely psychological perspective, in terms of present-centeredness, wider identity, and the capacity for love and compassion. If we allow for the *interplay* of psychology and spirituality, we enrich and expand our understanding of the human capacity for *psychospiritual* growth.

With such a wide range of definitions and approaches, our challenge is to find guidelines for understanding this territory. An inside perspective leads us to the framework of the spiritual journey, as experienced by the one who is on the journey. This is the territory we will explore in this chapter, with a focus on the themes of meaning, wholeness, and depth. An outside perspective points us toward the study of psychospiritual *development*, approached from an outside point of view. That will be the emphasis in the next chapter.

For each of these explorations I draw on both spiritual and psychological perspectives, and on approaches that embrace both. *Our capacity for spiritual growth is influenced by our psychological patterns, wounds, and gifts. Our capacity for psychological growth is likewise affected by our spiritual resources, betrayals, and inspirations.*

Prominent among these psychospiritual lenses are Jungian, transpersonal, and integral psychologies, each of which will receive its own basic introduction. It is my hope that the intricacy of the interplay will become increasingly clear as we unravel the themes and threads in what follows. In this chapter the Jungian lens is highlighted.

First I want to introduce the metaphor of the spiritual journey as an inner experience of spiritual growth.

## The Spiritual Journey

While drawing on spirituality as a resource may be relatively common, feeling that one is actually on a spiritual path may be less relevant to many clients. But becoming familiar with this territory can help us recognize the experiences that some clients do go through, and offering this perspective sometimes proves helpful to those who are struggling.

When we turn our attention to personal experiences of spiritual growth, we immediately find ourselves surrounded by metaphors. Ordinary language often fails to capture spiritual experience, and metaphorical language is needed in the attempt to express the inexpressible. We begin with the metaphors of path and journey.

In the words of transpersonal psychologist Frances Vaughan:

> The "path" is a metaphor of spiritual growth that appears in some form in all cultures, giving life a sense of purpose. . . . Metaphorically, a path suggests an intimate, personal journey. I walk a path by my own efforts. I may find companions along the way, yet their path is never identical to mine. A path is not a freeway. Riding a bus, a train or an airplane is not the same as exploring a path. Collective modes of transportation are efficient for getting to a predetermined destination, but

> the solitary path of the inward journey takes us into another dimension of consciousness where perception of the world is transformed.[4]

Descriptions of spiritual paths come from established religious traditions as well as from individual experience, but there are significant differences. One distinction is between paths of attainment and paths of surrender. In the former there is a clear goal, and steps or practices that must be accomplished in order to make progress. In the latter, there is said to be nothing to attain: you already *are* that which you are seeking. The first requires effort, practice and work. The second may be described as non-effort: opening to and resting in the deeper reality that is already present. This category includes some devotional paths (devotion to the Beloved Divine), as well as those characterized as nondual. While the attainment and surrender approaches differ in their emphasis, they are often complementary and fluidly interconnected.

We have encountered the notion of different personal and cultural styles. Through that lens we recognize that different paths emphasize different practices, such as the path of knowledge (jnana yoga, in the Hindu framework), devotion (bhakti yoga), and service (karma yoga). Kundalini yoga views development energetically, in relation to accessing and opening the chakras: the journey is essentially a vertical (but not linear or even) progression from the base of the spine to the highest chakra beyond the crown of the head. Saint Teresa of Avila, in the Catholic tradition, had her own way of describing the journey to what she called the *interior castle,* which suggests an inward journey of deepening rather than an upward journey of transcendence. For Zen Buddhists there are the ten ox-herding pictures that describe the journey to ultimate awakening and the eventual return to ordinary life.[5]

Here is another way to distinguish among six pathways, each of which has its own focus and aspiration:

- the way of sacred rite (with an emphasis on symbolic ritual enactments that represent participation in sacred archetypal patterns);

- the way of right action (emphasizing the effort to bring human life into conformity with the ultimate sacredness of all life);
- the way of devotion (cultivating a personal relationship to ultimate reality with an emphasis on wholehearted adoration and emotional surrender);
- the way of shamanic mediation (emphasizing altered states of consciousness accessed by mediators for the purpose of accessing supernatural help and guidance);
- the way of mystical quest (focusing on attaining a direct awareness of/union with ultimate reality, often through specific ascetic and meditative practices); and
- finally, the way of reasoned inquiry (the effort to transcend conventional patterns of thought through rational, dialectical practices, in order to access the ultimate Mind and Divine Wisdom).[6]

Each of these paths unfolds in its own distinctive way, with different practices and experiences as well as different markers of progress. Sharing this kind of model can help clients identify and name the orientation that speaks to them the most deeply.

As we shift from an emphasis on variation to a focus on possible commonalities, let's use a simplified synthesis of themes from various traditions, drawing on the metaphors of journey and path.

## *The Call*

Here we are alerted to the beginning of a journey that is felt to be spiritual. The recognition of the invitation may be clear in the present or may come with hindsight. We have some kind of *experience* that serves as a wake-up call, a shift in focus from the "trance" of everyday life. Something prompts us to question our normal, everyday sense of identity and perspective—the way we see reality. This may emerge through an experience of loss or suffering, a confrontation with death, a powerful dream, a vision, an encounter with some person or even a book, a pervasive discontent, or insistent longing. Buddhist teacher Jack Kornfield reminds us that "the most frequent entryway to the sacred is our own suffering and dissatisfaction. Countless spiritual journeys have begun in an encounter with the difficulties of life."[7] However the call comes, the seeker is born.

## *The Search or Preparation*

As with every part of the journey, there is no defined length of time to the preparatory process. It usually involves some kind of self-reflection and reevaluation of our lives. We peel back layers, and as we do so, we may be shocked to uncover our own shadow, the unacceptable parts of ourselves that have been hidden from view. Support and guidance can be of great help as we work with our egocentric patterns, pain and conditioning in our minds and bodies, and our resistance to change. Confusion, uncertainty, and self-doubt are likely to be constant companions. This is liminal space, typically a time of searching: exploring different religious or spiritual orientations, communities, and practices. Clients may turn to books or the internet, attend a variety of churches or spiritual gatherings, or even try to find a spiritually oriented therapist. On the other hand, it is not unusual for the search to come *through* the inner work of psychotherapy. The questions are similar no matter where the search takes us: "Where do I go from here? Who has been down this road before? Who has a map? How do I *do* this—what practices, strategies, tools can I use?"

## *The Struggle*

This part of the journey involves finding the courage to sustain deeply challenging work over a considerable period of time. Actual changes in habits, behaviors, and lifestyle are often called for, as well as challenging shadow work: we might describe this as a purging or cleansing process. In Kornfield's words, most people report that "their first years of spiritual practice involve uncovering the scales of the dragon. We directly experience these layers in the body, the heart, and the mind."[8] In the

Zen ox-herding pictures, the fourth image is called "Catching the Bull," suggesting the need for effort and self-discipline.

It can be very difficult to keep going alone, although people do it. Some are simply more solitary by nature, but many long for some kind of support or community. "Where is my tribe?" is the contemporary cry of longing. Where do people turn? Twelve-step groups, churches, study or prayer groups, yoga and meditation centers, an understanding therapist. Even one friend with whom to share the journey can make all the difference. Some give up. Some simply find themselves circling around this part of the path for a long time. Others eventually find their way through, and the path continues to open before them.

## *Initiation*

In time there may be a breakthrough or opening. This can happen suddenly or be a gradual process that is only recognized in retrospect. While initiation may come like "a slow spiral, a steady and repetitive remaking of inner being," often it "entails an intense, radical, and rapid change."[9] However it arrives, it heralds a new phase of the journey. It is appropriate to describe this experience as an archetypal rite of passage involving a transformation of consciousness, although it is rarely permanent.[10]

Jungians suggest that midlife is the major time of initiation, but there is also an initiatory aspect to the transition from adolescence to adulthood (rarely acknowledged in meaningful ways in our times). We may also think of moving into elderhood as a time of initiation. When there is meaningful acknowledgement at any of these junctures, something may be *seen and deeply known*. We have a new glimpse of reality, an expansion of consciousness, a recognition of a deeper Self. This cannot be forgotten, even though we may lose touch with it as we continue on the path. The Zen ox herder is depicted in the sixth image as riding the bull home in tranquility and joy. A Christian may have a powerful experience of being born again. The trap is the belief that this is the end of the journey and that we have arrived at our destination. For many seekers, more lies ahead.

## *Dark Night of the Soul*

Even after an initiatory opening, travelers often experience a falling back, a loss of the clarity and awareness that they had tasted. Such desolation is widely recognized as part of the spiritual journey, and may befall us more than once. We encounter a profound emptiness, aloneness, and flatness, rendered even more painful because of the contrast with the grace and joy that went before. This is the dark night of the soul described by Saint John of the Cross. Sharing this powerful image with clients can confer meaning and purpose on their deepest struggles, letting them know that others have endured what they are now experiencing.

Another line of inquiry may lead to an encounter with what are sometimes called the guardians at the gate or threshold. What do we sense is blocking our path, preventing our further opening and surrender? Not surprisingly, these guardians are often found deep within ourselves, in the form of fears, resistances, and blind spots: this is the territory of the unconscious.

## *Transformation and Integration*

Few make it this far on the journey. Relative changes are not unusual, but true transformation is rare. The latter involves a profound reorientation to a new sense of self and reality, an awakening that shifts everything. We are pointing to what psychologist Abraham Maslow calls the farther reaches of human potential, going beyond self-actualization to self-transcendence. Jungian psychology might frame this as the realization of the Self archetype through individuation. This is not just a passing experience or insight, but an enduring realization of the truth of one's Being, union with the Divine (God, the Beloved), the breaking open of the Heart. Ultimately, what is seen and known is virtually impossible to describe in words. The gate of awakening may be sought, but it is not so much achieved as encountered. We find ourselves there through what we might call grace. Kornfield quotes this saying: "Gaining enlightenment is an accident. Spiritual practice simply makes us accident-prone."[11] Paradoxically, absolute surrender, giving up on the whole search, can open the gateless gate (a Zen image) and allow the Divine to welcome us home.[12]

## *The Return*

The common assumption is that this is the pinnacle, the end of the path. But beyond even this radical awakening to a deeper Reality, personal accounts often describe a continuing journey. The remainder of the life may be dedicated to *integration* and *embodiment*. While the Zen ox-herding pictures portray the enlightened one returning to the village of ordinary life with "bliss-bestowing hands," in simplicity and egoless service, the experience is rarely that simple. There is typically a need for continuing inner work, which comes as a surprise.[13]

The process of integration is sometimes described as *waking down* or *waking inward*, into the deep spaces of the heart, and eventually into the instinctive territories in the gut—a descent through the chakras, if you will. Kornfield's description of this process is beautifully captured in his book *After the Ecstasy, the Laundry*. Adyashanti, an American spiritual teacher, emphasizes the vital importance of this ongoing work of integration into our bodies, our relationships, and our everyday dealings with the human world. Life challenges us to allow every bit of conditioning to be fully seen through and recognized for what it is.[14]

While it is unlikely that most counselors will encounter clients who experience this kind of transformation and return, I include these brief descriptions because I believe it is important to have a sense of where the path may be heading. In the midst of our professional concerns with everyday issues, having this glimpse of the larger picture, the farther reaches, can help us remember that each step matters. Small gestures of support and challenge may be part of a larger process that we cannot see.

## Reflecting on Enneagram Style Variations

Some of our Enneagram characters will relate more easily than others to the idea of a spiritual journey. Devin, for instance, describes herself as a seeker and talks openly about her long search. She cares that her therapist understands what this means for her. One of the ways her Nine pattern has manifested is in her difficulty with commitment: she can relate easily to a variety of pathways, and tends to fall asleep to her own deepest longings. At sixty-nine and feeling the pressure of having "limited time left," she wants very much to move forward.

Using the direct experience of her body as a guide, she revisits her own journey and realizes that she has skimmed over some essential inner work (the struggle). Growing up as a middle child with four siblings, for instance, she often felt insignificant and overlooked. Her parents' loud fighting terrified her, and her lifelong avoidance of conflict has limited her willingness to commit. As she turns her attention toward these patterns, she also acknowledges the ways in which her African American identity has been a complex source of struggle: while very familiar with the reality of racism, she has at the same time explored spiritual approaches that have largely separated her from more traditional African American paths. She feels very alone on her path. "Where do I belong, and who is the one who is searching?" But she sees the importance of addressing these psychospiritual patterns and feels ready.

How might this notion of a spiritual journey be helpful to Janice, the Romantic Four? She relates strongly to the experience of the struggle. Not only does she feel discouraged and unsure of her destination, she feels very lonely and longs to share the journey with even a few others. She eventually recognizes that her approach has been rather haphazard, and since she wants to continue growing, she begins to evolve a more consistent form of practice. For her this means meditation, in order to be still and listen to a deeper voice, and commitment to journaling and working with her dreams. We talk about what spiritual growth means to her, and where she is headed. Janice describes her purpose in terms of getting more in touch with her soul or higher self, fulfilling her destiny, and serving others in whatever way she can. She feels called to a path of the heart, ultimately a path of love. The hardships and challenges can now be understood as part of the journey, and she draws comfort and strength from this perspective.

For Charles, the Perfectionist One, the situation is quite different. While he has been a faithful Episcopalian, he has connected mostly with the externals of church attendance and participation. Nevertheless, his faith in a creed and in the moral dimensions of being a "good Christian" has been an essential aspect of his identity. As his grieving process unfolds, I eventually frame his loss as a possible call to a spiritual journey, as part of his search for meaning. This interpretation makes sense to him since he feels the loss of his taken-for-granted faith in addition to the loss of his wife.

He is not experiencing a dark night of the soul in the classic spiritual sense; the true dark night experience usually appears much later on the journey, after substantial spiritual growth. But it is helpful to frame his loss of faith in this language. He immediately feels the power of the image and finds comfort in some contemporary writings on the dark night of the soul.[15] The words of Saint John of the Cross, as he encounters them in these sources, begin to open up feelings and perspectives that were missing in Charles's earlier focus on doing what was right. He gradually finds himself probing new depths of his own being, and authentically contemplating new questions: "Who am I? What matters in my life? Where am I going, and what is my purpose now?" In this process, his grief eventually finds its place in a larger landscape.

Marissa relates easily to the idea of being on a spiritual journey, even though she has very little idea of what that might mean at first. As a young Enthusiast (Seven), she recognizes her cancer as the call. Much of our work involves her search for some way through, for meaning and direction. This includes an exploration of herself, her strengths and vulnerabilities, but also the parts of herself that she disowns (such as sadness and fear). Her search leads to a profound source of help that was always close at hand but not recognized or appreciated, in the form of her grandmother. This deepening relationship brings her into contact with her Native American roots, and within this context, she finds the support she needs to face her fears and engage in deeper psychospiritual work (the struggle).

As counselors, our agenda is not to move a client along the spiritual path. While we are often involved in teaching (psychoeducation), we are not spiritual teachers (although in some transpersonal psychology circles, questions may arise about the dividing line).[16] But we can create a space where clients feel their experiences are witnessed and appreciated, and we can also introduce frameworks of understanding that offer perspective and guidance. We can create conditions for the possibility of growth.

## Metaphors of Growth and Transformation

Since ordinary language often falls short of conveying spiritual experience, becoming familiar with common metaphors can be valuable. Ralph Metzner, a clinical psychologist, draws on a wide variety of sources in his comprehensive exploration of spiritual metaphors.[17] If we are familiar with such images, we can both recognize their appearance in conversations with clients and introduce them appropriately, sometimes with powerful reverberations.

Probably the most well-known metaphor is the *transformation from caterpillar to butterfly*, which evokes a profound sense of how radical this change really is. How astounding: at first we can only crawl, then we are able to take flight. Of critical importance is the in-between, where we spin a cocoon and withdraw into its darkness. In that darkness, the structures of our being *dissolve,* and somehow, mysteriously, we emerge as a winged creature. No longer bound to surfaces, we are free to fly above them and to share our beauty wherever we pass.[18]

Another widely used metaphor is *awakening from the dream of reality* that is our highly conditioned way of experiencing life. Waking up from a dream state suggests that we emerge from a world that is now seen to be unreal, into a startling experience of clarity, "seeing through" the dreamlike images to which we have been accustomed. In some traditions, *awakening* is used as another term for enlightenment. This is the metaphor that most enlivens Devin's spiritual search and serves as a magnet for her commitment.

A similar experience is evoked by the metaphor of *lifting the veils of illusion*. Removing the veils which have clouded our vision, we begin to see in a whole new way. A deeper Reality is uncovered, and we see "what is really real" for the first time. This may not be a one-time experience: we may well find the veils lifting again and again.

Through another metaphoric lens we focus on the passage *from captivity to liberation*, emphasizing the experience of being freed from the chains of habit and conditioning. We are no longer bound by the constraints of beliefs, painful emotions, and deep-rooted personality patterns. Freedom and liberation bring entirely new possibilities for living; these are themes which have a strong appeal for Marissa.

The metaphor of *purification by inner fire*, on the other hand, emphasizes the intensity and pain of this transformation. Everything that stands in the way of experiencing the Truth of our Being is burned away, and we emerge cleansed and purified. For some, fire is not merely a symbol but is also reflected in experiences of intense heat and energy in the body. Charles is particularly drawn to this metaphor because it reflects the devastating and transformative power of his grief.

Moving *from fragmentation to wholeness* suggests the healing ("whole-ing") of our splintered, fragmented selves. This includes the process of bringing the contents of the unconscious into conscious awareness. The integration of unconscious and conscious aspects of the psyche is central in Jungian psychology.

The classic metaphor of *dying and being reborn* points to the experience of letting go of the old self entirely, and only after that total surrender, discovering that something new and unexpected emerges. Such is the caterpillar's process. Moving *from darkness to light* picks up the theme of seeing more clearly as well as opening to a radical new reality. Light is widely used in spiritual literature as a metaphor for the Sacred and Divine.

*Returning to the source* evokes the powerful sense of coming home. After this whole arduous journey, one experiences a joyous recognition, a remembering—"Ah yes . . . *This*!" This is the metaphor that carries the most meaning for Janice, and it shows up in her dreams. Finally, it is important to point out that all these metaphors speak to the arc of the entire spiritual journey, not just a phase labeled "transformation."

We also need to acknowledge the metaphor of the *hero's journey*, made famous by mythologist Joseph Campbell. This classic story describes the adventure of the archetype known as the Hero, who hears a call to adventure. At first he refuses the call (as do many of us). Eventually (usually with the help of a wise mentor), he leaves home to meet the trials, battles, and tests that await him before returning home, transformed, bringing a gift or treasure to share with others. The metaphors of journey, pilgrimage, and path all speak to essential aspects of our experience: leaving the habitual and familiar, movement, encountering unknown territory and challenges, seeking, facing (inner or outer) enemies, and finally returning home.

On the other hand, Zen Buddhism emphasizes the vital importance of recognizing what is *already present*, which may be overlooked when we focus on journeying to another destination. What we are seeking is not far away, at the end of strenuous effort, but right here, where we are. The tale of the Alchemist captures this experience of journeying away from home to find the treasure, only to discover that it has been hidden at home the whole time.[19] T.S. Eliot's well-known lines from his poem "Little Gidding" reflect a similar theme: after all our explorations we often find ourselves back where we began, but with deeper understanding and awareness.[20]

Developmental psychologist Sharon Daloz Parks suggests that the hero's journey captures a typically *masculine* process of transformation. The alternative she offers is the metaphor of *home*, which may speak more to the experience of women (or the archetypal feminine). The image of home and homemaking is viewed "as a metaphor for the development of meaning and faith," inviting us into "the increasing embodiment of truth, compassion, and justice in our midst," deeper "abiding" and "dwelling together."[21] Here the emphasis is not so much on the solitary seeker, but on holding a nurturing space for the human family.

The emphasis on homemaking, embodiment, and relationship is a valuable and thought-provoking challenge to familiar, habitual ways of framing spiritual growth. I am reminded of Robert Wuthnow's distinction between a spirituality of *seeking* and a spirituality of *dwelling*. Can the kind of transformation we have been talking about unfold here and now, in the context of being fully home and offering the authentic space of home to others? Perhaps this is what some spiritual teachers are pointing to, in a more radical framework, when they invite us to experience the truth that we are not *at* home, we are home *itself*. Home is always already here.

There are also spatial metaphors, so commonly used that we can fall into the trap of overlooking their metaphoric nature.[22] They are relevant not only to the theme of the spiritual journey but also to the whole subject of psychospiritual development. Metaphors of ascent are common: the path leads upward, up the mountain, up to heaven. The means of ascent may be a path, but it may also be a ladder (Jacob's ladder, for instance). An ascending spiral is another alternative that softens the rigidity of the ladder image. Our destination promises a higher perspective, a larger view of human territory, and brings us closer to the reality that is sensed to be above *and* beyond. Has the ancient mystery of the celestial realms—the Sun, Moon, planets, stars—pulled human beings in this direction for centuries? The problem is that it is only too easy to equate "up" and "higher" with "better," which can feel problematic to some. This association can also contribute to what we call the inflation of the ego—which is definitely *not* what the spiritual journey is about.

References to descent are often reserved for descriptions of the difficult or dark parts of the journey. Myths about hell realms situate them underneath the earthly plane. We fall into despair. Or we hear that we must go down in order, eventually, to go up toward the light. But there are also positive connotations to "down." Some experience falling into grace. Mystics speak about dwelling in the depths, and the metaphor of the Ground of Being directs our attention toward the mystery that is always present and does not require a flight to heaven.

Notice that the spatial metaphors of up and down, ascent and descent, are also associated with light and dark. While terms such as enlightenment, illumination, and "seeing the light" are familiar to many, and we have already explored experiences of dark in connection with suffering, the capacity to appreciate paradox introduces another whole possibility. Some who have had profound mystical openings, which are inherently inexpressible, draw on paradoxical language, such as "dazzling dark" or "luminous darkness." In this context, endarkenment is a gift. Descriptions such as these point beyond any familiar geography, and cannot be understood logically.

Contrasting the ascent to the heavens with the embrace of the earth below can also lead us to an appreciation of the lowly, the terrestrial, the human and embodied. As we saw in chapter 2, this downward embrace (a "descending spirituality") may be described as more "feminine," while the upward thrust (an "ascending spirituality") is associated with the archetypal masculine.

Metaphors of ascent and descent, light and dark, do not have to be mutually exclusive. If a client is interested, I sometimes recommend a beautifully written book by John Tarrant entitled *The Light Inside the Dark*, which offers a guide to the interior voyage that embraces *both* movements of "descent into the night" and "climbing into the light."[23] His approach is unusual in that he draws on two perspectives that are rarely found together: Zen Buddhism, which he characterizes as oriented to the upward movement of spirit, and the psychological tradition of C. G. Jung and James Hillman, which emphasizes descent into the dark of the soul and the unconscious. The beauty lies in Tarrant's embrace of both movements in the spiritual journey.

## Reflecting on the Personal Journey

Have you experienced some kind of inner journey in your life? Whether or not you have described it as a spiritual journey, I encourage you to reflect on your experience. Are there any metaphors that come close to describing your process? Have there been distinct phases of the journey, or chapters in the story? When did the path begin, and where are you now? Could you create a visual image or a musical impression of this journey? If none of these metaphors fit your experience, how else might you describe the unfolding of your life?

For a deeper dive, I encourage you to write your own spiritual autobiography. There are many ways to frame such an endeavor—the story of your life as a spiritual journey. Here are some questions to help you explore:

- What struggles have you had in your relationship to spirituality and/or religion?
- How have you tried to develop and sustain yourself spiritually over the years, whatever that means to you?
- Have there been spiritual gifts that came through dark times?
- What spiritual transformations have you experienced, if any?
- What have you learned or come to realize about who you are?
- What are your deepest longings and values?
- What do you hold sacred?
- Where do you currently stand in relation to spirituality and to religion, and how do you envision your direction of growth?

I place an emphasis on metaphor in relation to the theme of spiritual growth because when we listen for metaphors that appear in our clients' conversations, we open up rich territory. As we explore these metaphors together, we often discover depths and possibilities that may be missed if we pay attention only to the surface of what is said. At times it is also appropriate to suggest a new metaphor for a client's experience. When we do so, it is in the spirit of a tentative offering so that we may explore its potential value together. Understanding the central role of metaphor helps us to appreciate the subtlety of this psychospiritual process and the challenge of finding language to convey our perceptions and experiences.

Having considered some broad perspectives on metaphor and meaning-making, let's now focus on some central ideas from Jung and James Hillman, who studied with Jung and founded the field of archetypal psychology. Their work is invaluable for understanding the interplay of psychology and spirituality in relation to the spiritual journey.

## Jung's Psychospiritual Map

How is spiritual growth also a psychological process? How is psychological growth also a spiritual process? A primary source of insights is found in the depth-psychological work of Carl Jung. Although Jung's work may be familiar to many, reviewing and highlighting some key ideas may provide significant insights in relation to these questions.

Jung's real interest was not "the treatment of neurosis, but rather . . . the approach to the numinous," a term which suggests the holy or the sacred.[24] Swimming upstream against the modern insistence on the physical realm as the fundamental reality, Jung understood the psyche to have objective reality and autonomy. The psyche (the Greek word for *soul*) consists of the contents of consciousness, but even more importantly, embraces the realms of the unconscious. (It is crucial to clarify that this interpretation of the term *soul* is not the same as the traditional religious meaning of the term, which points to something like the individual spark of the Divine within each of us.) While ego-consciousness plays an essential role as the center of the field of consciousness, it remains secondary. The unconscious psyche is primary and offers us access to the numinous, which lies far *deeper* than ego. In part, the human journey involves bringing some of the contents of our personal unconscious into consciousness, but for Jung it is the collective unconscious of humanity, accumulated over eons, that holds the real riches.

Drawing on the intense experiences of his own midlife confrontation with the unconscious—his initiation through a descent into the depths of the psyche—Jung spent the rest of his life exploring such territory as the collective unconscious, archetypes, and the imaginal realm through which we encounter hints of the numinous.

In order to appreciate what depth psychology has to offer, we need to look more closely at several key concepts.

## *Archetypes and the Self*

Defining the concept of an archetype is difficult. Archetypes may be characterized as both images and instincts. Jung's own thinking about archetypes evolved over his career, but simply put, he approached them as embracing a spectrum. At the spiritual end, they entail universal images that represent deep mythic structures within the collective unconscious. At the biological end, they represent deep predispositions or energetic patterns of human behavior. In both instances, archetypes exist prior to, and exert influence on, consciousness.

In Jung's words, archetypes are "a priori structural forms of the stuff of consciousness." They account for the "collective component of a perception," the "forms in which things can be perceived and conceived," shaping all human experience. In addition, "as an attribute of instinct they partake of its dynamic nature, and consequently possess a specific energy which causes or compels definite modes of behavior or impulses."[25] More simply put, archetypal images have a power of their own, and convey meanings that are *beyond the personal.* When we encounter an archetype in a dream, for instance, it is imperative that we recognize its independence and objectivity. Otherwise we fall into the trap of identifying personally with the archetype, a dangerous move described as *ego inflation*. Having learned from his own experience, Jung cautions us to remain anchored in the conscious ego even as we explore the depths of the unconscious, or we will get lost.

The primary archetype, which emerged for Jung over several years through drawing and painting and eventually through a pivotal dream, is the *Self.* The Self is "the magnetic center of Jung's psychological universe [whose] presence pulls the ego's compass needle to true north."[26] Descriptions of the Self are paradoxical and mysterious. Often symbolized by a circle, the Self is both the whole and the center. It is transcendent, lying beyond the personal psyche but also connecting the psyche with the larger reality, with Being itself. The Self is Wholeness, the Eye of God, represented throughout human history by circular images called mandalas, which convey unity and totality. The mandala is, in a sense, equivalent to the fundamental God-Image. (Clients may spontaneously create mandalas of their own if invited to draw or paint.)

The Self acts upon us, drawing us toward unity through these symbols of wholeness and moving toward integration within the psyche. Although it remains a mystery, the Self can be *experienced.* The spiritual journey is, in essence, this movement toward wholeness, unity, and totality. The challenge is for the ego to develop a healthy relationship with the archetype of the Self. Whereas some spiritual paths (Eastern in orientation) emphasize the dissolving of the ego in the Ultimate Reality or realizing that the ego has never been separate from it, Jung insisted that the Western psyche needs to maintain a strong ego. He warns repeatedly that losing this anchor can lead to psychosis.

With or without using Jungian language, introducing this theme of the Self to some clients can help frame their experience in a meaningful way. Even when the larger movement toward wholeness is not immediately apparent within the challenges of daily life, opening to the possibility offers meaning and purpose. The sense of a universal force or pattern may begin as a matter of faith, and evolve into a powerful orienting principle through the direct experience of dreams and images.

Jung describes this spiritual journey toward wholeness as a process of *individuation.* Let's take a closer look at the meaning of this term.

## *Individuation*

Individuation involves becoming "a unified but also unique personality, an individual, an undivided and integrated person."[27] This is a journey of growth in which the personal and collective unconscious are (substantially, but never totally) brought into consciousness. The goal of the soul's journey is *integration.*

This integration involves a process of *compensation.* The one-sidedness of the conscious realm (ego) needs to be countered and balanced by engagement with the unconscious. Such encounters often take place through dreams and active imagination (which we will explore shortly).

Jung sees individuation primarily as the work of the second half of life. While the first half of life typically involves the ego's process of creating an identity and negotiating a relationship with the forces of social conformity, midlife introduces a new and essentially inward movement focusing on the ego's unrealized relationship with the unconscious.

This inner work requires us to face difficult and painful emotions, since we have to come to terms with our *complexes*, and it is through emotion that the unconscious complexes are triggered into action. Complexes are core instinctive *patterns* that are initially activated by particular experiences. We can think of complexes that are readily identifiable, such as an inferiority complex or a hero complex, but often they are more subtle: whenever we are in the grip of a pattern, such as discomfort in crowds or test-anxiety, we may be contending with a complex. Each complex is associated with particular emotions, memories, perceptions, and wishes, and has a basic theme associated with the initial experiences. Each complex is also likely to be associated with an image, which has its own inner coherence, wholeness, and autonomy. This is important, because much of the work of individuation involves learning to pay conscious attention to images that emerge from the unconscious, and then to engage deeply with them. The complexes need to be met and worked through.

In this process we are not simply pushed from behind by our history and patterns (complexes), but also pulled and *drawn forward* by the Self, by the image of the unique individual we are called to be. We are guided by this image, and from the perspectives of both Jung and archetypal psychologist James Hillman, we are wise to pay attention to this calling, this guidance. This emphasis on purpose (instead of cause) turns much of psychological theory upside down.[28]

Jung also frames the call to individuation in these words:

> The meaning of my existence is that life has addressed a question to me. Or, conversely, I myself am a question which is addressed to the world, and I must communicate my answer, for otherwise I am dependent upon the world's answer. That is a suprapersonal life task, which I accomplish only by effort and with difficulty.[29]

The call to grow toward individual wholeness may be experienced in the form of questions: Who are you? What is your gift? What do you offer to the world? Especially important here is Jung's caution: do not be dependent on the world for your answer. The deeper truths do not come from the world, but from listening to the voices of the personal and collective unconscious, from the connection with the Self.

There is no doubt in Jung's mind that the work of individuation is arduous and not for everyone. For most, differentiating from what he calls "the herd" is too challenging. The pull of conformity is strong, and few become conscious enough to go alone and be their own company, although he believes that this is the only path worth following. In Jung's words we find the metaphor of the journey in its classically masculine and solitary form as a lonely path into uncharted territory. "It may be that for sufficient reasons a man feels he must set out on his own feet along the road to wider realms."[30]

## *Shadow*

The Self is not the only archetype that matters in the process of individuation. Readers may be familiar with the archetypes of Persona, Shadow, and more controversially, Anima and Animus. The journey into the depths of the psyche involves encountering and relating to these basic archetypes, as well as allowing ourselves to be addressed and challenged by the images associated with our complexes and other archetypal images.

Of particular importance to those interested in psychospiritual growth is the Shadow. Shadow refers to those unconscious aspects of our personality which the conscious ego does not recognize as itself. These are kept out of consciousness because they hold a negative charge. They are rejected and repressed as unacceptable and dark. Some shadow dimensions of ourselves may actually be positive, and these are sometimes referred to as golden or bright shadow aspects. For instance, someone who has very low self-esteem on a conscious level may have a shadow aspect which represents self-confidence. More typical shadow aspects are selfish, greedy, aggressive, critical, pleasure-focused, controlling, or hard-hearted—and generally socially unacceptable. We each have our own core cluster of such traits, which we keep out of our awareness but often criticize in others (projection).

Bringing shadow elements into conscious awareness is an essential aspect of the journey toward integration and wholeness. You probably know, or know of, people who consider themselves spiritually evolved but clearly display shadow characteristics. Shadow may also lure us into mistaking concrete objects of desire for the Holy, which is the soul's deepest longing. We may find ourselves acting out our shadow preoccupations with food and drink, sex, or drugs. We may substitute worship of an abusive teacher for our devotion to the Beloved. The task of bringing shadow elements out of the dark is facilitated through dream work and active imagination, as well as by exploring our strong criticisms of others.[31]

## Reflecting on Enneagram Style Variations

The archetype of the Self offers Janice (Romantic Four) an orienting principle that helps her pay attention to her inner process in new ways. She begins to look for ways in which the Self may be appearing in her dreams, drawings, and musings, giving them new meanings. As she develops the inner sense that her experience has significance, despite the times of feeling lost or discouraged, she finds the strength and will to keep going. For instance, we have already seen that in her recurring image of traveling alone across a desert-like terrain, she is sometimes accompanied by the figure of a wise woman. Later, an image of a circular community of dwellings appears in the distance and becomes her destination: this is a mandala-type image. She senses a welcoming home, but also recognizes with a feeling of awe that this is no ordinary place. She senses a movement toward "feeling whole," and wholeness emerges as a new theme with deep emotion for her, given her history of feeling broken.

Janice also appreciates the invitation to recognize the influence of a particular complex in her own life. Growing up with two siblings, she was consistently labeled as the emotional one. Her parents, her younger brother, and her older sister were all more matter-of-fact and intellectual in their personality styles, leaving her as the carrier of emotions in her family. She has several pivotal memories from her childhood that are charged with painful feelings. Her youthful interpretation of this difference between herself and her family was that feelings were weak, and she was, therefore, the weak one, the wounded and incapable one, the one never likely to make much of herself. She experienced the weight of this judgment in her heart area, and struggled with it every time she tried to strike out on her own and make something of her life. In her attempt to go back to school and use her creative talents toward a new career, she is encountering the power of this complex as part of her spiritual journey. We work with the images, feelings, and body sensations that surround this complex until eventually it loses much of its compelling power.

For Charles (Perfectionist One), the theme of individuation proves to be very valuable later in his healing work. It is not necessary to import a lot of theoretical detail into the exploration, but he has the maturity to approach the process of self-exploration with seriousness. He is searching for purpose, and the idea of a calling resonates with his Episcopalian background. This also begins a process of questioning his notions of right and wrong: perhaps he no longer needs to measure his worth by the standards of others (the herd), and is being invited to discover his own path. Naturally, part of the work is exploring his shadow. Much to his distress, he discovers the disowned parts of himself that are selfish, immoral, and generally "bad." Integrating this unconscious material is slow, painful work, but as his pattern of self-judgment begins to soften, he can listen more openheartedly to the subtle whispers of the unconscious.

As an Enthusiast Seven, Marissa's natural inclination is to love the vast scope of the mind, and to reach up for the light, for joy and freedom. She is not comfortable diving down into the dark, meeting the shadow, or experiencing some of the frightening images that visit her in dreams. But with small steps and a lot of encouragement, along with her grandmother's support and her growing connection with her Native American ancestry, she is gradually able to open to a larger reality that includes darkness—just as the natural world does. She is young, so this is not the major turn toward individuation that may come in midlife. But gradually, she finds herself learning about a new dimension of interior experience, reaching from the mental level of understanding down into the domain of feelings, emotions, and sensory experience.

This psychospiritual perspective on growth and transformation is a natural fit for some clients. For others, there are valuable elements that help the clients focus on neglected aspects of their experience, or that enrich and broaden an existing inclination. As therapists, we can draw on basic aspects of Jungian work without being trained Jungian analysts, though a referral may be appropriate if deeper immersion feels right for the client.

So far we have emphasized the metaphors of depth and downward movement that are a natural feature of the Jungian perspective. Let's take a brief look at the tension between "up" and "down" in the form of the relationship between spirit and soul.

## *Spirit and Soul*

The movement into the depths of the psyche is reflected in Jung's description of his own experience: "In order to seize hold of the fantasies, I frequently imagined a steep descent."[32] (By *fantasies* he means images, imagined encounters, and experiences.) This descent is into the territory of the unconscious, which ultimately brings us into contact with the wholeness of the Self.

James Hillman, who developed what he calls archetypal psychology, is a passionate lover of the depths of soul. He also has some critical things to say about the upward thrust toward "spirit." This is particularly relevant to our exploration because the orientation of transpersonal psychology (to be introduced in later chapters) is often understood to be upward to the domain of spirit.

For Hillman, spirit is oriented to peaks, and the journey to spirit is up toward the mountaintops, to the high and light places. He characterizes spirit as "humorless," anti-historical, metaphysical, impersonal, and dry. Soul, on the other hand, is at home in the moist valleys, dark and heavy, historical, particular, full of humor and humility, expressing itself through images. If we neglect soul, he warns, we forget to ask *who* is going up the mountain: "For it is not the trip and its stations and path, not the rate of ascent and the rung of the ladder, or the peak and its experience, nor even the return—it is the person in the person prompting the whole endeavor."[33] This "who" is, like everything else, shaped by psychic images, and to bypass these images is to "close the door on the person who brought one to the threshold in the first place."[34] We will miss something essential, and we will get tripped up.

Although he speaks provocatively on behalf of soul as the neglected aspect, Hillman does believe we need both spirit and soul. He concedes that finding their connections *is* the ultimate work, both psychologically and spiritually. In this he finds himself more or less on the same ground as John Tarrant, although their styles are very different. In Tarrant's sympathetic and poetic exploration of both spirit and soul, he describes the "seductive" nature of spirit's path toward awakening, when "the veils that obscure our view are lifted and our oneness with God and the universe is revealed."[35] Attending to spirit, we walk a path of reverence and deep witnessing. And yet, this does not define the whole of life's journey. We need to find our way through the "valley world" as well, allowing ourselves to touch and be touched by the world. For this we need soul, which is tangible, human, always losing its way, loving and learning. Soul brings *meaning* to our experience, embraces all the vulnerabilities, longings, and sorrows, and inhabits "the brokenness of the world."[36]

This soul-oriented approach to the journey may be very appealing to some clients. It may be particularly useful to those who are tempted to "go up" in a spiritual bypass of the psychological experiences of shadow, complexes, and emotional pain. Here are Tarrant's words:

> Every journey toward wholeness involves the interplay of spirit and soul. Neither is sufficient alone, for we are hybrid beings and cannot confine life to a single purpose. . . . Spirit forgets the necessity of imperfection, and that within our very incompletion is the opening where love appears. . . . Identification with

> the spirit, then, is not the goal of the inner work; such identification can have disastrous consequences because it leads us to think of ourselves as right, as immune from ordinary failings.[37]

From this perspective, the journey is full of ups and downs: descents into night, ascents into light. If we forget spirit, we get lost in a maze. We miss the profound gifts of silence, vastness, spaciousness, emptiness, Reality. We no longer have a sense of the limitless mystery. If we forget soul, we are shocked, mortified, and disoriented by our inevitable return to the ordinary world. Ignoring soul means that we are unprepared for this gritty encounter. The embrace of the depths also prepares us for the dark night of the soul and reminds us of the need for *embodiment* after awakening. Both ascending and descending paths are valuable. The uniquely Jungian telling of the spiritual journey story orients us to the depths of the psyche and the gifts of the soul's imaginal path.[38]

Imagination plays a central role in this kind of work. What are its unique offerings?

## *The Role of Imagination*

Much of the work of making the unconscious conscious may be described as imaginal in nature. It's important to understand that *imaginal* is not the same as *imaginary*. *Imaginary* is a somewhat derogatory term pointing to something that is unreal in the physical or rational sense. *Imaginal*, on the other hand, describes a *way of knowing*, alongside knowing through the senses or through reason, which are the pathways of science. As described by Islamic scholar Henry Corbin, imaginal knowing offers access to *a specific order of reality*.[39] This is the meaning that is intended here.

Material from unknown sources in the unconscious (personal or collective) often presents itself to the conscious ego in the form of images. (Let's not be too literal about this term "image." What appears is not always visual. Sometimes in a dream, for instance, we may encounter only a sensation, words, or a musical phrase.) In his autobiography, Jung articulated "the crucial insight that there are things in the psyche which I do not produce, but which produce themselves and have their own life."[40] These "things" are autonomous and inhabit their own worlds within the psyche: the inner self is multiple, not singular. We meet various aspects in our dreams and reveries, *in symbolic form*. The more we accept the invitation to translate emotions into images, and the more consciously we engage with the images that appear to us through active imagination and dreamwork, the deeper we travel toward the archetype of the Self and therefore toward individuation.

But imaginal knowing can be helpful throughout the spiritual journey. When we first encounter the call, it may be a dream that captures our attention. When we are trying to find our way through the struggle or the dark night of the soul, an image may appear that seems to hold a mysterious key. There is value in dedicating time and energy to engaging with the images that appear.

Since we do not place much value on imaginal work in the modern world, learning to work with images usually involves opening new pathways of exploration and developing new skills. There are contemporary guides to this work that are very helpful.[41] As we learn to recognize these symbols and images as aspects of our own psyches, we are called upon to meet them on their own terms, not ours. To interact with images that appear in dreams or daydreams, we need to set aside quiet time to explore them: closing our eyes, picturing the image, engaging with it, asking questions, developing a relationship. It might also mean doing spontaneous writing as an imagined dialogue unfolds, or alternating writing with the dominant and nondominant (imaginal figure) hand.

Creative modalities such as art, dance, music, drama, and poetry are also powerful avenues through which to engage with these imaginal figures. Caution may be needed in working with some clients in these ways. Jung realized that these forms of deep engagement can run the risk of leading the individual too far from reality. So if one is not a trained Jungian or art therapist, it is wise to tread carefully and move slowly.

Since dreams are the most common way in which images present themselves to clients, the following approach to dreamwork may prove helpful as a practical synthesis (drawn from various sources).[42]

## *Suggestions for Working with Dreams*

Begin with: "I have no idea what this dream means."

Stay open.

**Associations**

- Describe the dream in present tense.
- Notice your body as you narrate the dream.
- Listen for the beginning, the landscape, the ending.
- Elements to pay attention to: setting, characters, mood, action. How does the story unfold? Look for rhythms and patterns.
- Generate associations around all these. What do they remind you of? What do your body sensations remind you of? Some images may be personal, others may be archetypal or images that have a collective source.
- Focus on images that seem the most significant—and also those that seem the *least* significant.
- Compare how the dream-ego responds and how the waking-ego responds to the dream.
- What title would you give the dream?

**Amplification**

- Work with a particular image: open it up.
- Bring in stories, myths, other dreams you have had.
- Open up the sound images, sensations, moods—make a sound or make music, explore movement.
- Give the image expression through drawing, painting, sculpting, or poetry. If you use clay or Play-Doh, try working with your eyes closed and allow the image to come forth. Write a poem back to the dream; write the dream *as a poem*.

**Animation**

- Allow the image to have its own life, to be present, here and now, as an embodied presence. Who is visiting? What does the image want? Why now? What needs your attention?

- Allow the image to become vivid to your senses, to reveal its essential quality; it may change in form, develop, or evoke a response in you.
- Look into the eyes of the image (if it is a being and if this is permitted); enter into a dialogue with it.
- You may develop an ongoing relationship with certain figures; imagine a "dream council," in which these figures become companions and advisors.
- Create an "altar" where representations/symbols of these figures can be assembled.

Helping clients explore their dreams can lead in unanticipated directions. (Our own dreams may also hold imaginal information relevant to our work with clients.) If we think we know where we are going, we need to stop and start again. Never presume to know what something means, and refrain from interpreting dreams *for* clients. Explore together, in a "what if" way. In this kind of work we are moving in the territory of soul. Rules and formulas will lead us further away from the depths.

For many, being on a spiritual journey probably means bumping into the following realization over and over again: *it is essential to surrender to not-knowing.* We *do not know* where we are going or what we need. We may be conscious of certain themes and experiences, but there is much more that is not in our conscious awareness. If we can allow ourselves to be addressed, to be brought up short, challenged, guided, even surprised, we acknowledge the power of unconscious forces arising from our personal patterns and also from dimensions beyond the personal.

## Reflecting on Enneagram Style Variations

Janice (Four) gravitates naturally to imaginal work, and engaging with her dreams proves to be a powerful avenue to insight and growth. We bring active imagination to the desert journey of her dream. She dialogues with the wise woman and later draws a mandala of the sacred community. Our attention naturally falls on the ways in which unacceptable parts of her own psyche (shadow) may play a role in her interpretations. For instance, a dark figure appears in one dream. He is pursuing her and she feels threatened by him. Reentering the dream and courageously turning to engage in an imaginal encounter with him, she eventually senses that he speaks for the hopeless part of her that feels completely unworthy and wants her to stop this journey "because it will lead to no good." Then he unmasks himself, and beneath this shame is an angry energy that urges her to turn back and take revenge on those who so wrongly belittled him. She listens and tries to understand. He softens a bit. She is finally able to persuade him to accompany her on her journey, bringing valuable gut energy to help her face the challenges ahead.

Charles's (One) more intellectual and rational bent does not dispose him to giving dreams and imagination a central role. Eventually, however, he finds rich solace in reading sacred texts and allowing thoughts and images to arise spontaneously in his contemplations (*Lectio Divina*).[43] He gradually opens up to exploring prayer in deeper ways that allow for the role of images. This kind of work can appropriately be incorporated in counseling as part of psychospiritual growth. If Charles is motivated to go deeper, referral to a spiritual director would be appropriate.

Marissa (Seven) is delighted to participate in dreamwork, since dreams and visions are deeply meaningful in her ancestral Native American ways. However, respect must be paid to her traditions, as imparted to her by her grandmother. Her primary guidance comes from that source of teaching, and I am careful to check in with her whenever we consider doing dreamwork and active imagination in session. She is also strongly motivated to learn more from both inner and outer sources as she begins to engage with images of cancer as teacher.

Finally, let's return to Devin (Nine). She has explored dreams periodically in her life and is open to returning to this work with greater focus and commitment. She starts keeping a dream journal. We work with dreams in our sessions, emphasizing her somatic experience as we do so. After some time, she begins to encounter images that make her particularly uncomfortable—angry figures, a volcano. These explorations prove to be both powerful and frightening as she begins to own some long-buried anger (shadow for her) and feel it in her belly. In this anger is her life energy, her capacity for action and commitment, but this aspect of the work cannot be rushed. Eventually she finds herself drawn to the path of Sufism (the mystical sect of Islam), in part because it embraces psychological aspects of the inner journey and values dreamwork.[44]

We need to be aware that for some clients, such as more conservative Protestants, the depth psychology approach is unlikely to be useful. Their traditional emphasis on literal interpretation of scripture and more prescribed forms of prayer makes these imaginal perspectives highly suspect as sources of temptation.

## The Unconscious: Some Questions to Ponder

What *is* this mysterious thing we call the unconscious? Contemporary research suggests that there are many cognitive processes that operate outside of conscious awareness but still play an important role in decision making, problem solving, and critical thinking. In that context, "unconscious" has a much more straightforward and brain-based meaning. When we shift to a traditional psychodynamic perspective, I suggest caution about relying on overly concrete, geographical metaphors of the unconscious as a repository, a hidden iceberg, or even a deep ocean. Instead we might simply say that the term points to forces over which the conscious self—the "I" that I am aware of, know, recognize—does not have dominion.

As we have seen, one kind of unconscious content includes the recurring or persistent patterns (complexes) in our lives to which we are blind. These are personal patterns whose outlines we may at first perceive only dimly, if at all. Eventually we may begin to recognize them as parts of ourselves, as familiar companions on the journey. They are dynamic and powerful. They play an important role in shaping our path, the apparent detours and dead ends, the times of feeling lost, even the flavors of our openings and revelations.

From a soul or spirit perspective, we may speak about another source of unconscious forces that is less shaped by personal biography. From this unknown origin come many forms of help and guidance, some of which we welcome and some of which we would rather avoid or ignore. These are the quiet whispers (the intuitive thoughts, the gut feelings) and, from Jung's perspective, the images that invite or compel our attention. The powerful pull of the deep Self may be a way of characterizing one of these mysterious forces. Some of these may have a personal flavor, such as Hillman's notion of our soul-companion, which he calls our *daimon*; this inner guide carries the image that holds our destiny. Other influences may be seen as collective sources that have their origins in the accumulated history of humanity's inner travels.

But Jung's account of the unconscious also omits two important possibilities. One is a potentially crucial distinction between a lower and a higher unconscious, pointed out by Italian psychiatrist Robert Assagioli and also by contemporary philosopher Ken Wilber. For instance, the accumulated images and teachings of the collective unconscious of humanity may *not* be full of wisdom for us in our time. Some of them may be limited by the frameworks of the past, confining us to smaller or more limited worlds of possibility because they arise out of earlier realms of human experience and development. In addition, we may experience insights that emerge from a *higher* unconscious, suggesting a pull from the future or from realities beyond the human (transpersonal).

I also part with Jung in his insistence that we must remain within the confines of the psyche, that we cannot know anything outside of the psyche.[45] This perspective limits us to experience in the human realm. If we remove that constraint, then we are free to consider sources of guidance or information that are from dimensions, realms, or levels of reality beyond the human psyche. (When such guidance does come for Jung, he interprets the source as an imaginal manifestation within the psyche.) This possibility, of actual (although indescribable) dimensions of reality beyond the human, enlarges our perspective immeasurably. Even though we may not know or *be conscious of* the sources themselves, we may become more conscious of them as our awareness evolves beyond the personal level. (Chapter 8 focuses on such dimensions of growth and transformation.) We also need to be discerning and perhaps to seek guidance we trust: some believe that not all such trans-personal sources are benign or truthful.

To stretch our conceptual framework, let's look at a different interpretation of the unconscious from the perspective of Buddhist and transpersonal psychologist, John Welwood. Taking issue with Jung's view of meditation as withdrawal from the outer world and surrender to the unconscious, Welwood suggests that the unconscious is not a kind of container that is separate from consciousness:

> Conscious and unconscious are not two separate regions of a psyche, but rather two different modes in which the body-mind organism structures relatedness. Unconscious process is a holistic mode of organizing experience and responding to reality that operates outside the normal span of focal attention.[46]

His alternative model begins with the dynamics of figure and ground, where these are understood as "continually shifting features of the experiential field." The unconscious ground has four levels:

- the situational ground of felt meaning (the implicit felt sense of the immediate situation);
- the personal ground (how patterns of past experience and accumulated meaning shape our present consciousness, behavior, and worldview);
- the transpersonal ground (the ways in which the body-mind organism is attuned to larger, universal qualities of existence);
- the open ground (pure, immediate presence to reality prior to identification with the body-mind organism).[47]

The conscious/unconscious relationship may then be approached as descriptive of the individual's two-sided connection with reality. Meditation, as understood from this Buddhist point of view, has the potential in advanced practice of being pure naked awareness of the open ground, clear and transparent, viewed as beyond (deeper than) duality. Ultimately, "I" am not separate from "reality." Self and world interpenetrate.

It may not be necessary to choose one particular framework for approaching the unconscious. The purpose in offering different points of view here is to open up possibilities and discourage overly concrete thinking. We are moving in subtle territory, and our grasp is necessarily limited. Working with clients' experiences (as well as your own) helps to develop a feel for the territory.

## Reflecting on Enneagram Style Variations

Let's review the characters in relation to the themes of this chapter. Janice is like many Enneagram Fours (the Romantics) in being drawn to depth and unafraid of leaning into the dark places. She is at home with creative imagination and following her own unique path, and is naturally introspective. You may recall that her favorite metaphor of transformation is returning to the source. This longing for home has a familiar feel to her as a Four. Overall, Jungian-oriented therapy is a good fit for her. However, it is also important to recognize that she may have a tendency to get lost in the longing for what is missing. She needs to be reminded to focus on what is *present*.

Viewing Charles through the lens of the One, we have to watch for perfectionism and for tendencies to interpret his favorite metaphor of purification by fire in a self-punitive way. But his conditioned motivation (perhaps a complex) is being challenged: he questions how a loving God could be so harsh. The search for meaning can lead him into a broader, deeper exploration of his religious tradition and his vision for the future.

Marissa, as an Enthusiast Seven, initially finds new territory exciting. While she has a tendency to be attracted to the next shiny viewpoint, her melanoma has clearly brought her energies into focus. From this point of view, a depth-psychological perspective is a good fit for this time in her life, inviting her to look inward, meet the difficult feelings that are present, and explore the unconscious through dreams and images. This movement toward more focus is important, but if overdone, will generate too much frustration at the sense of limitation. The deeper work, of being present with the dark, needs to be done in small doses.

For Devin (the Nine, Peacemaker), going deeper within is a valuable movement since Nines are often out of touch with their core. Like some other Nines, she is also at home with images and imaginal work, so this, too, makes for a good fit with depth psychology. The somatic dimension is particularly important for her since this grounds her experience when she encounters shadow material, a complex, or an imaginal figure.

If you have a sense of your own Enneagram pattern, I invite you to reflect on your response to this chapter through the lens of your own style.

## Closing Thoughts on the Psychospiritual Journey

In exploring the spiritual journey as a subjective experience, we have encountered a variety of descriptions. We've come to realize that we cannot fully understand the spiritual journey in purely rational or objective terms, and we naturally find ourselves drawn to metaphors over and over again. The connection with metaphors and images should come as no surprise: we are moving here in territories of *meaning*.

The person on a spiritual journey is a psychospiritual being, with psychological patterns in place. These patterns, such as complexes and shadow aspects, lie deeper than conscious awareness until life events and experiences bring them to light and we are compelled to confront them. At the very least, such psychological work is part of the invitation to healing, even if the journey is not explicitly recognized as a spiritual one. Whether or not our clients are able to accept the invitation depends on many factors, among them their life circumstances, the availability of help in developing awareness, and the intensity of the internal and external obstacles they encounter. The patterns themselves are not likely to go away, although their influence may diminish as clients travel further along the path.

Sometimes help comes from sources unknown to them, beyond their conscious awareness and beyond the human psyche. When they feel the pull and guidance of such mysterious forces, we can invite them to explore surrendering control and offer our encouragement for this venture. (The client's egoic stability is an important consideration here.) This relationship with forces beyond the personal and psychological domain is what characterizes the experience of the journey as a spiritual one, as opposed to a purely psychological process.

If, as psychotherapists and counselors, we do not personally relate to such possibilities, we can nevertheless find ways to enter into our clients' worlds and support them in exploring their own meanings. We can feel our way with respect and curiosity. But if we shut the door on their deepest longings and fears, we may miss openings for healing and growth.

At this point let's balance our approach by shifting the focus from a subjective or interior perspective to one that is more objective and exterior.

## CHAPTER SIX

# Consciousness Evolving: Development, Identity, and Perspective

As a lifelong student of human development—a teacher of young children, a learning disabilities specialist, an academic professor, and a counselor—I have always been fascinated by the ways in which we try to make sense of human development over the life span. As we noted at the beginning of the preceding chapter, there are stage models that focus on childhood and adolescence, and controversies over the applicability of such stage models to adulthood. Developmental psychology searches for ways to explain the interactions of nature and nurture. One of the strategies for dealing with the complexities of human development has been to divide the territory into research specializations, such as cognitive, moral, social, and emotional development. Psychodynamic lenses differ significantly from structural-developmental perspectives. If you are looking for universally accepted conclusions, you will not find them here. But there are generalizations that can be useful, and we can draw on them to help make sense of our observations.

Little attention has been given to what we are calling psychospiritual development: the ways in which psychological development helps to shape our relationship to spirituality and religion, and the ways in which our spiritual/religious development can influence our psychological development. The mutual influence is substantial, but also fluid and enigmatic—hence my fondness for the term *interplay*. Contributions to our understanding come from Jean Piaget's theory of cognitive development, Erik Erikson's theory of psychosocial development, Jane Loevinger's work on ego development, and the field of moral development studied by Lawrence Kohlberg, Carol Gilligan, and others. However, James Fowler's work on faith development is the most directly related, so we will begin there.

## Fowler's View of Faith Development

Fowler derived his theory from interviews of 359 individuals, from three to eighty-four years old, mostly white and Christian, conducted between 1972 and 1981. The sample was clearly limited, and the research is dated, which is important to consider. But I want to draw attention to his definition of faith, not in relation to a religious tradition or belief, but in these terms:

> Faith is a person's or group's way of moving into the force field of life. It is our way of finding coherence in and giving meaning to the multiple forces and relations that make up our lives. Faith is a person's way of seeing him- or herself in relation to others against a background of shared meaning and purpose.[1]

Fowler also drew on theologian Paul Tillich's approach to faith as having to do with matters of "ultimate concern." Whether we are religious or not, our faith "shapes the way we invest our deepest loves and our most costly loyalties." Faith has to do with "how to put our lives together and what will make life worth living."[2] Fowler goes even further, suggesting that we consider *faith as imagination*, as an imaginative process that "grasps the ultimate conditions of our existence, unifying them into a comprehensive image in light of which we shape our responses and initiatives, our actions."[3] His view opens doors to larger frameworks of understanding.

He reminds us that a developmental perspective gives us two things: first, a view of the dynamics of change and transformation, and second, a view of periods of equilibrium and continuity. Together these two aspects make up a pattern over time, a pattern which is only visible from the outside. From the interior, we are aware of our experiences and their meaning for us. It is challenging to step outside of this framework to see the structural pattern that is being formed. For that we need some distance. These patterns of change and equilibrium are the subject of stage theories of development.

We can picture Fowler poring over his interview transcripts for hours on end. Eventually he begins to see themes and patterns, which he then describes as stages of faith development. While influenced by Piaget and Kohlberg, Fowler ultimately found their models to be too focused on cognitive and rational structures. (Erikson's theory was helpful in balancing this formal emphasis.) Because he understood faith as involving both reason and passion, his theory embraces both structure (formal capacities for knowing and valuing) and meaningful content (what he calls the structuring power of particular symbols, beliefs, practices, and experiences). So there is room here for both the external view of structural patterns and some of the interior view of particular sources of meaning. This matters if we want to take seriously the interplay of psychological and spiritual dimensions.

What follows is a brief summary of Fowler's stages. Then we will consider a number of other related stage models, each with its own particular descriptions and labels.

**Infancy: Undifferentiated Faith**—This is really a pre-stage, laying a foundation of trust, courage, hope, and love that may be jeopardized by threats of abandonment, deprivation, and unpredictability. This is the arena of Erikson's basic trust, which creates a foundation for the stages that follow.

**Stage 1: Intuitive-Projective Faith**—Typical of ages two to seven, this stage is characterized by imagination, fluid thought patterns, and ways of knowing dominated by sensory perception. Imitation is prominent, and the actions and stories conveying the faith of key adults are powerful influences. Fears (arising internally or fed by adult taboos) become part of the imaginal experience. The point of view is egocentric, but late in this stage, we find the beginnings of self-awareness. *Transition*: the emergence of concrete operational thinking, in Piaget's terms.

**Stage 2: Mythic-Literal Faith**—The stories and beliefs of the child's family and community now become his or her own. Interpretations of these stories, myths, and beliefs are literal and concrete. Rules and moral attitudes are understood literally. The development of concrete operational thinking allows for the development of a linear, narrative approach to meaning, which gradually replaces the imaginative fluidity of the previous stage. As the capacity to *take the perspective of the other person* increases, considerations of fairness and reciprocity become dominant. This stage is characteristic of the school-age child, but also some adolescents and adults. *Transition*: The experience of clashes between stories as well as potential disillusionment with teachers and teachings. Encounters with different views of what is meaningful, opening the way to deeper reflection (increasingly possible with the development of formal operational thinking). An emerging capacity for additional perspective-taking in which "I can see you seeing me, and see me as you see me," leading to "I see you seeing me seeing you."

**Stage 3: Synthetic-Conventional Faith**—This stage is typical of adolescents and many adults. With a growing sense of belonging to larger communities beyond the family, the individual's meaning-making has a more interpersonal flavor. Faith offers a strong sense of belonging as the values of significant others take on increasing importance. In this sense, it is a conformist stage. Beliefs and values are often absorbed from others rather than explicitly chosen or reflected upon, although there is usually a coherent orientation. Authority is typically entrusted to leaders or to the consensus of the group. The individual develops a personal myth, consistent with the group orientation, which provides a sense of identity and purpose. *Transition*: Clashes or contradictions among authority figures or between traditional and emerging paradigms. Leaving home, emotionally or physically, which may lead to a reexamination of beliefs and identifications.

**Stage 4: Individuative-Reflective Faith**—The individual begins to take more responsibility for his or her beliefs, attitudes, and commitments. This typically involves an experience of some new tensions: between group norms and personal values, between subjective, unexamined feelings and objective critical evaluation, and between recognition of the relative and the longing for an absolute. A new sense of self and a new worldview begin to emerge from the web of interpersonal roles and expectations. Individual identity is consciously and explicitly owned. Symbols and myths often become secondary to conceptual meanings, leading to the description of this stage as "demythologizing." The capacity for critical reflection is a new strength. There may also be overconfidence in the rational mind, which can bring arrogance and underestimation of the power of unconscious factors. *Transition*: Disturbing inner voices that disrupt the neat self-image and categories. The emergence of deeper images and energies that make existing meanings feel flat. Experiences of disillusionment, along with recognition that life is more complex than rational categories can explain.

**Stage 5: Conjunctive Faith**—A reuniting of symbols and concepts now becomes possible. The meanings and myths that were discarded in favor of rational analysis are reclaimed in a more flexible framework of faith. There is a growing capacity to engage with paradoxes and live with apparent contradictions. The deeper self and the deeper roots of social traditions (religious, ethnic) are recognized and embraced. The truths held by others can now be approached with more understanding and openness. The individual's own truths (or those of his or her group) can be compelling while also being recognized as relative and partial glimpses. These shifts can come with increasing maturity, although sometimes they do not unfold at all. The pitfall may be a kind of paralysis, an inability to commit or move in one direction because of the appreciation of paradox and relativism. *Transition*: Fowler's words are worth quoting here: "But this stage remains divided. It lives and acts between an untransformed world and a transforming vision and loyalties."[4]

**Stage 6: Universalizing Faith**—Fowler describes this perspective as exceedingly rare. The key development is the emergence of a truly universal outlook in which the direct experience of a transcendent, unified reality makes all lesser commitments, to nation, religion, even oneself, transparent and insubstantial. Those who embody this kind of faith (Gandhi is Fowler's exemplar) are often described as martyrs, more revered after their deaths than before. Other developmental approaches and research studies suggest that there are intermediate stages between 5 and 6—stages that were not apparent in Fowler's sample of interviewees.

## Developmental Basics

Bearing in mind Fowler's broad definition of faith, we can perceive an unfolding of *qualitatively* different ways of making meaning, of viewing and valuing one's self and the world. Each stage has its own coherent pattern, which is the lens through which we experience everything. We can't see the structure or pattern we are in, because it is what we *see through*. It is our *worldview*. We may be able to understand the complexity of the next stage intellectually, but we are usually approaching that complexity through our present lens (which is not visible to us).

These stages unfold in an invariant sequence. The evidence for this comes from developmental psychology research as well as from religious/spiritual teachers and from students of cultural and historical change. Sometimes this sequential movement is represented by the image of a ladder. A more elegant image suggests that development proceeds in a spiral movement. Whatever the image, it is vital to recognize that invariant sequence does not mean rigidity. Development itself is fluid, complex, and intricate.

How long individuals remain in a particular stage can vary, of course. They may come to rest at a particular stage for various reasons, having to do with their cultural surroundings (holding environment), their life conditions, and their own biological givens (nurture and nature). It is also important to recognize that not all changes are developmental. We go through many changes that do not entail a structural shift. These may be described as additive, incremental, or horizontal. They are transitions rather than deep transformations, and we deal with them all the time in our rapidly changing world. Losses, gains, shifts in focus and context, expansions, contractions: these are the stuff of life, of both our joy and our suffering. On the other hand, how we understand and approach such changes is likely to be shaped by our developmental stage, as well as by our personality style, cultural style, history, relationship to unconscious forces, and more.

We will explore other descriptions of stage development, with different names and emphases, but mostly, we will find common themes and a shared framework of understanding. Sometimes these are called stages, sometimes levels or, more fluidly, waves. Before presenting a composite sketch, however, I want to highlight several important characteristics of this developmental approach. Grasping these essentials will help make sense of the whole perspective.

## *An Outside Perspective*

As we have noted, stage descriptions are inferences drawn from an outside perspective, based on what is said (in interviews, for example) and what is done (observed behaviors). Unlike maturational theories (see Erikson, Levinson) which emphasize biological age and the demands of typical life tasks, structural theories follow in Piaget's footsteps and focus on the *basic ordering principles* which shape a view of world and self. These principles are not evident from an inside perspective: that is, we are rarely aware of the principles which characterize our current stage. In the words of an expert on adult development and spiritual direction, "the ordering system acts like an unperceived horizon defining what one sees and how one fits these pieces together into a coherent whole."[5]

Harvard developmental psychologist Robert Kegan, a major theorist in the field of adult development, introduces the idea of a subject-object structure in development. In any given stage, we are seeing *through* the lens of "subject," with which we are more or less fully identified.[6] How we see ourselves-and-the-world is not available to us as an object of observation or reflection. Only as we begin to move into the next stage can we begin to see our worldview from the outside, as an object. We can then look back and see the patterns that shaped our understanding. The practical implication is that a therapist may be able to discern the shape of a client's stage and choose appropriate ways of interacting, but the client is not typically aware of this pattern until well into a transitional phase. In a nutshell, "subject" at one stage becomes "object" in the following stage. We can then *see* what was invisible to us before because we were fully inside it. This is a crucial aspect of stage development.

## *A Dynamic and Fluid Process*

Second, stage development theories inevitably focus on observations of equilibrium. But human beings are dynamic systems, in constant interaction with their environment. Development is complex and messy, and stages are best viewed as evolutionary *truces*, in Kegan's language. A useful lens is the notion of a center of gravity, suggested by Jane Loevinger and more recently by Ken Wilber.[7] At any given time, depending on context, each of us is organizing our identity and worldview through a range of lenses—one developmentally earlier, one more central in the present, and one into which we are currently leaning. Under pressure, we may regress. Under optimal supportive circumstances, we may stretch beyond our characteristic limits. Stages have fluidity, overlapping like waves. The boundaries are not rigid, but about 50 percent of the time, we are operating from the stage which is our center of gravity.

## *Multiple Intelligences*

A further complication has to do with the existence of different *kinds* of human intelligence. Just because someone seems to be operating from a particular stage of cognitive functioning, we cannot assume that their emotional or moral intelligence is at the same level. This notion of multiple forms of intelligence has several well-respected sources in psychology, with Howard Gardner being perhaps the most widely recognized.[8] Elaborating on Gardner's proposal, Wilber's integral theory suggests that these various aspects of development—cognitive, moral, emotional, values, interpersonal, spiritual, kinesthetic—are likely to show uneven development. He refers to these as *developmental lines*. When we study developmental theorists, we can readily see that they emphasize different lines: Piaget highlighted the logical-mathematical line of cognitive intelligence, Kohlberg the moral line. Fowler focused on the spiritual or faith line, but some theorists question whether there *is* a distinct spiritual line. We will explore that question shortly.

## *Subpersonalities*

There is an additional source of complexity. Most of us can relate to the experience of having different parts to our personality: "Part of me wants this, but part of me wants that." Also described as *subpersonalities* or ego states, these parts may themselves be operating at different stages of development. We may have one or more young parts—a wounded child, or an innocent child, for instance—who approaches the world through an earlier developmental lens than our controller, perfectionist, or skeptic subpersonalities. Since we are not usually conscious of these parts at any given moment, we are now introducing the role of unconscious dynamics into our developmental picture. This is messy and complex indeed; the metaphor of waves seems much more appropriate than that of a ladder.

## A Contemporary Description of Developmental Stages

We will return to a consideration of developmental dynamics shortly, but first I would like to introduce a composite description of the major developmental stages, drawn from several sources and going by slightly different names. The primary sources are transpersonal and integral theory, along with the work of Harvard developmental psychologist Robert Kegan. I will lay a foundation by offering a very brief introduction to the transpersonal and integral lenses.

Transpersonal psychology has its roots in the late 1960s, influenced by William James (1842–1910), Jung, Aldous Huxley (who died in 1963), and others. Abraham Maslow had already voiced criticisms of behaviorism and psychoanalysis (known as the First and Second Forces in Psychology) and played a major role in the development of humanistic psychology (the Third Force). But his work was not done. He and Anthony Sutich, one of the cofounders of the Association for Humanistic Psychology, began to be dissatisfied with that framework as well. The missing piece for them was the spiritual dimension of life, which was being brought into focus by the influx of Eastern spirituality, mysticism, meditation, interest in indigenous cultures, and the psychedelic experimentations of the times. In 1967, Maslow and Sutich, along with Stanislav Grof, James Fadiman, and Sonya Margulies, created a working group to consider new possibilities. Grof's term "transpersonal psychology" was embraced, and the Association of Transpersonal Psychology was soon born.

With an emphasis on bringing together the wisdom of the world's spiritual traditions with the best of modern psychology, the field has focused on the study of nonordinary states of consciousness, transpersonal experiences, and the development of the human being beyond (*trans*) the personal level. From a transpersonal perspective, the essence of human beings is *consciousness*, the Ground of Being; and human development is the evolving of consciousness.[9] Since the 1960s, the field has seen a growing interest in embracing the personal and everyday dimensions of life as well as the transpersonal. I would describe this as a movement toward integration.[10]

Ken Wilber was an early contributor to the transpersonal movement, but he began to branch out in new directions. Eventually, he consolidated a perspective which he called integral theory. The acronym AQAL points to the basic premise of the integral perspective. All levels (AL) means that human development spans from conception to the far reaches of the transpersonal. All quadrants (AQ) stipulates that life always appears in four dimensions, the interior and the exterior of both the individual and the collective. In addition, integral theory recognizes the importance of *states* of consciousness, *lines* of development (multiple intelligences), and *types* or styles (such as the Enneagram). The aim of integral psychology is "to integrate the enduring truths of premodern and modern approaches to psychology and consciousness," which involves coordinating and integrating the research findings about all the levels in all four quadrants.[11] In this chapter we are exploring developmental levels; the four quadrants will play a role in the next chapter.

Since we are interested in psychospiritual development, it makes sense to think in terms of a web or bundle of relevant skills, abilities, and orientations. The stage descriptions that follow incorporate considerations of faith, cognition, ego, values, and moral development.[12] Initially, it is helpful to frame these perspectives in first-person language, in order to include the subjective dimension to some degree. For each stage a more objective explanation will follow. (I encourage you to focus on the descriptions themselves rather than allowing yourself to get caught up in critiquing the stage titles.) In this numbering system the combined numerals simply indicate transitional stages.

**Stage 1: Sensorimotor-Undifferentiated, Reactive**

There really is no "I" in this early stage of infancy. The primary developmental tasks have to do with differentiating the physical body from the surrounding world, learning to manage sensory input and self-regulation, and distinguishing people from objects. (In the next chapter we will look at a transpersonal perspective that suggests more may be going on in this stage.)

**Stage 1/2: Naïve**

*I am what I feel.*

The self (six to twenty-four months) is fused with emotional energy. A transitional stage, this period is the relational context within which development unfolds. Sensorimotor intelligence is applied to self and other. The infant-caregiver relationship is the primary crucible for the development of self-regulation, basic trust, and secure attachment.

**Stage 2: Intuitive-Projective, Magical-Impulsive**

*I am drawn to images and symbols. They are the source of my faith, my fears, and hopes. There are magical things in the universe, and taboos and rituals that I must observe in order to be safe. I am strongly influenced by the examples, moods, actions, and stories of those I look up to around me, the leaders in my tribe. The world I live in is fluid, and my perceptions and imagination shape my experience.*

Typical of the two- to four-year-old child, this stage may also have a magnetic draw for adults at times, particularly for those who inhabit the affiliative/relativistic stage (see 4/5). There is a felt merging of the mental, emotional, and physical worlds (which is lost in the Rational/Achiever worldview—see stage 4). Part of this fluidity is a tendency to act on impulse. While impulsivity and magical thinking can definitely be a problem for adults, the gifts in this stage include a sense of wonder, possibility, and emotionally flavored intuition. With an emerging sense of a "me" (at Piaget's preoperational level), urges that are experienced as unacceptable or shameful begin to be pushed down into unconsciousness. These may find less healthy forms of expression at some later point.

**Stage 2/3: Opportunistic, Self-Protective, Egocentric**

*I know that there are rules, but I only follow them if they are good for me. Otherwise, I do what I want, and try to avoid getting in trouble. If something goes wrong, it's usually someone else's fault. I focus on the present, on what's right in front of me. I don't worry about what might happen in the future. The world I live in revolves around me.*

Another transitional stage, this is a normal but typically brief pattern seen in older children, but sometimes in adolescents and perhaps about 5 percent of adults. Cognitively, we are looking at some preoperational and early concrete-operational thinking, with an inability to take the perspective of another person. What has meaning is concrete, immediate, and focused on the individual's interests. There is an emphasis on power and access to supernatural elements for the purpose of self-protection. Morality tends to be at a preconventional level (focused on one's own needs, without much consideration for others), reaching into the early conventional stage.

### Stage 3: Mythic-Literal, Conformist

*I now take on for myself the stories, beliefs, and observances that symbolize belonging to my faith family. I believe in them literally and absolutely, and believe that my salvation depends on my observance of the moral codes that are part of the truth that has been given to us. There is only one truth, one path, and one purpose for my life, which is obedience to the will of God (etc.) as given to us by our faith leaders, whose authority is absolute. My personal relationship to God/Allah/Deity is a driving force in my life.*

There is now a more solid mental self (concrete-operational), differentiated from the emotional and physical self, and a new ability to narrate one's own experience. There are internal scripts that define what is right and wrong. But it is essentially the group's story that is taken as one's own. Sacred texts are interpreted literally, often with a focus on a few select segments. Social and moral roles and rules are understood as givens and shape the meanings that govern life for these older children and early adolescents (as well as about 10 percent of adults). Hierarchy is respected in the group to which one gives allegiance. This stage is often described as *ethnocentric,* with "ethno" referring to any group with which one is identified. There is an in-group and an out-group, with little recognition of individual differences. The membership group may be traditional or nonconformist, based on peer group, family, religion, nationality, ethnicity, sexual orientation, and so forth. Fairness and reciprocity matter within the boundaries of the group, and "our God" is likewise seen as fair. (If something goes wrong, it implies that the individual has done something wrong or bad. Guilt keeps the individual in line.)

**Stage 3/4: Conventional, Traditional, Interpersonal**

*I am still embedded in the rules and roles that have been given to me by my parents, my faith community, and my society. My relationships are central in my life, but are more complex than they used to be. I am aware that I am also an individual with my own personality traits. I often find myself caught between my own needs and the expectations of others. Because I am increasingly aware of my own thinking and experience, I often feel quite self-conscious. But I am comforted by my personal relationship with God, who knows and loves me.*

Another transitional stage, this characterizes mid-adolescence and is also estimated to describe about 37 percent of the adult American population. Early formal operations are now available, making it possible to think about the future, acknowledge one's accountability to others, and understand that others have their own perspectives. On the whole, however, those whose center of gravity is at this stage still find themselves enmeshed or fused with their interpersonal relationships. They cannot stand outside their own values and beliefs in order to critique them. Some people at this stage find themselves seeking and questioning (particularly in adolescence), while others are very set and certain in their spiritual beliefs (especially if they are a bit older and chose not to question the beliefs established at the Mythic, Conformist stage.)

**Stage 4: Rational, Self-authoring, Individual, Modern Achiever**

*When I begin to feel constrained or disillusioned by the conformist/conventional worldview, I begin searching for my own way. I am more able to reason abstractly, to consider alternative possibilities, and to think about thinking. As I think more for myself, I am no longer embedded in social systems. Individual mastery, problem solving, goal-oriented planning, and achievement are important to me, and I like being acknowledged for my successes. I am more scientific in my approach and also appreciate systems of thought that highlight individual rights. My view of the world is more relativistic. There are no absolutes any more. I distrust authority and take responsibility for making my own meanings. I am the author of my own life.*

This stage is estimated to be characteristic of about 30 percent of the adult American population. With the full development of formal operations, there is an increasing capacity for critical reflection on one's identity and meaning structures. This is sometimes described as a demythologization process, characteristic of the modern mind. Myths, symbols, and conventions that were once important lose their significance. In their place, reason and individual conscience play prominent roles in decisions. We may view atheism or agnosticism as expressions of spiritual orientation at this stage. Emotion and intuition tend to be dismissed as guides for action, and there is often a lack of connection with bodily experience. The influence of unconscious motivations is disregarded. Individual rights are respected, and the circle of care and compassion expands beyond one's own group to all people (shifting from ethnocentric to world-centric). At the same time, the ability to step fully into other perspectives is typically lacking. We may describe this as tolerance, or simply agreeing to differ. No one person or group has "the truth," but rational approaches are still privileged. Individual striving and achievement are prized, and hierarchies based on achievement command respect.

Some models propose that this is a more typically masculine path in our culture.[13] From this perspective, many women move out of Conventional/Traditional (stage 3/4) into a subjective mode that is still oriented toward personal meaning, but more influenced by an intuitive inner voice than by a rational way of knowing. When this evolves into a reason-based, procedural mode, it is often as a result of formal education. But even within procedural knowing, there are two possible flavors. One is *separate* knowing, which is much like the individual/achiever form described above. The other is *connected* knowing, which converges with Carol Gilligan's work on moral development. (Critiquing Kohlberg's research as biased toward males, Gilligan found that female moral development emphasized care and relatedness over individual rights.)

**Stage 4/5: Affiliative, Relativistic-Sensitive, Postmodern, Pluralistic**

*In this way of making meaning, I am capable of even more cognitive complexity. I can criticize systems of thought, see patterns, and consider alternative possibilities and paradoxes. What is emerging more strongly now is an orientation toward relationship. I have an intimate connection with both the object of knowledge and my partners in dialogue. I like to share experiences and don't like debate and argument. I value harmony and empathize with other points of view. I like to think of myself as tolerant and accepting of everyone's viewpoint. All truths are relative and emerge in a particular cultural and historical context. Honoring diversity matters a lot to me. In my faith/spirituality, the power of symbols, myths, and rituals is now reintegrated with conceptual meanings, and I am open to the voices of my deeper self and my personal unconscious.*

Here we are looking at mature formal operations and early postformal operations. Estimated to describe about 10 percent of the adult population, this *postmodern* stage emphasizes the importance of *context*. Truth depends on the point of view of the observer. With increased empathy, psychological-mindedness, and ability to take multiple perspectives, this stage brings the potential for significant expansion and deepening of spiritual perspectives. A world-centric orientation may even embrace all beings in what is sometimes described as a *cosmo-centric view*. Social engagement and activism may emerge from this sense of interconnectedness. Hierarchical structures of any kind are typically rejected.

There are some limitations to this way of knowing. For example, Relativists are often not very tolerant of those who view the world from a conformist/conventional perspective. While they can see the possibility of a universal, inclusive human community, they are still wed to their own perspective and well-being. They tend to have difficulty dealing with the inharmonious elements of difference of opinion and negative emotions, especially anger. So it is easy to fall into a pattern of "being nice." In groups of like-minded others, avoidance of conflict sometimes means that very little actually gets accomplished. Awareness of multiple perspectives can also lead to a new kind of identity crisis, a paralysis of overprocessing, or an exclusive reliance on intuitive knowing over rational considerations. Related to this latter point is a postmodern tendency to revere the perspective of stage 2, the Intuitive-Projective, Magical-Impulsive stage. The rejection of modern rationalism often leads to a nostalgic longing for the prerational worldview that is associated with both the innocence of childhood and the premodern cultures of indigenous peoples. We will examine a critique of this view (described as the pre-trans fallacy) in chapter 8.

### Stage 5: Integrative, Integral, Authentic, Multiperspectival, Self-Actualized

*I can now naturally make room for people who inhabit all the prior stages. I am at home in a global, big-picture view of all these complex systems, understanding that they are in flow and that a certain amount of chaos and change is natural. I deeply appreciate paradox and dialectical processes. I embrace such apparent opposites as mind and body, reason and emotion, masculine and feminine, conscious and unconscious, self and other. I am at home in life and in myself, and am able to bring forth my gifts in an authentic way, often in service to others.*

With a solid foundation in postformal cognition, people whose center of gravity is in this stage probably make up about 5 percent of the adult US population. This stage is just beginning to emerge in the population. (Current research suggests that Fowler's final stage of Universalizing Faith was too global. Perhaps his interview sample was too limited, or we are seeing the more recent emergence of two possible stages between the postmodern relativistic perspective and the truly transpersonal stages.) The Integral stage is characterized by a deeper openness to other spiritual traditions and perspectives. In addition, the illusions of earlier stages (that the self will triumph over suffering, loss, death, or that the Mystery may eventually be penetrated and understood) fall away, leaving the individual with a new sense of existential isolation and uncertainty.

**Stage 5/6: Ego-Aware, Paradoxical**

*I am often able to access a witnessing perspective, clearly recognizing that the "I" with which I have been identified for so long is just a construct. I see that the ego filters everything I experience, so that even the notion of authenticity comes into question. There is a reality that is deeper than this incessant inner conversation, and I clearly experience this freedom at times. I cannot describe it in words, and I find myself going back and forth between my identification with my personal ego and this vast, silent Ground of Being or Divine. But it is evident to me that life is full of apparent paradoxes and contradictions, and that somehow there is an underlying harmony, symbolized by the yin-yang symbol. I am open to seeing and exploring whatever presents itself as part of "me," and I find myself increasingly able to trust an intuitive knowing about what is needed.*

Much of the evidence for this stage comes from the research of Susanne Cook-Greuter, who developed a rigorous research tool using the Sentence Completion Test.[14] Estimated to describe less than 2 percent of the adult US population, this stage is rare, and the data is only suggestive at this point. But if we are trying to understand human development, and especially the interplay of psychology and spirituality, we need to pay attention to these relatively unusual patterns. They may point to emerging possibilities for human beings. It is important to realize that those at this stage can feel torn between the world of everyday reality and the deeper reality they experience. This tension may be accompanied by a sense of aloneness, since there are few people who share or even understand their perspective. The striving of ego gradually drops away, but they are still in a transitional space in terms of the spiritual journey.

## *Is* There a Spiritual Intelligence?

Is there indeed a separate line of spiritual intelligence? Contemporary thinking on this issue is divided. Gardner did not include spiritual intelligence in his list because he considered it too difficult to define and assess, although at a later point, he considered the possibility of an "existential intelligence."

Author Cindy Wigglesworth offers a thought-provoking introduction to this territory, and she has even developed a self-assessment tool.[15] Beginning with her own definition of spirituality as "the innate human need to be connected to something larger than ourselves, something we consider to be divine or of exceptional nobility," she describes spiritual intelligence as "the ability to behave with wisdom and compassion, while maintaining inner and outer peace, regardless of the situation."[16]

Paying attention to both inner experience and outer behavior, she describes four main areas of spiritual intelligence: Self/self Awareness, Universal Awareness, Self/self Mastery, and Social Mastery/Spiritual Presence. Within each of these arenas are five increasing levels of skill, suggesting that these skills can be developed with practice. Viewing these areas as steps beyond the model of emotional intelligence proposed by Daniel Goleman[17], Wigglesworth suggests a four-quadrant model (shown on next page).

Skill 1, awareness of one's own worldview, may begin with simply being able to describe one's own beliefs. This capacity can be present in very basic form at early developmental stages. For instance, someone whose center of gravity is at stage 2/3 (Opportunistic, Egocentric) may simply say, "You just have to look out for yourself." A more developed articulation of beliefs comes into play with the experience of belonging to a group and taking on the group's beliefs (stages 3, Mythic-Literal, and 3/4, Conventional). But it is not until stage 4 (Rational, Modernist, Self-Authoring) that there is likely to be a broader awareness *that* one has a worldview, and this awareness comes into full flower in stage 4/5 (Postmodern, Relativistic).

| **QUADRANT 1**<br><br>**Self/self Awareness**<br><br>1. Awareness of Own Worldview<br>2. Awareness of Life Purpose<br>3. Awareness of Values Hierarchy<br>4. Complexity of Inner Thought<br>5. Awareness of Ego self/Higher Self | **QUADRANT 2**<br><br>**Universal Awareness**<br><br>6. Awareness of Interconnectedness of Life<br>7. Awareness of Worldviews of Others<br>8. Breadth of Time Perception<br>9. Awareness of Limitations/Power of Human Perception<br>10. Awareness of Spiritual Laws<br>11. Experience of Transcendent Oneness |
|---|---|
| **QUADRANT 3**<br><br>**Self/self-Mastery**<br><br>12. Commitment to Spiritual Growth<br>13. Keeping Higher Self in Charge<br>14. Living your Purpose and Values<br>15. Sustaining Faith<br>16. Seeking Guidance from Higher Self | **QUADRANT 4**<br><br>**Social Mastery/Spiritual Presence**<br><br>17. Being a Wise and Effective Teacher/Mentor of Spiritual Principles<br>18. Being a Wise and Effective Leader/Change Agent<br>19. Making Compassionate and Wise Decisions<br>20. Being a Calming, Healing Presence<br>21. Being Aligned with the Ebb and Flow of Life |

*Figure 6.1 The Four Quadrants and Twenty-One Skills of Spiritual Intelligence. Used with permission.*

Although Wigglesworth's model does not come out of a strictly academic approach to developmental psychology, and there are certainly questions about embedded assumptions, it is a useful beginning for those interested in understanding and nurturing psychospiritual growth. Therapists might listen to a client's talk with these stages in mind.

The focus in Wigglesworth's model is on the question: "Who or what is driving your life?" The overall trajectory of development is seen as moving from a life driven by the ego (self-centered, short-sighted, small-minded) to one guided by the Higher Self (the aspect of ourselves characterized by wisdom, compassion, selflessness). Regardless of whether we agree that spiritual intelligence is a separate line, this shift in orientation from self to Self is consistent with many metaphors of transformation and descriptions of the spiritual journey, as well as with the overall direction of development in stage theories.

Transpersonal psychologist Frances Vaughan takes a similar but somewhat broader view. She suggests that spiritual intelligence calls for multiple ways of knowing and for the integration of the inner life of mind and spirit with the outer life of work in the world. It can be cultivated through questing, inquiry, and practice, and may be enriched by spiritual experience. Spiritual maturity, in her view, is expressed through wisdom and compassionate action in the world.[18]

There are some similarities here—the emphasis on both inner capacity and outward action, as well as the possibility of intentionally cultivating spiritual intelligence. What is also striking is the relevance of other lines of intelligence, such as emotional and moral: cognitive capacity is important, but other capacities are also significant. Among these we might consider intuitive, aesthetic, somatic, and contemplative capacities, some of which open us to the experience of nonphysical realities. Spiritual intelligence is a rich resource.

We opened this chapter with a description of Fowler's stages of faith, and then stepped back for a wider view of human development. Now that we have a composite description of the major developmental stages, and have considered the possibility of spiritual intelligence, it's time to allow for some personal reflection. We will then tackle more complexities and critiques of this developmental perspective.

## Personal Reflection on Development

Levels of development are alive in you—but it can be very hard to get perspective on your own. It is easier to see them in others, based on a kind of developmental intuition. Reflect on some individuals you know—perhaps clients. Where do you think their center of gravity falls, and why do you think so? What have you observed in their behavior, ways of speaking, and so forth? You can also reflect on what you see in our social/

cultural/political world: how might the notion of levels of development help you understand what you see there? Finally, try to sense where your own center of gravity might be. And remember this is an uneven process, and we fluctuate with context, mood, and more.

## A Deeper Look at Developmental Dynamics and Variations

Let's consider some common critiques of the developmental perspective, as well as some common metaphors for the developmental process; the latter are significant because they imply different patterns of movement. Then we will take a closer look at the dynamics of moving through stages, which will help us recognize the kinds of problems that can arise in the course of development. Finally, we will focus on a crucial distinction between healthy and unhealthy versions of each stage.

### *Objections and Critiques*

The first issue that usually presents itself is a red-flag objection to the study of adult development, i.e. that it is biased and judgmental. If later stages are viewed as somehow "better" or "higher," then they must be *valued* more highly. Surely all human beings are equal in their fundamental value or spiritual essence? Of course. That is not in question here.

Following are some of my own responses to this challenge. First, the objection comes primarily from the postmodern/relativistic perspective, which is very uncomfortable with the idea of privileging any one perspective over another. As soon as we introduce the concept of *privilege,* we step into the highly sensitive territory of cultural diversity and power inequity. Any form of hierarchy is suspect. Once this concern has emerged in human consciousness, its importance needs to be recognized and embraced in any developmental approach.

The risk of biased judgment certainly exists, and any tool may be misused. We have seen clear evidence of the abuse of a hierarchical lens in colonial and Western-oriented writings of scholars in anthropology and religious studies, for instance. But prejudiced, unwise use of the hierarchy concept does not necessitate the avoidance of all hierarchical lenses. Any contemporary use of a hierarchical framework needs to be committed to the awareness, sensitivity, and responsibility that are the fruits of those earlier distortions. The blanket avoidance of all possibilities of hierarchical organization becomes its own kind of self-limiting prejudice.

A developmental lens can help us relate to a range of perspectives with *more* understanding and compassion, not less. We can appreciate that any framework of meaning has its place in human life. We can see how a particular worldview unfolded, and how it makes coherent sense to those who inhabit it. There is a growing capacity to approach those who hold a particular perspective in a more respectful and skillful way, not assuming that everyone sees the world the way that we do. This is very helpful in working with clients.

It's also important to highlight a crucial distinction between oppressive (or dominator) hierarchies and growth (actualization) hierarchies. We recognize the former in any system that values "power over," emphasizing domination, oppression, and exploitation. Actualization hierarchies, on the other hand, point to the unfolding of potential, the process of growth itself. We see the latter in the natural world, in the development from atoms to molecules to cells to organisms. In humans, healthy development involves an *increase* in both complexity and the capacity for caring and understanding—represented in widening circles from egocentric (me) to ethnocentric (my group) to worldcentric (all human beings, all life on the planet), and eventually to cosmocentric (the whole cosmos). Every new level, if it emerges in a healthy way, both *transcends* (reaches beyond) the preceding level and *includes* (embraces) it. A growth hierarchy actually points to a *lessening* of oppression and domination. The recognition of this potential invites us to consider human development as a process of transformation, with increasing depth and scope as it unfolds.

## *Metaphors and Movement*

The familiar image of a ladder of development does not seem very useful, and from a postmodern perspective may be simplistically arrogant. An alternative metaphor is that of a labyrinth, suggesting the sometimes confusing, back-and-forth experience of the developmental process.[19] Many people prefer the metaphor of waves of development, which allows for a better sense of the fluidity in the developmental process.

Related to the notion of waves is the image of a developmental *spiral* or *spiral cone*. A spiral gives us the vision of both ascending and expanding cycles, with an element of dynamic flow as well.

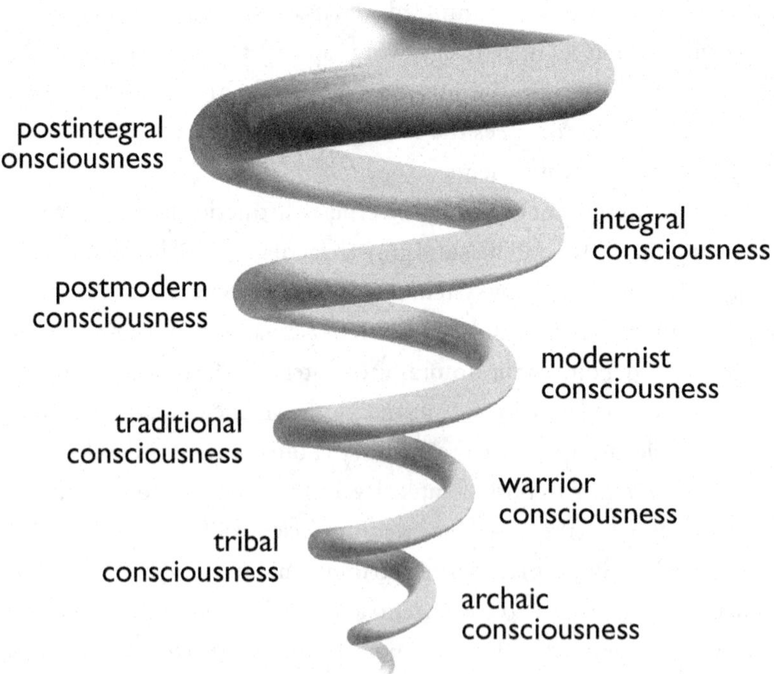


*Figure 6.2 Spiral of Development in Consciousness.*
*Used with permission of Steve McIntosh.*

A different version of a spiral is suggested by Michael Washburn, a transpersonal philosopher and psychologist whose theory works toward integrating transpersonal psychology and the psychoanalytic tradition, especially Jungian thought. He proposes that development (that is, individuation) unfolds in a particular kind of spiral movement which always involves a *return* to the deep unconscious in order to integrate its transformative power before moving on to a higher integration. Washburn describes this as "regression in the service of transcendence."[20] His model is worth exploring for those who are particularly drawn to Jungian psychology. My own sense is that we *may* need to regress or revisit past stages of development in order to heal or rework problematic aspects associated with those stages. Counselors may well find themselves facilitating this kind of work. I do not, however, see this return as absolutely *necessary* for consciousness to evolve in everyone. For our purposes, we can recognize that all these metaphors entail recognition of fluid movement and the complex and messy aspects of human unfolding.

However, I want to highlight the point that higher is *not* necessarily better. In particular, therapists are not in the business of getting people to move to the next stage. What is important is the *fullness and health* of each stage. Fullness has to do with how wide a scope of application there is: Do we see our personal relationships through this particular lens but not our professional world? How broad is the reach of our current-stage view? Have we extended this perspective across the full territory of our lives? This horizontal expansion is known as translation, which is distinct from the vertical movement through stages, known as transformation.

## *The Stages of Moving Through Stages*

As we evolve, there are three primary phases in each stage: fusion, differentiation, and integration.[21] The term *fusion* refers to the phase in which we are totally embedded in a particular framework of meaning, identity, and perspective. This is a time of *identification*. As noted earlier, we are not able to reflect on this lens, although we may be able to describe what we believe in intellectual terms. (In other words, our lens is not an "object" to us.) At some point, if particular internal or external factors exert a push-pull, life no longer works or makes sense within this framework. We may, for example, experience a series of powerful dreams (internal pressures from unconscious sources), or a significant loss, or a new educational challenge (external pressures). Then a process of differentiation begins.

*Differentiation* from a stage may be relatively gradual and smooth, but can also be a very uncomfortable, unsettling, even frightening process. This may also be described as a process of *disidentification*. As the old self and framework of meaning crumble, there is less and less to hang on to. We may even describe this as a liminal state and a kind of death, of the old self and old world. There may be waves of crisis, followed by relatively quiet periods. In any case, the phase of differentiation is often prolonged. As it draws to a close, and the next stage gains a foothold, there may be an outright rejection of the earlier stage. This sometimes takes the form of actual distancing from the people and concrete embodiments of the old worldview, or intellectual rejection, or both. If the stress of leaving the old behind feels like too much, the differentiation process may be abandoned, and the earlier stage reembraced.

This reembrace is described as *fixation* or *fusion*. It represents a kind of retreat, either temporary or permanent. Fixation may also take place when a part of the client's personality is fixated at an earlier stage because of some traumatic experience. As clients begin to gain a larger developmental perspective, they may be able to bring that traumatized part into conscious awareness and draw on healing resources, thereby integrating the part into their ongoing growth.

In the final phase of *integration*, we see a rebirth into a new sense of self and a new worldview. This involves not only substantial movement into the next stage, but also inclusion of the prior stage. A healthy process of development involves an enlarged capacity to embrace what went before, not as a source of total identification, but as a capacity for understanding or "visiting," if you will. Rather than rejecting the prior identity and worldview, we can remain aware of their boundaries and qualities and are able to include them as part (as "object" rather than "subject') of a new self, of a new whole. Under certain circumstances, such as the pressure of stressful life conditions, we may also find ourselves re-inhabiting that perspective for a while. Healthy development involves this kind of expanded repertoire and flexibility. The phrase that is often used to describe healthy development is "transcend and include."

If integration does not take place, there may be fewer healthy responses to the developmental challenge: ongoing *repression* of the former perspective or radical *dissociation* from it.

## *Healthy and Unhealthy Versions*

The Jungian concept of shadow holds a prominent place in the psychospiritual theory of development. At each stage there is unconscious material that I (the generic subject) have not owned or consciously experienced as mine. When I have not recognized shadow as part of the "I" that I identify with, I usually project it out there, onto other people: "*You* are so critical." "*They* are selfish and power hungry." Remember that in Kegan's language, the "I" (the subject) of the former stage becomes the "me" (object") at the new stage. But if I have not *owned* the shadow aspect of myself, and have projected it onto another person, it is not part of the "I" at all, and is not available to become the new "me." It is an object, over there.

Since healthy development entails making the unconscious conscious, I first need to become conscious of the projected shadow (it) as *part of "I."* I need to re-own it. Only then can transcending the "I" mean transcending a complete "I" (that has integrated the shadow). Otherwise the shadow "it" just gets carried along from stage to stage, perhaps dressed in new clothes, but never actually becoming part of the developmental growth process.[22] This is less than healthy development. (If you find you need to reread this section in order to sort out what is "I" and what is "it," you are not alone. But it is worth untangling.)

What other considerations might lead us to distinguish between healthy and unhealthy versions of a particular stage? Let's look at possible examples from stages 3 (Mythic-Literal), 3/4 (Conventional, Traditional),

4 (Rational, Modern), and 4/5 (Relativistic, Postmodern), since they are the most prevalent in contemporary culture.

In a healthy version of stage 3, the individual develops a new sense of personal self that goes beyond emotional impulses to include awareness of social roles and moral rules. Appreciation of, and sacrifice for, one's membership group can be significant. The God-Image, the image in which the Self or Ultimate is clothed, may at this stage take the form of a benevolent Parent. An unhealthy version, which we might describe as extremist, takes a radically negative stance toward out-groups. In this case, an individual may act upon his or her judgments with violent impulses carried over from the prior stage (Opportunistic, Self-Protective, Egocentric). There may also be a tendency to absorb negative scripts of guilt and shame from the in-group, believing that God must be punishing him or her with painful experiences. This is an example of a harsh and punitive God-Image.

A healthy Traditional (stage 3/4) perspective includes the ability to plan for the future, take responsibility, and take a third-person perspective on one's own thinking. Interpersonal relationships are important, and a rich personal relationship with the Divine is possible. The God-Image is usually nurturing and benevolent. While loyalty is to one's own God/religion, and others may be considered wrong, the individual at this stage may nevertheless do good work in the world with a loving heart.

A less healthy version might take the form of total enmeshment with relationships, such that modern society's expectations of us as individual, independent deciders and actors lead to painful stresses and strains. Likewise, there can be a kind of stagnation or paralysis in relation to the fixed beliefs and ideals of the Mythic-Literal stage, resulting in an extremist condemnation of other belief systems. Self-condemnation and guilt may also prevail (linked to a judgmental God-Image).

A healthy Rational, Modern perspective (stage 4) brings new abilities to reflect critically on one's own thinking. Ethnocentrism is largely left behind, and there is a more flexible approach to rules and norms. The individual begins to carve out his or her own life path. What is of ultimate concern in this stage may have nothing to do with religion, but there may be a pursuit of truth in scientific or rational terms.

Sam Harris, a contemporary philosopher, neuroscientist, and self-proclaimed atheist, has written a book called *Waking Up: A Guide to Spirituality without Religion*, in which he explores the experience of self-transcendence. In his view, such experiences have real value as reflections of the mind: they suggest that our ordinary sense of self is illusory, and direct our attention to the cultivation of emotions such as compassion because they contribute to our lives.[23] He speaks about spiritual transformation from a rational modern perspective.

Possible challenges and pitfalls may result from an overreliance on reason, such that intense emotional or sensual experiences are circumvented or the feelings of others are minimized and judged. Likewise, without a sense of mystery or depth, life may begin to feel flat and meaningless. In the wake of a total embrace of demythologization, a dry sense of alienation and disenchantment may predominate: "God is dead." We might describe the God-Image (if one can use this term) as empty, or perhaps as represented by the laws of reason. Condemnation of all traditional religious perspectives may be taken to an intolerant and extreme form of atheism.

Finally, a healthy version of stage 4/5 (Relativistic, Postmodern) typically involves a caring sensitivity to the truths and experiences of others. There is now an ability to reconnect with emotions and bodily experience, as well as with the mysteries of spiritual life. The God-Image at this stage often reflects this experience of mystery and depth. Self-awareness likewise deepens. An openness to multiple perspectives may take the form of identifying as spiritual but not religious, with a commitment to following a non-dogmatic spiritual path. Interreligious dialogue typically comes from this level. At the same time, there may be strong judgments of people who inhabit a conventional or traditional perspective. The questioning of all values (since everything is relative) can also lead to a kind of cynicism and rejection of all spiritual paths. Alternatively, reluctance to evaluate any perspective at all can lead to a naïve embrace of any and all spiritual beliefs without discernment. It may be difficult to commit to a course of action if there are differences of opinion. The God-Image may become so fluid that its compelling power is lost.

In these scenarios we see what can happen when characteristics of a stage take an *extreme form*. Fusion with problematic aspects of a prior stage may also prevail. Useful aspects of the prior stage may be totally rejected (dissociation). Characteristics of the current stage (the center of gravity) may be so enthusiastically inhabited that any possibilities for balance disappear, at least for a time.[24]

The Integral perspective (stage 5) is still relatively rare, so it is challenging to assess its healthy and unhealthy aspects. We can certainly find positive aspects in the ability to fully embrace all previous perspectives while being grounded in one's own path. This often seems to combine with a healthy willingness to engage in action that might benefit the world. A less healthy possibility might be a kind of arrogance: "Why can't others see that every point of view has its place? Why can't they appreciate the inevitability of paradox?" This may be accompanied by a sense of isolation that makes it difficult to act. In addition, it is quite possible to be operating from an Integral perspective only in the cognitive line of development, comprehending the complexities on an intellectual level but not actually living from them.

## Possibilities and Questions

With an essential understanding of psychospiritual development, we are now in a better position to understand potential reasons why some counselors, therapists, and psychologists have been uninterested in (or hostile to) considering spirituality and religion in their work.

One possibility is that some view the world from a Modern or Postmodern perspective, rejecting any and all conventional/traditional forms of religion. What is overlooked in this dismissal is the possibility of engaging with spirituality and religion in healthy ways at all levels, and also of approaching spirituality from different perspectives: Conventional, Modern/Rational, Postmodern/Pluralistic, and Integral.

Again, we need to remind ourselves that human development unfolds in a fluid, untidy way. The basic structures are identifiable, but an individual's course through them may involve fits and starts, with pauses, detours, and wanderings. There are still so many questions, and we still have so much to learn. For instance, what are the possible interactions between an individual's developmental stage and the developmental center of gravity of the surrounding culture? Is there a kind of gravitational pull, such that moving into the next stage might be more difficult because it would make one uncomfortably out of step with one's surrounding social or cultural context? Do we all begin at the beginning? Is it possible that some people move very rapidly through early stages because of innate gifts, or perhaps because of reincarnation? The latter subject is almost never discussed in professional psychology circles, but remains of interest to many in the general population.[25]

Let's take a look at our Enneagram characters through the lens of developmental stages.

## Reflecting on Enneagram Style Variations: Developmental Perspectives in Action

In midlife, Rob (Eight, Challenger or Asserter) is restless and searching. He has strong opinions, distrusts authority, and clearly sees himself as the author of his own life. Individual mastery, problem solving, goal-oriented planning, and achievement are a focus for him, so overall he fits in stage 4 (Rational, Modern). It is important not to confuse style and stage: the Eight pattern also has some resonance with stage 2/3 (Opportunistic, Egocentric), but we have to consider the overall picture of worldview, values, and cognitive development. In Rob's case, these suggest that his center of gravity is considerably beyond the focus on the immediate present, and he is able to take other perspectives (even though, as an Eight, he often believes he is right).

At his developmental stage, psychodynamic exploration of the unconscious can be effective, and we can make good use of cognitive therapy that challenges some of his core beliefs. Insight into his own life narrative is possible, and he is able to gain perspective on different parts of himself.

One part, for instance, wants emotional intimacy, but he has not been able to create that in his marriage: vulnerability is frightening for another deep part of him. He is able to explore a dialogue with these two parts.

He becomes aware that *some* of his dissatisfaction has less to do with specific circumstances and more with a feeling of boredom. As an Eight, he seems to have a meaningful connection to point 5, the Observer or Investigator. While this can signal stress for an Eight and devolve into an unhealthy withdrawal, in Rob's case this move seems to offer a healthy interest in learning new things. When his friend introduces him to a Buddhist meditation group, he is curious about this path. He sees a possibility for more balance, while also appreciating the practicality and the absence of "religious stuff." This emerging interest in Buddhism may begin to open the door to the Postmodern stage, as he experiences mindfulness, meditative states, and teachings that tend to undermine faith in thoughts and even in the ultimate reality of the separate self. Currently, mindfulness helps him to be present and manage intense feelings of aggravation and impatience.

Devin (Nine, Peacemaker) has been exploring spiritual paths for much of her life. Because she easily appreciates multiple perspectives, we might guess that she inhabits the Postmodern/ Relativistic stage (4/5). But deeper listening is called for because the affinity between this stage and the Nine pattern can be confusing. (In both there may be an "anything goes" viewpoint, so that it is difficult to take a stand.) She is often unsure of what feels true to her and where to focus. So she needs to ground her explorations in direct experience, rather than remaining in the realm of ideas. For instance, she has recently been having some deep meditations involving heightened spiritual awareness and profound love. There is more evidence of Postmodern tendencies in her ability to revisit these experiences, dropping into the felt sense of her body while maintaining an open awareness. She begins to feel more centered and more spacious at the same time.

She also displays a growing appreciation of paradox: she wants to be rooted in her own truth even as she realizes, paradoxically, that there is no one truth. This theme also applies to her identity as an African American woman: this is who she is, and yet she is somehow more than this. This emerging appreciation of paradox and her desire to become more rooted in her own spiritual experience may be pointing to glimpses of the Integral stage. It is important to appreciate that not all stage-shift processes are precipitated by crisis. Sometimes there is a gradual unfolding, so subtle that it is not until later, with hindsight, that the individual recognizes the shift in identity and perspective that has taken place.

In the wake of his wife's death, Charles (One, Perfectionist) finds himself challenged to open to new ways of making meaning, ways that are more fluid, more connected to the body, emotions, and direct experience (hallmarks of the Postmodern stage). We might guess that he primarily inhabits the Rational stage. However, since he has never questioned the basic assumptions of his faith, his *faith development* may be centered in the Conventional, Traditional stage (3/4). We are reminded of two important notions: that of different lines of development, and that of a center of gravity (with some aspects at prior or later stages). One more possibility: since he fits the Perfectionist pattern, he may naturally orient toward notions of right and wrong without necessarily inhabiting the Conventional, Traditional stage. We always need to be alert for potential confusions between stage and style.[26]

When we are unsure of a client's developmental stage, we can try different approaches and see what proves the most useful. It is clear that supportive grief work is essential for Charles, but when meaning-making emerges as a focus, can he engage in creating a more complex narrative (Rational, Self-Authoring)? Is he open to active imagination work? How much awareness is he able to bring to his moment-to-moment experience? If I try some of these approaches and they are a stretch for him, we may be working just beyond his center of gravity.

In the midst of intense grief, too much of a stretch may not be helpful. I *don't* want to offer too much challenge while he is still so vulnerable. So I begin by helping him reflect on a simple narrative of his life journey. When he falls into a problem-solving mode ("How do I get better?"), which is a Conventional-stage tendency, I listen, and then try reflecting his concern back to him in terms of a part: "Part of you really hates feeling so uncertain and lost. You want this fixed." Working with different parts of himself allows him to acknowledge doubt, shame, and imperfection without feeling overwhelmed. This provides a foundation for him to explore his long allegiance to the Episcopal Church, which he begins to recognize as having been primarily anchored by his wife. Now there is more space for him to find his own way.

At the age of thirty-four, Sienna (Two, Giver) is struggling with her allegiance to her traditional Christian church. She seems to present a good example of stage 3/4 (Conventional, Traditional), seeking a security that was missing in her nontraditional and rather chaotic upbringing. The betrayal by her pastor, a revered authority figure, has had a profound impact on her. Such a relational trauma (remember that Two's are relationally oriented) may precipitate movement into the connected knowing version of the Rational, Self-Authoring stage (4). This kind of development is often triggered by disillusionment, leading to a questioning of faith and a greater capacity for critical reflection.

But exploration of her painful feelings needs time, and she is strongly motivated to find ways of affirming her faith in God and in her religious community. What unfolds is a *wider application* (translation) of her current developmental stage, as her need to understand sexual abuse (a religious authority figure taking advantage of a parishioner) expands to include a social interest in the experience of women in other church communities.

Her faith continues to offer her comfort and strength. Her desire for healing reaches back to her relationally unstable childhood as she begins to see a possible connection between her early longing for relational security and her adult experiences. She also starts to acknowledge her pattern of focusing on the needs of others, and tentatively experiments with asking her fellow church members and family for what *she* needs. Her Enneagram Two pattern is becoming healthier. Her sense of self-and-world may also be reaching into the next stage: she is beginning to think and feel more independently, taking the initiative to connect with women outside her immediate faith community.

Linn (Three, Achiever) is forty-two, Korean American, and a successful businesswoman who seems to be at home in the Rational, Modern worldview. Having experienced a traumatic car accident in which an oncoming vehicle veered into her lane and hit her car head-on, her first task has been healing her bodily injuries. However, as we have seen, even more disturbing is her near-death experience, which has thrown everything she valued and believed into question. She finds herself in what is sometimes called a state of spiritual emergency, without the tools to process her NDE or to cope with the apparently intuitive abilities that have appeared in the wake of the accident. Scared and confused, reluctant to talk to anyone, she finds her way into therapy because she is wondering if she has lost her mind.

Without much trouble we can understand part of her process as the experience of a powerful nonordinary state of consciousness. This radical encounter opens a glimpse beyond the Rational, Modern, Self-Authoring stage into the wide and fluid landscape of the Postmodern, Pluralistic stage. She is no longer able to place total trust in her rational, scientific worldview or in her sense of herself as an autonomous individual. Her experience of leaving her body and encountering profound connection with a nonphysical reality has thrown everything into question. She is truly in a liminal space, not yet seeing the way forward but sensing the frightening possibility of multiple truths and perspectives. The therapeutic work needs to be supportive and gentle, providing a larger framework of understanding to validate her experience and confirm her sanity. At the same time, she needs authentic understanding of the vacuum she is experiencing in terms of her identity and worldview.

Janice's pluralistic, experiential, intuitive style (Four) suggests that she is at home in the Relativistic, Postmodern stage, or perhaps the connected-knowing version of the Modern, Rational stage. We see clear evidence that she is not bound by a commitment to objective rationality. She values harmony, empathizes with other points of view, and honors diversity of all kinds. Symbols and myths are significant sources of guidance, and she is open to the voices of the unconscious. Her impatience with the Conventional, Traditional point of view is a tendency that may persist in both the Rational and Relativistic stages. This might also fit the Romantic tendency of the Four, so we have to be cautious about assumptions. Again, there are subtle interactions between style and stage, and it is too easy to fall into a preference for one or the other as an exclusive interpretive lens. We find ourselves once again in the territory of complex and messy.

Because of his intellectual gifts, we might initially wonder if Kyle (Five, Observer) is centered in the Postmodern developmental stage. Developmentally that would be somewhat unusual for his age (twenty-two), so he may simply be experiencing glimpses into that stage. It is more likely that his center of gravity is in the Rational, Self-Authoring stage, supported by his own cognitive gifts. He is a questioner and a lover of knowledge, but there is an affinity between the Five pattern and the Rational stage, so it is important to look for other possibilities.

For instance, his development seems uneven, with cognition leading some of the other developmental lines. This seems a likely hypothesis, as his emotional and interpersonal lines of intelligence turn out to exhibit strong conventional, interpersonal characteristics of stage 3/4 (feeling self-conscious and caught between his needs and the expectations of others, in typical adolescent style), and at times the opportunistic, egocentric characteristics of stage 2/3 (focusing on the present and "what works for me"). The therapy process needs to give broad attention to his social anxiety with peers, even though it might be easy to get sidetracked by his displays of knowledge and enjoyment of adult-level intellectual conversation.

Gabriela (Six, Loyal Skeptic), fifty-two years old, has been struggling for some time with her allegiance to the traditional Catholic Church of her Mexican American heritage. Her new experiences in graduate school and in her women's group are intensifying her questions as she transitions from stage 3/4 (Conventional, Traditional, Interpersonal) into stage 4 (Rational, Self-Authoring, Modern Achiever). She struggles with the clash between these newly emerging perspectives and her loyalty to family and church. As a Six, she often feels conflicted and full of doubt. Losing her foundational sources of security is an enormous challenge, and her journey is plagued by fears. Counseling sessions could easily end up focusing on these questions and new ideas, but it is important to ground the work in emotional and somatic experience. She needs to find ways to reclaim and reinterpret sources of comfort and strength from her past, and eventually learn to place more faith in her capacity to think for herself. Is this a spiritual journey? Definitely. And framing it as such may be helpful for her.

Facing a serious illness has served Marissa (Seven, Enthusiast) as her call to her own personal spiritual journey. She is questioning her traditional Christian framework of meaning and launching into her own search: "Who am I? What really matters?" She seems to be transitioning from the Conventional stage (3/4) to a feminine subjective perspective, reflecting critically on her own beliefs and discovering the significance of her own experience. We may view this as the connected style of moving into the Rational, Modern stage, as reflected in Marissa's embrace of her own intuitive knowing and her deepening sense of connection to the natural world. These dimensions of life, inspired by her reconnection with her Native American ancestry, emerge as sources of healing for her. So for her, approaching the Modern, Self-Authoring stage does not involve a wholesale rejection of traditional perspectives or a total embrace of rational knowing.

Rejoicing in this newly emerging form of freedom, she seeks out internet sources, books, and people who can point the way. As she begins to experience herself as the author of her own life, she also begins to tell the truth, to herself and her family, about her sexual identity as a gay woman. This is a profound transition: she needs steady understanding and support as she finds her way in this new territory.

Clearly, the information we have in these vignettes does not allow us to make definitive judgments. We can, however, see the possibility of making informed hypotheses, which can in turn help us pursue certain avenues of inquiry that may prove fruitful. When we have a sense of clients' developmental levels and personality styles, we are in a better position to shape therapeutic approaches that fit the individual. We are more likely to understand and meet clients where they are, and to guide the process in appropriate directions.

## Developmental Pushes and Pulls

In the stories of our Enneagram characters, we can recognize the role of *catalysts* for development, which often seems to be pushed by life events and conditions. Similarly, the experience of transformation on the spiritual journey is often precipitated by experiences such as a dark night or existential crisis. Human beings sometimes manifest a kind of inertia, a tendency to keep going in the same direction unless moved by an external force. (Perhaps that statement applies largely to adults, since development typically unfolds quite naturally in childhood?) On the other hand, from a larger perspective, when we look at the continuing emergence of new stages in human history, *something* seems to keep unfolding. This is often described as the ongoing evolution of consciousness. Carl Rogers's theory of self-actualization also emphasizes this natural urge in all life to expand, develop, and mature. In contrast to the *needing to be pushed* perspective, we observe that people often *seek out* persons and situations that offer a degree of novelty and complexity.

Those persons and experiences that offer just the right amount of novelty and complexity (not too much or too little) are sometimes called "pacers." If we hypothesize that culture creates a center of gravity that favors a particular developmental stage, then consider this possibility: "To move beyond that point requires a new pacer cogent enough to counteract the historical-cultural forces working to keep persons in line with the reigning system."[27] So adult development is not only pushed but also pulled, and influenced not just by individual factors but also by cultural forces. Recall, too, our discussion of the Self as a powerful archetype that draws us forward in our spiritual journey. There may be forces at play in our developmental process that a rational perspective cannot explain. And of course, we each have *our own lenses* that shape what we see and what we consider relevant in this exploration.

## Spiritual Journeys and Spiritual Development

Is there a relationship between the spiritual journey and spiritual development? Remember that the spiritual journey is an interior perspective, with a focus on personal experience. (We may describe others as being on a spiritual journey even if they are not aware of it. But in the context of this exploration, I have linked the term to a subjective experience of being engaged in an unfolding spiritual process.) Descriptions of psychospiritual stages, on the other hand, take an exterior perspective on structural patterns. How might they be connected?

Beginning the spiritual journey requires some basic self-awareness and capacity for reflection. The lens of the journey is probably not relevant until stage 3 (Mythic-Literal, Conformist). In contemporary Western culture, the prior two stages—Intuitive-Projective, Magical-Impulsive and Opportunistic, Self-Protective, Egocentric—are relatively rare in adulthood. While individuals in later stages may visit or draw from these two earlier stages, it is unlikely that those at either the Magical or Egocentric stages would describe themselves as entering on a spiritual journey. That requires the more stable sense of self and the ability to narrate one's own experience; these develop in stage 3.

Let's revisit the brief description of stage 3:

> *I now take on for myself the stories, beliefs, and observances that symbolize belonging to my faith family. I believe in them literally and absolutely, and believe that my salvation depends on my observance of the moral codes that are part of the truth that has been given to us. There is only one truth, one path, and one purpose for my life, which is obedience to the will of God (etc.) as given to us by our faith leaders, whose authority is absolute. My personal relationship to God/Allah/Deity is a driving force in my life.*

An adult who has been living in the Opportunistic-Egocentric mode might, for instance, find herself in the midst of an experience (such as a loss, an addiction crisis, or a terrifying dream) that shakes her deeply. This may serve as the wake-up call. The search that follows may lead to membership in a new family group, perhaps in AA or a religious group, and the stories, beliefs, and observances of this faith family become the framework of meaning that offers salvation and purpose. The ongoing work of changing habits and dealing with challenges is then part of this journey, and the preparation may open into a significant initiatory experience (being "reborn," for example). This may be followed by a time of feeling lost in the dark, and the path may have many ups and downs. These are likely aspects of the journey in stage 3 (Mythic-Literal) and into stage 3/4 (Conventional, Interpersonal). The possibility of shifting into an authentic experience of *transformation* is not likely to occur until later in the development of consciousness.

What about those whose center of gravity is in stage 4 (Rational, Self-Authoring) or stage 4/5 (Relativistic, Postmodern)? The perspective and focus of attention shift, so the *content* of the experiences may now be quite different. But the experience of a call, a search, preparation, and the struggle of working on the self all continue to be relevant. Similarly, initiations and dark nights clearly have their place. The challenges and openings may precipitate movement into the next developmental stage, but not always.

It is from the evolutionary truce of the Relativistic, Postmodern stage, however, that it first becomes possible to open into a more compassionate embrace of all the earlier worldviews, into the mystery of paradoxical and dialectical perspectives, and into deepening disidentification from the limited egoic self. These capacities expand and deepen with movement into stage 5 (Integral, Multiperspectival). Let us acknowledge that, while the experience of deep transformation *may* occur at any point in a lifetime—who are we to impose time boundaries on the Mystery?—the movement from a life grounded in the separate self (ego) to a life grounded in and as Spirit (Self, God, Goddess, the Divine, Godhead, Oneness) is more likely to be the fruit both of a developmental and an experiential journey over time.[28]

## Closing Thoughts

What is our relationship to these waves of evolving consciousness? As counselors, we *support* people where they are, working toward the healthiest possible manifestations of a given perspective. This includes encouraging its expansion to multiple aspects of a client's life (translation). We also offer *challenges*. At the right time, we gently challenge stories, metaphors, and points of view that may no longer be useful or sufficient. We open doors, point to possibilities, and invite. Sometimes we get to witness what we might describe as a transformational shift into a new developmental wave. It is, however, rare to see a shift from one center of gravity to another within the framework of a therapeutic relationship, unless the relationship endures for a long time. More likely is a scenario in which a client is already beginning to question and reach beyond a given perspective, and the therapist can support that process. Finally, I suggest that it may be difficult for us to recognize and appreciate the essential aspects of a wave of consciousness that is beyond our own horizon.

On a personal level, awareness of these possible perspectives may serve as a pacer, an invitation, a call. Indeed, all the material we are exploring may be described as "psychoactive" (expanding that term's relevance beyond the physical effect of drugs). An encounter with Jungian ideas can have a profound impact on the psyche, and engaging with ideas about the evolution of consciousness can exert an influence on the unfolding of our own consciousness.

## Chapter Seven

# Obstacles and Openings to Psychospiritual Growth and Transformation

We have so far delved into variations in personal and cultural styles, the role of spirituality and religion in suffering and healing, perspectives on the inner experience of spirituality across a lifetime, and approaches to psychospiritual development. That is a vast territory.

This chapter has a narrower focus. We will explore life circumstances and experiences that may serve as both obstacles and openings to psychospiritual growth, while also bearing in mind the role of spiritual resources in mitigating difficult circumstances. Life challenges *may* also turn out to be doorways. While we cannot consider all the possible variations, we can at least recognize some meaningful differences. I have selected three areas that are familiar in counseling and psychotherapy: attachment and early experience, trauma, and depression and grief. In addition, we will consider the dynamics of subpersonalities (ego states) and the role of the body. There are, of course, other areas which would be relevant (addiction, for instance) but which I have omitted here in the interests of brevity.

First, however, we need to be alert for clients' self-judgment if they find themselves unable to "break through" a painful pattern or experience into some new way of being in the world. We also need to be alert to our own subtle judgment of *their* inability to move forward. Finally, self-judgment may play a part in our own work. Countertransference is to be expected: we can all find ourselves feeling stuck, frustrated, or inadequate. This too is part of the journey. Drawing on spiritual resources to help endure suffering may be just what clients need, and more than enough, without expectations of significant growth. Compassionate presence is always the foundation.

We will begin with a framework that allows for multiple perspectives.

## Four Territories and Perspectives

Debates among different lenses abound in the field of psychology, as in every field. Freud's and Jung's perspectives differ significantly from those of behaviorism and family systems theory, and multicultural psychology diverges from neuropsychology. I want to introduce a scheme that makes room for, and even encourages, all these points of view. Each perspective on human reality has its own truth, *and* each is partial.

We begin by recognizing that each individual "I" has subjective ("inside") experiences: perceptions, thoughts, emotions, moods, images, memories. "I" have an individual interior life that no one else can actually observe. In order to find out what I am experiencing and what it means to me, you need to communicate with me in some way. This is a familiar perspective in psychotherapy and will be our focus.

Each individual can also be considered objectively, in terms of genetics, neurological patterns, biochemical functioning, and behavior. These can all be *observed* through some exterior means, whether they involve scientific equipment or human senses. Through this lens the person is viewed as an object or "it."[1]

Neither of these perspectives is complete, but each has valuable information to offer. Furthermore, as many psychologists, philosophers, and poets remind us, we do not exist in isolation. We are social, relational beings. We come into human life in the context of relationships, without which we do not survive. Our relationships also have interior dimensions that cannot be understood simply through external observation. These include shared meanings and values, shared language, cultural stories, and worldviews. Whether we are focusing on a two-person relationship (mother and child, lovers, partners, even enemies) or a group relationship (family, religious, political, or cultural), we need to take an "intersubjective" perspective in order to appreciate the interior experience of the relationship (the "we"). If we want to understand these meanings, we need to do more than simply observe from the outside. We need to engage in communication, dialogue, and interpretation.

It is also possible to observe collectives from the outside. We can take an exterior point of view and analyze *patterns of interaction* in family systems, ecosystems, technology networks, organizations, and economic or political systems. Observation of these objective dynamics can be challenging. Because we, as observers, also bring our own interior filters—individual and collective—to the task, we need to exercise caution in our conclusions. Such is the wisdom of the postmodern perspective. Nevertheless, we can gather information from an exterior perspective (not requiring dialogue or interpretation), and this information can be tremendously useful. We might describe this as an "interobjective" point of view, looking at collectives as "its."

These four perspectives also point to four fundamental dimensions of reality. The following diagram gives us a view of their interrelationship:

This diagram comes from Ken Wilber's integral theory[2] and has been widely adapted in a number of other fields, including health care, business, and ecology. For our purposes, the four-quadrant model will serve to orient us to a range of viewpoints that are not always associated with spirituality. Indeed, in some religious views, the worldly plane is considered separate from Spirit or the Sacred, or even as a source of temptation and corruption. Other orientations embrace earthly existence as the expression or play of the Divine. But often the interplay of psychology and spirituality is approached primarily in terms of the upper left

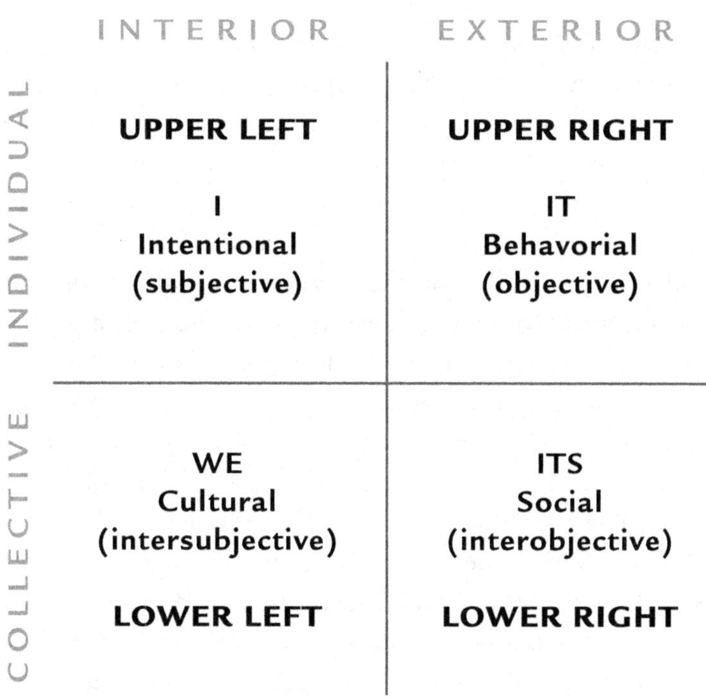


*Figure 7.1. Wilber 4 Quadrants*

quadrant of individual subjective experience, with some consideration of the lower left, cultural or relational experience and meaning.

In psychospiritual life there is a significant interplay among *all four* of these dimensions: within each quadrant there are factors that may serve as resources or impediments to the spiritual journey or to psychospiritual development. A richer understanding becomes possible when we consider potential obstacles and opportunities through this multidimensional lens. Let's begin with the lower quadrants.

## *Lower Right Quadrant: Collective Systems*

The systems within which our lives and journeys unfold play a powerful role. Socioeconomic context, for instance, provides or limits access to basics such as physical safety and health as well as to educational and employment possibilities. The political system within which we live may limit access to learning and expression, or offer an experience of empowerment. Every workplace has its own collective patterns, as does every neighborhood. Education may open doors to new perspectives and possibilities, but educational systems that are stagnant or oppressive have a very different effect. Living in rural or coastal areas may offer possibilities for spiritual connection with nature that differ from those available in an urban environment. The community support systems offered by religious institutions are widely recognized as providing a significant buffer against physical illness, loneliness, depression, and anxiety.[3] Families too can be viewed from the outside, in terms of their observable patterns of communication and interaction. Family therapists know that the patterns that exist at the level of the family system can have a huge impact on the lives of individual members.

While this book does not emphasize this perspective, it is crucial to acknowledge that psychospiritual experience and development do not occur in a vacuum. If we want to understand the interplay of psychology and spirituality, we need to be aware of the ways in which this interplay unfolds within the context of multiple collective systems.

## *Lower Left Quadrant: Relational and Cultural Meaning and Experience*

Here we find the domain of shared meaning. Culture is the most obvious dimension: the meaning and interpretation of spiritual /religious experiences (indeed, of *all* experiences) are shaped by cultural worldviews, stories, and myths. We absorb these in our psyches and even in our bodies as we live within the language, the gestures, and the taken-for-granted "realities" of a particular culture. It is from our cultures that we learn what is "real" and what is not, what gives life meaning and what threatens meaning. Time itself takes on different qualities in different cultural contexts and historical periods. The experience of growing up is different in Japan, Chile, Egypt, Russia, Zimbabwe, and Great Britain. And for the increasing number of people who, by choice or necessity, are bicultural or multicultural (immigrants, refugees, expatriates), there is an even more complex interaction of cultural realities. If we want to understand someone's experience, we have to consider the contexts of meaning in which their lives unfold. This requires *communication*. Simply observing a communal ritual—a dance of whirling dervishes, an initiation ritual, a Catholic Communion—will not tell us what is going on. We have to ask, converse, and then interpret what we hear.

This collective domain also includes our shared experience in interpersonal relationships. Whether we are talking about a couple, a family, or a religious community, the meanings that are taken for granted are the inevitable container within which individual psychospiritual experience evolves. What counts as a loving gesture or a hostile one, what is understood as growth or decline, what is viewed as normal or pathological—these are defined within shared frameworks of meaning.

If I (upper left) find myself turning toward new sources of consolation or inspiration, this may violate tacit agreements in my (lower left) relationships, leading to possible relational challenges. If a family shares an implicit agreement about what emotions are acceptable, and one member often expresses an emotion that is not on the acceptable list (such as sadness or anger), this may create a difficult dynamic that would be missing in a family with a different set of shared norms around emotions. Moral values within a religious community are also part of this quadrant, whether they are explicit or taken for granted. Often it is only when an implicitly shared belief or value is *violated* that we first become aware of its existence and its power.

A subtle example of this intersubjective understanding is found in the dance between an infant and his or her primary caregiver: There is a palpable "we" in the synchronicities and turn-taking of smiles, movement in and out, pitch variation, and eye gaze. When the "we-ness" is violated, through a lack of response, gaze aversion, mis-timing, or too much energy, the infant often shows signs of distress.[4] Consistent experiences of such violation can result in relational trauma and insecure attachment.

Again, there is a natural interplay among quadrants. Individual experience/meaning ("I") and shared experience/meaning ("we") are intermingled: an individual's "private" experience is inevitably saturated with collective meaning. Even the experience of a hermit in the mountains may be facilitated by villagers who recognize the importance of the spiritual quest and bring food for sustenance.

## *Upper Right Quadrant: Body, Brain, and Behavior*

Looking at the individual from an objective exterior perspective, let's begin with the physical body. I suggest that the body plays a central role in psychospiritual life, despite the historical disparagement of the body in some religious traditions. Differences in body structure and function can shape many aspects of experience. Genetic factors potentially contribute to developmental disability, ADHD, susceptibility to some forms of mental illness, and even addiction. Physical impairments, disabilities, diseases, and injuries may be obstacles that result in limited options, but can also serve as incentives to overcome the challenges and grow.

Sensory factors are another consideration. Unusual acuity in hearing or vision, for example, can contribute to a capacity to be present to immediate experience, to the "now," and this can enrich spiritual life. On the other hand, unusual sensitivity can also be overwhelming and painful, resulting in withdrawal.[5] Blindness (or visual impairment) and deafness (or hearing impairment) create significant obstacles, but may also invite a deepening of alternate ways of knowing. Helen Keller is a classic example of someone who was able, with help, to transform an obstacle into an opening.

A traumatic birth, a major surgery, sexual or physical abuse, a physical attack or accident, all affect the body and the brain. Such experiences may serve as barriers or opportunities in the realm of psychospiritual growth, often both. The individual and shared *meanings* associated with these experiences (the two left quadrants) also play a crucial role in how we respond to them.

Consideration of physicality brings us to the complex territory of neurophysiology and neurobiology. Neuroscience represents an upper right quadrant perspective that is playing an increasingly important role in psychology. Whether we are talking about emotional arousal, the neural underpinnings of empathy, or the general role of neurochemicals (serotonin, dopamine, oxytocin), we cannot afford to overlook the importance of this source of individual variation in shaping psychospiritual experience. The effects of antidepressants, the repercussions of serious insomnia, the influence of the brain on gender development, and the role of diet: these are among the variables that require consideration. And we are not simply talking about the brain: some intriguing perspectives on the "brain in the gut" and "the brain in the heart" widen our lens considerably. We will touch on these later in this chapter.

Behavior, of course, also plays a crucial role in the upper right quadrant. The field of psychology has been strongly influenced by behaviorism's emphasis on the objective exterior perspective. In the world of contemporary psychotherapy, cognitive behavioral approaches emphasize a combination of mental and behavioral dimensions (upper left and upper right quadrants). Observable behaviors (even at the micro level) play a crucial role in shaping the mother-infant relationship and therefore attachment. Exercise affects brain chemicals in ways that can alleviate depression. In the West, we have been slow to recognize yoga's positive influence on states of mind, but many in the East have long recognized the psychospiritual power of physical practices.

In therapy we pay attention to clients' observable behaviors, from shifting posture to gestures and subtle movements of the face or hands. These movements both reflect and shape internal experience. Our understanding of the client's experience may be enhanced when we wonder out loud about a particular facial expression, or simply bring the client's attention to a movement and see what unfolds from that noticing. Sometimes if we ask the client to make the movement intentionally or in an exaggerated manner, new insights emerge. Here again we are talking about interactions between the upper left (subjective "I") and upper right (objective "it") quadrants.

Many people struggle with establishing and maintaining healthy behavior patterns, such as eating well and going to bed at a reasonable hour. The lack of such healthy routines can negatively affect emotional experience, and psychological stress in turn may make the establishment of such routines more difficult. On the other hand, fasting and late-night meditation may be embraced as meaningful spiritual practices and contribute to psychospiritual growth.

Religious traditions build on an essential foundation of moral and ethical behavior. What *counts* as ethical may vary (involving the shared meanings in the lower left quadrant), but certain kinds of behavior are expected and encouraged. There may be sanctions for violation of these behavioral norms. Whether we are talking about the Ten Commandments, the Buddhist Eightfold Way, or charity as the Third Pillar of Islam, the one who is on the spiritual journey is taught that behavior matters.

Other forms of behavioral practice are also significant. Consider contemplation, meditation, prayer, and chanting. While these are focused on interior subjective experience, there are usually physical aspects as well. Meditation may involve slow walking. Bowing or kneeling before an altar or holy person is common. Ritual actions are an aspect of prayer in numerous traditions: for instance, the Islamic *Salat* (the five daily prayers), Christian Communion, lifting the hands in praise, the fingering of prayer beads, or bowing before an altar.[6]

Any behavioral practice may also be carried to an extreme. For instance, an intensive fast may be harmful to physical and mental health. An extreme focus on meditation may draw attention and energy away from managing daily life and attending to its responsibilities. This can be a challenging issue for therapists: when clients make spirituality a priority, their lives may look out of balance from a secular perspective. Gandhi undertook a "fast unto death" for the sake of his people. Numerous spiritual teachers (Jesus, the Buddha) have spent varying periods of withdrawal from everyday life, in the "wilderness." When is a practice "too much," and who is to make that judgment call? As counselors, we may need to consult with others who are more deeply familiar with a client's path.

Conventional science suggests that the relationship between the two upper individual quadrants is causal: physical processes (upper right) produce effects in subjective experience (upper left). Integral theory suggests that we view the relationship between the two upper individual quadrants as *correlative*. A subjective experience has correlates in the objective field. This is a crucial aspect of the quadrant model: all four aspects of human experience are always present. One is not *reducible* to the other; each perspective has some truth, but is partial. This position flies in the face of long-standing contentions that one perspective offers the ultimate explanation (known as quadrant absolutism).

Psychiatrist Daniel Siegel suggests a model called the Triangle of Well-Being, pointing to the ways in which mind, brain, and relationships are interconnected. This is his version of the co-emergence of the upper left, upper right, and lower left quadrants. Siegel's work in the new field of interpersonal neurobiology reflects a clear recognition of this interconnection.[7]

## *Upper Left Quadrant: Individual Experience and Meaning*

When we turn our attention to the upper left quadrant, we come at last to the territory that is most familiar to those interested in psychology and spirituality. Here we find the subjective interior experience of individuals, which cannot be "observed" from the outside, only understood (to some extent) through dialogue and interpretation of meaning. This is the lens that focuses on the "I": this is how *I* interpret experiences in my life; this is how *I* give meaning to what happens.

We know from cognitive behavioral theory that an individual's thoughts and beliefs shape their emotional experience as well as their behavior. Mindfulness approaches point to the crucial role of awareness (observing thoughts, as opposed to getting "caught" by them) in regulating our emotional responses and inviting greater peace of mind. Where we put our attention plays a powerful role in shaping our subjective experience. Here we are also in the territory of Jungian psychology, dreams, metaphors, and images. How I envision myself on my spiritual path, how I find meaning in dark times, how I "imagine" my sources of help: these are all aspects of this dimension.

There may also be forces that belong to more than one quadrant. Archetypes, in Jung's view, share both psychic (upper left) and physical (upper right) aspects and act on both a psychic and material plane. He uses the term "psychoid" to describe this dual nature.

In what follows we will focus on several kinds of inner experience which figure prominently in therapeutic work and also have implications for the interplay of psychology and spirituality. Hopefully these examples will illustrate ways in which experiences that we usually classify as psychological may serve as both obstacles and openings to spiritual growth. (These have corresponding aspects in other quadrants, but they will receive less attention here.)

## The Quality of Attachment and Early Experience

Infant-caregiver attachment is a relational phenomenon (lower left quadrant) with neurobiological dimensions (upper right quadrant) and implications for individual subjective experience (upper left quadrant). The subject of attachment plays a prominent role in contemporary psychotherapy, with ongoing exploration and lively debate. The history of attachment theory unfolds from the observations and theoretical contributions of John Bowlby, the Strange Situation research of developmental psychologist Mary Ainsworth, and more recently, the longitudinal research of Mary Main. The premise of all this research is that our early patterns of attachment to caregivers form the foundation for our relational life in adulthood. Following is a brief summary of the essential attachment patterns in adulthood.

**Secure Adults:** These are people who formed an emotional attachment to a consistent, sensitive, and responsive caregiver before the age of two. They grew up with the capacity to value relationships, and feel at home with both intimacy and independence. They also have the ability to reflect on their relationships: their working models of relationship (expectations and beliefs) are flexible, open, and self-aware.

**Anxious/Ambivalent/Preoccupied Adults:** Growing up with a caregiver who was preoccupied and insecure about relationships, these people are anxious about relationships. They want a great deal of availability, intimacy, and responsiveness from others. They are often very emotionally expressive, but because they lack confidence in their own self-worth, they are highly sensitive to any lack of responsiveness from other people and worry about abandonment. They have multiple and often contradictory working models of relationship that reflect the conflicting experiences with their caregivers: sometimes responsive, sometimes detached, and sometimes intrusive. Relational life can be emotionally overwhelming.

**Dismissive/Avoidant Adults:** These people probably had a caregiver who was detached or unavailable, minimizing the importance of relational connection. For people with this pattern, independence has a high value. They like to feel self-sufficient and avoid vulnerability as much as possible. They may consciously minimize the importance of attachments, period. There is a defensive flavor: "I don't need anyone." In relationships they curtail intimacy, may see themselves in a more positive light than the other, and are likely to hide or control their feelings. Again, their working models tend to be contradictory. On the one hand, the self is experienced as "good, strong, and complete, while others are untrustworthy needy, and inadequate." But a less conscious model views the self as "flawed, dependent, and helpless, while others are likely in response to be rejecting, controlling, and punitive."[8]

**Disorganized/Unresolved Adults:** Caregivers of those with this pattern usually have experienced unresolved trauma or loss. This attachment pattern is engendered by the often overwhelming sense of feeling endangered by an attachment figure on whom one's life depends. These are people who get overwhelmed by emotions such as fear and anger, feel constantly threatened from within as well as from the outer world, and tend toward dissociation. Any working models of relationship are disorganized and dangerous.

Main contends that we internalize rules of attachment from early experience. These become working models to live by in terms of our relationships, communication, emotions, and overall security in the world. They also help shape the "relatively stable internal points of reference known as the *self.* This is the part of the human being that *experiences* life—but also shapes it—nonconsciously as well as consciously."[9] The self, from this perspective, includes a somatic dimension (rooted in early attachment relationships), an emotional dimension (rooted in "felt security," which is connected to the body), and a representational dimension (grounded in emotional experience that is primarily unconscious). These internalized representations play a significant role in our adult lives. The more secure our early relationships, the more we are likely to respond to life's ups and downs with flexibility and openness, adapting to change and relying on an internal sense of basic safety.

Object relations theory adds an emphasis on two fundamental aspects of these mental representations: differentiation and integration. Differentiation allows us to maintain healthy psychological boundaries, and a differentiated sense of self enables us to act independently, without feeling defined by others. An integrated representation of ourselves, on the other hand, gives us the capacity for balance and complexity so that we can tolerate even conflicting feelings, such as anger and love.

In *Attachment in Psychotherapy*, clinical psychologist David Wallin suggests that our capacity for reflection and mindfulness emerge "through a relationship in which experiencing the attachment figure as a secure base makes it safe for us to explore the world, including the internal world."[10] If we have grown up without much experience of existing as a person in the mind and heart of another, we may have difficulty making sense of our subjective experience. Self-regulation then faces significant challenges: we are apt to feel overwhelmed by internal experience, or cut off from it.[11]

These observations suggest that our experience of somatic boundaries and of our relationship to the other contributes to a self-representation which we know as "ego." In the next chapter we will explore the difference between the self-representational ego, with which we *identify*, and the functional ego, which is associated with vital and necessary executive functions.

For now, we can simply appreciate the significant influence of attachment patterns on our sense of self. Insecure attachment can be challenging in terms of psychospiritual growth: a preoccupied tendency, for example, keeps the focus on personal needs and deficiency, while a dismissive orientation devalues relatedness and promotes "spiritual bypassing." (This is a topic we will revisit in chapter 9.) Even a religious "attachment" to a Divine Being can be filtered through one of these lenses and hence distorted. But healing and insight are possible. A healthy relationship with a therapist offers the possibility of what is known as "earned attachment," which can then begin to flow into spiritual life. And the constraints of these deeply ingrained patterns can also be softened by spiritual resources. At some point, struggling with the constraints of insecure attachment may also initiate psychospiritual openings beyond the personal.

If we step outside of the psychological literature on attachment into a less mainstream perspective on infancy, we encounter stories about actual recall of prenatal and perinatal experience. Many counselors might argue that it is impossible to have such early memories. This is generally true, although the concept of implicit memory (procedural or sensorimotor memory that is not conscious) offers a partial explanation. However, apparent recall is sometimes possible through an altered state of consciousness.

Jenny Wade, a transpersonal psychologist, draws on research from such fields as perinatal psychology and clinical hypnosis. In her view, "the evidence suggests a mature, physically transcendent source of consciousness that coexists with the immature consciousness originating from the fetal body."[12] The reported memories range from the time of conception, sometimes through attempted abortions, to *in utero* experiences and the birth process. Strangely, there may be both an *in utero* vantage point and one apparently observing from outside the mother's body. The narratives display complexity and insight. What is of particular interest is the extent to which such stories have been validated when researchers checked them against what parents and medical personnel recall.

Contributions to this literature have also come from years of work by transpersonal psychiatrist Stan Grof, initially in legal research with LSD and subsequently through the consciousness-altering technique known as Holotropic Breathwork.[13] (Briefly, this involves a combination of hyperventilation, music, and bodywork.) Grof reports that he was able to confirm the accuracy of many reports of perinatal and birth memories.

While I have not obtained verification, I have been impressed by similar accounts I have heard from some of my own clients when engaged in deep experiential work. These comments and narratives often display emotional authenticity and depth, as well as insight into the dynamics of the relationship with the mother in particular. Sometimes there is awareness of the mother's feelings about the pregnancy. Along with spontaneous expressions ("I don't want to be here," "She isn't happy about me," or "I feel loved . . . wow"), there is likely to be a felt sense of discomfort, pain, and fear—or relaxation and ease.

Such early experiences (if they occurred) may be part of the legacy we carry with us as we grow up, a kind of tacit orientation. Those experiences that were difficult may present hidden obstacles to be struggled with or eventually overcome. When brought to awareness, they offer a possibility for healing as well as an opening to possible dimensions of self and reality that have been obscured by everyday reality. "Who was feeling this?" "How did I know that?" "Amazing . . . Somehow I saw where I was headed." In the process, a larger perspective on life may become available, as well as a capacity for deeper self-compassion.

These broad brushstrokes suggest the potentially crucial role that early psychological and somatic experiences may play in spiritual life. I am not saying that we are always pushed by the past. In chapter 5, we considered the idea that we may also be "pulled" by archetypal or transpersonal forces. But the relational patterns created by past experiences are too significant to overlook.

Psychotherapists who are open to such possibilities can learn to help clients access and process these kinds of experiential glimpses and insights. As clients struggle to interpret and integrate their experiences, they need a mature, informed perspective, a secure holding environment, and an empathetic response. They need a safe, grounded space in which to feel into potentially spiritual interpretations, including: "I don't know. It's a mystery." If therapists overlook the clues, convey skepticism, or shut down the exploration, an opportunity for secure connection and deeper self-understanding may be missed, and an opening for psychospiritual growth may be overlooked.

## Reflecting on Enneagram Style Variations: Dismissive and Preoccupied Attachment

Let's look at two of the characters we have been following. Charles (One) has never had much social connection outside of his marriage and does not have close relationships with his three adult children. As he works with his grief and loneliness, and searches for meaning in deeper layers of his faith, he is also encouraged to explore his family of origin and early memories. He does not remember much. When he begins to get in touch with his body sensations (for the first time in his life), he initially finds a kind of deadness or emptiness. Paying close attention to his descriptions of his interactions with others, as well as to the images that present themselves in contemplative reading, I discern signs of a dismissive-avoidant attachment pattern. He describes his mother as rather distant and intent on having well-behaved children, his younger sister as cute and ingratiating, and his father as preoccupied with work. Charles's anger at God suggests a God-Image that is uncaring at best, punitive at worst.

It feels important to keep focusing on somatic experience as well as the "working models" that he expresses in words. Despite his obvious loneliness, for example, he sometimes says, "I don't really need people." This is clearly a defensive move: he believes people are likely to be disappointed in him and leave, especially if he is imperfect. With practice he is able to sense his defensiveness and resentment in body tension (which I describe to him as armor). When invited to imagine a secure and warmly loving connection, he remembers his relationship with a nurturing aunt. This memory is accompanied by a sensation of softening and opening in the area of his heart. Revisiting this experience often may develop new neural connections so that he can eventually access this resource within himself. The therapeutic relationship also offers him a felt sense of being fully seen, empathically welcomed, and appreciated. It becomes a container, a holding environment, in which he can begin to feel an "earned secure attachment."[14]

I am suggesting a gradual journey, not a miraculous shift. It is a journey which also begins to open Charles to a more meaningful relationship with God, one in which he starts to feel cared for and loved rather than judged. His spiritual life, for the first time, is expanding beyond rules and morality (the Enneagram One focus) to embrace a deeply meaningful relationship with the Divine. In the process of becoming familiar with Saint John of the Cross and experiencing his own heart, this emerging relationship with the Divine can now include, without being eclipsed by, the dark night in which the way forward is obscure. The opening to an unconditionally loving God in turn begins to suggest new possibilities for his relationships with other people. He senses, very tentatively at first, that even after the loss of his wife, he may not be condemned to loneliness forever. As we focus on connecting with his three adult children, he remembers playing with them when they were children and begins to experience moments of simple joy. He feels a pull to reach out to them.

Sienna (Two) grew up in a very fluid environment, with a free-spirited mother who moved frequently and had numerous partners. About her father, Sienna knows only that he was African American. She was able to stay with her very nurturing grandmother for periods of time, and speaks of her grandmother as her "rock" (in the same way she describes her church). When this metaphor is highlighted and explored in therapy, she realizes that the rest of her early relationships with adults felt more like "quicksand" or "watery waves."

The picture that unfolds is of a somewhat preoccupied attachment style, mitigated by at least one secure attachment. We can see evidence of her search for strong relationships in her family and in her church community. Thankfully, her husband and children appear to offer the kind of security she craves. But the betrayal by her pastor has been devastating, reactivating old fears of abandonment and memories of instability. Exploring the felt sense of this precarious sense of connectedness helps her to understand her Enneagram pattern of trying hard to meet others' needs so that she will be loved.

Connecting with inner resources—her grandmother, her own soul, Jesus—is a step toward experiencing a stronger center in her own being. A very important resource turns out to be her Angel, whose love and guidance, she realizes, have always been present. This kind of work, grounded in bodily experience, serves as a foundation for the deeper work of gently turning toward the insecure feelings of her childhood. This shift in attention unearths anger and fear. With the help of her inner resources, she slowly develops some ability to meet and explore these difficult feelings.

How far someone is willing to go in this kind of healing work depends on numerous factors, including the strength of the therapeutic relationship and external circumstances. In Sienna's case, when her church community begins to engage actively in healing their shared wound through praying together and reaffirming their faith, this offers her the opportunity to hold her insecurity in a larger context. She can recommit to her spiritual path with a stronger sense of self and greater self-awareness, and an interest in the experiences of other faith communities.

## Trauma

Trauma is also a central theme in contemporary psychotherapy. The word itself is derived from the Greek word for "wound." Recognition of the overwhelming impact of war on veterans (originally described as shell shock or battle fatigue) opened the door to research in the twentieth century, but our lens on trauma has widened significantly.

One intriguing new development, for instance, is the identification of *moral injury* as an aspect of war trauma. This term refers to the experience of transgressing (or witnessing transgression of) one's deeply held moral code, which may be rooted in religious or spiritual beliefs, or in cultural or group-based norms. Moral injury in war may result in "aversive and haunting states of inner conflict and turmoil."[15] Here is a clear recognition of a psychospiritual dimension.

Many counselors and psychotherapists acknowledge both big *T* and little *t* forms of trauma. Increasingly, we recognize that, while too many people do indeed experience Trauma in the form of combat, natural disasters, and violent attack—where there is an actual threat to survival—many more carry the effects of small-t trauma in their bodies and psyches from a variety of less commonly recognized sources.

There are single events, such as car accidents and getting lost in the mall at age three. There is also a range of experiences that endure over time, such as physical and sexual abuse, social shunning in middle school, school failure due to learning disabilities, parental neglect due to alcoholism or self-preoccupation and narcissism, sibling scapegoating, and taunting. The growing literature on trauma suggests that this lens is playing an increasingly important role in psychotherapy, without necessarily falling under the formal heading of posttraumatic stress disorder.

Traumatic experiences are extremely disturbing and usually overwhelming. Individual variations exist: what is experienced as traumatic by one person may not have the same intensity for another. In our discussion of spirituality as a resource in the context of suffering, we also saw that some people are more resilient than others in the wake of trauma.

When we include the interrelationship of the four quadrants, the picture takes on even more complexity. Traumatic events impact the brain and body (upper right), and our response to them is also influenced by preexisting patterns in our neural networks (strengths and vulnerabilities, including attachment-related patterns). The systems within which we live (lower right) can make a huge difference: our access to health care, for instance, and the reliability of our social support system. Finally, traumas are experienced within frameworks of shared intersubjective meaning (lower left) in terms of the larger culture, smaller webs of relationship, and intimate relationships. We also know that the availability of perceived support (what we *feel* as support) makes a significant difference in our ability to cope with trauma and loss.

What role might trauma play in the spiritual journey? It depends, of course. Severe trauma, or trauma that overwhelms an individual's inner resources, can shut down the capacity to seek out or process new experiences. A person may become enclosed in a kind of reactive loop of arousal, focused on survival at both the psychological and physiological levels, unable to see or move beyond the immediate context.

In terms of treatment, cognitive behavioral therapy is widely used. There are also other approaches such as EMDR (Eye Movement Desensitization and Reprocessing), Brainspotting, Somatic Experienceng, and Sensorimotor Therapy that emphasize the direct experience of trauma in the body. These approaches follow what psychiatrist Bessel van der Kolk calls a "bottom-up" rather than a "top-down" approach, emphasizing the crucial effects of traumatic experience on the reptilian brain (brain stem and cerebellum) and the limbic brain (which regulates somatosensory experience, emotion, and memory). The neocortex, the most recently developed area of the brain, can then be involved more effectively in cognitive information processing, self-awareness, executive functioning, and conceptual thinking.[16] The argument is that top-down trauma work, which begins with a focus on cognitive processes (the client's thinking, which then affects emotions), leaves out the critical and enduring impact on the body and brain.

Spiritual resources can play a significant role in the passage toward healing from trauma, especially when approached through direct felt experience rather than beliefs or ideas. Clients may find themselves sensing the company of an inner guide, Higher Self, Essence, Soul, or a spiritual teacher. They may be drawn to the image or memory of a place in nature that evokes a spiritual connection. Someone may spontaneously find that a profound spiritual surrender opens the way to a direct experience of a "self" and a "reality" beyond the physical, which in turn permeates and transforms the wound. And there is the therapeutic relationship itself, which can be a vehicle of healing and offer an opening to the spiritual dimension of life.[17]

Bringing to mind such images, memories, or sacred words may be soothing to the nervous system and calming to the centers of emotional arousal. This kind of resourcing work can eventually make it possible for the client to process the traumatic experience itself. Peter Levine's somatic experiencing approach incorporates this principle directly in his notion of *pendulation*, which describes a gentle movement back and forth between resource experiences (calming, comforting) and traumatic experiences (arousing, distressing). This pendulum movement allows the client to process the trauma within a "window of tolerance," avoiding the hyperarousal of fight or flight and the hypo-arousal of the freeze response.

For someone who is committed to a spiritual path, trauma is likely to play a significant role. When old traumas are ignored, they usually resurface in less than desirable behaviors, such as angry outbursts or fearful withdrawal. But they may also lie dormant until they resurface on meditation retreats, when attention is focused inward for prolonged periods. The response to such memories in those contexts is shaped by the particular path or discipline, but whatever the approach, it is important to remember that these memories are not only a matter of images and beliefs: they live in the body. Skillful attention to the body is needed. Van der Kolk finds that yoga, for instance, can be very helpful in trauma healing.

On the other hand, when old traumas are met and investigated with compassion and skill, they can be sources of deep insight not only into the human condition, but also into the spiritual realities that shine through even the darkest experiences. From this perspective, trauma has the potential to be a doorway beyond the personal.

## Reflecting on Enneagram style Variations: Trauma and Spirituality

Linn (Three) has suffered the trauma of both a car accident and a near-death experience. Since it is the NDE which is especially disturbing to her, and since she feels she cannot tell anyone about it, she needs an open and supportive listener. She needs to be reassured that she is not crazy, but more than that, she needs to be heard with an open mind and heart. If a counselor is unfamiliar with this phenomenon, consultation and research are essential.

While much of the scientific literature still attempts to find purely neurobiological explanations for NDEs (upper right quadrant bias), there is a growing and respectable literature on NDEs that goes beyond the popular first-person accounts that are widely available.[18] Regardless of the counselor's personal beliefs, it is essential that Linn be able to explore what the experience means to her, and all her questions and confusions, in a context of safety and compassion. She needs to know that she is not alone: many others have shared similar experiences.

As she begins to tell her story, she conveys an attitude of distance from the experience, but this soon dissolves into deep emotion. She describes the strange sense of feeling herself leave her body at the moment of impact, and looking down on the crash. There was no fear, and no pain. She watched with something like quiet detachment as other cars stopped and people ran over to help, but then felt herself floating away from the scene and entering a kind of dark passage. She was aware of "traveling" through the dark for a while, until suddenly she was overwhelmed with an unimaginably beautiful light and a profound experience she could only describe as love, "but not an ordinary love." As she talks, there are tears running down her cheeks. There was, she says, no sense of time, only a timeless peace. At some point she found herself viewing a flashback of her entire life, and feeling a "presence" that gently pointed to a need for more "opening." Suddenly she was being pulled back. She knew she was having to return to her body, and describes a deep longing to stay in this other reality. When she found herself back in her body, she was simultaneously aware of both physical pain and indescribable grief.

She retells the story a number of times, gradually remembering more subtle aspects. Each time, we sit quietly with the feelings. She sees her characteristic tendency to reach for rational answers and practical solutions (the Three likes something to *do*), but something has been so deeply touched that she finds herself unable to settle for familiar strategies. Eventually we consider the possibility that her typical ways of knowing may have reached their limits. Framing the situation in this way proves helpful, since she has also been frightened by the emergence of other ways of knowing, including intuitions that often turn out to be valid. These have made her question her sanity. With support, she begins to realize that she may never have certainty about what is "real," and needs to learn to live with unknowns. This is part of the developmental shift that we discussed in the preceding chapter. Some somatically-oriented work can be helpful: "When you remember this powerful experience, what do you notice in your body?" Such gentle, quiet explorations help Linn to *feel* herself more deeply.

This process can eventually lead to a focus on the trauma of the accident and the medical aftermath, which involves following Linn's lead, encouraging her to attend to and trust her own felt sense. Rather than leaving the physical/emotional trauma buried in her neural networks, overlaying it with positive thoughts and beliefs, it is possible to turn towards it together in a bottom-up way, pendulating with new inner resources and emphasizing body awareness. It can be helpful to anchor her experience in the present with some sensory input (such as tapping, bilateral music, or slow movements). Such a process gradually diminishes the traumatic elements and clears the way to a deeper sense of her own *being.* "I am here." She feels a desire to explore what this means: who is this "I"?

As she is increasingly able to be present in her body and to trust what reveals itself there, she finds herself more at home in what she calls her essence, and even more surprisingly, open to the paradoxical experience that she both *is* and *is not* her body. A whole new world is unfolding: she finds herself reflecting often on the last part of her near-death experience, the invitation to more "opening." Her identification with the self who is a doer and achiever begins to feel incomplete, even inadequate. At some point she may be drawn to exploring NDEs more deeply. She may simply need to rest for a while. Either way, she will probably need ongoing support in integrating her experience and her emerging intuitive abilities. We cannot predict the timing of the process, but her trauma has opened a door.

If we focus for a moment on the lower quadrants, we also take into consideration that immigration itself can involve trauma. Immigration patterns continue to play a huge role in our world. Immigrants themselves typically experience uprooting, loss, new language and economic challenges, cultural, racial, and religious prejudice. In response, many families hold more tightly to their religious roots as a resource. Growing up in her immigrant family may have created a background of trauma for Linn, who turned away from her parents' faith traditions as one way of distancing from this traumatic field.[19]

When Rob (Eight) tells his life story, several important aspects come to light. He was the younger of two brothers, and always felt "less than." His father was highly critical, angry, and verbally abusive, especially when he drank (which was often). But his older brother could do no wrong in his father's eyes. Rob's mother was quiet and unable to stand up for him, although she was caring and did her best to provide support as long as she did not cross her husband.

Rob suspects that by the time he was born (four years after his brother), his father was having an affair. But his parents' marriage lasted until Rob was in eighth grade, at which point they divorced. His brother was a rather independent eighteen-year-old then, and went off to college, leaving Rob home alone. The divorce settlement stipulated that Rob would go to his father's every other weekend, an arrangement which Rob fought, especially after his father remarried and gained two younger stepchildren (who were favored). As an adolescent and young adult, Rob found some escape through drugs, including LSD. He recognizes that he has an addictive tendency.

Rob's experiences with his father felt traumatic and left him feeling vulnerable. He longed for his father's love and approval but buried his pain under a facade of self-righteous anger and bravado. He presents himself with a strong and confident energy to ward off any hint of weakness.

Building trust takes time, but he is eventually willing to look below the surface. When we begin to go deeper, we find a number of traumatic memories that form a kind of template. They start in infancy (a vivid sensory experience of being shaken by his father when Rob was "crying too much") and continue through an intense fistfight with his father in ninth grade.

Working with these memories, he slowly begins to encounter the intense emotional pain and vulnerability that are at the core. While he is familiar with the sensation of rage in his gut, he now opens more to uncomfortable sensations in his chest. When he is eventually able to turn mindfully toward the pain, instead of the "weakness" he has battled against, he finds an authentic courage that he did not really believe he had. He contacts his *heart.*

This is work that cannot be pushed, even though Rob's pattern is to want to blast through it all at once. Over time, he touches a new openness to feelings, although he is cautious about where he reveals this heart quality in his life. He reenters couples therapy with his wife, and finds he is gradually becoming more patient with his daughters. His experience of learning to be present is supported by beginning classes in Buddhist meditation, and he appreciates his deepening connection with the friend who suggested this exploration. A new doorway opens up, one that leads him in an unanticipated direction: he now finds himself on a spiritual path.

## Depression and Grief

Depression is, as we know, a common reason for seeking help from both doctors and psychotherapists. "Feeling depressed" can mean many things, so it is always important to ask questions about what that means to each individual. What does that feel like? What do you experience? How often, or when is it more acute during the day? How does it affect your body? Your mind? Your behavior? Your relationships? Your work? For some it is deep and debilitating, making ordinary functioning next to impossible. For others, it comes and goes, more like a mood, but is still disturbing and persistent over time. For someone who is used to feeling upbeat, like an Enneagram Seven, any temporary but unfamiliar sense of "being down" or discouraged may be described as depression. Grief itself may be experienced through the lens of depression.

Traditionally, clinicians have attempted to differentiate between endogenous and exogenous depression, or clinical and situational depression. The attempt to locate a primary cause (biochemical or experiential) highlights the debate between proponents of the upper right quadrant and those of the upper left. If we start with the hypothesis that both are usually involved, then we can acknowledge that a depression triggered by a significant loss, for instance, also affects our neurobiology. We may also be more vulnerable to such a depression because of neurobiological factors, whether they originate genetically or through early traumas. Or there may be an "endless loop," in which a biochemical vulnerability to depression in turn affects our self-image and damages our relationships, both of which intensify the brain's responses.

Grief and depression can clearly be major obstacles that immobilize us. We may find ourselves feeling lost, stuck, off course. My particular interest here is in exploring how these profound experiences may also serve as openings into a deeper, larger spiritual life. I want to share an approach that I have found to be a valuable resource, for professional and sometimes clients as well, offering a perspective that illuminates the shadows.

Miriam Greenspan, a psychotherapist, has written a book called *Healing through the Dark Emotions,* which was a staple in my Loss and Grief class for many years. Describing herself as Jewish and also Buddhist in orientation, Greenspan invites us into a deeper relationship with grief, fear, and despair. These are emotions that we usually label as "negative" and try to avoid. With moving stories and powerful emotional exercises, she encourages the reader to see these dark emotions afresh, to experience the gifts that they offer if we can learn to be fully and skillfully present with them. She relates despair to clinical depression.

> This is how they describe their emotional state: *I've descended into a dark abyss. There's an empty hole inside me. I'm trapped in this dark place. I don't feel I'm really alive. I'm wandering through a desert. Nothing makes sense.* The imagery of descent, stasis, emptiness, captivity, sterility and darkness vividly

> communicates the interior landscape of despair as a place of inner paralysis, abject loneliness, spiritual barrenness, and existential meaninglessness.[20]

These words echo our earlier exploration of spirituality and suffering, and also remind us of the power of images. Greenspan suggests that depression is "unalchemized despair" that may well have its correlate in the brain but also has a great deal to do with the loss of meaning. We may be talking about the loss of a loved one, the loss of self due to violence, abuse, or emotional neglect, or the loss of a sense of purpose in the world.

When I first came across the writing of William Styron, essayist and novelist, I was stunned by a comment that came late in his book *Darkness Visible.* Only towards the end, after chronicling his long, dark descent into depression, does he mention his awareness of a possible connection with the death of his mother when he was thirteen.[21] Not everyone will find such a link between loss and depression, especially since the loss may be "unremembered" by the mind. Some losses are carried in the body, in implicit memory, or in patterns that were created very early in life. This link to early loss does not exclude the role of biochemical factors. But loss and loss of meaning are worth searching for as originating or influencing elements in depression. And loss of meaning is essentially a spiritual experience.

Greenspan argues that in the modern West, we have somehow lost the awareness that life necessarily has a dark side. We are often unwilling and poorly equipped to take the journey through the dark in order to say *yes* to all life. Offering specific exercises and practices for the "alchemy of despair" and the opening to faith, she extends this invitation:

> Don't be afraid of your despair. Be gentle with yourself. Take your time with this journey. Let despair guide you to the self you need to birth, the meaning you need to make, the world you need to serve. Let it reward you with a resilient faith in life.[22]

Without invoking any particular religious or spiritual framework, Greenspan invites us to consider grief and despair as gateways into what is essentially a spiritual journey. The journey begins with cultivating the intention to meet and tolerate the experience, then focuses on the importance of bringing attention and support to the body. We are invited to tell a wider story, looking for the context of our despair/depression in the world around us. Helpful practices include mindfulness, focusing on beauty in nature (however small), dialoguing with despair, walking with despair (exercising), creating from despair, and connecting with others.

In the end she encourages us to discover that surrender is the way to transformation. Surrender has been the path all along, but now it becomes even clearer. In a similar vein, cultivating the ability to be present with grief is often what is most needed: the way out is the way through. This is not what most people want to hear. It is certainly not what is encouraged in mainstream Western culture, and it is not always what is called for in a particular case. But I have seen this often enough in my own work to appreciate the essential value of this path.

So what can help us to bear the pain of grief and the weight of despair? Whatever serves as a spiritual resource: prayer, chanting, meditation. When Greenspan talks about the three basic prayers—"Thank you; help me; I surrender"—I am reminded of Thomas Merton's words: "Prayer and love are really learned in the hour when prayer becomes impossible and your heart has turned to stone."[23] The presence of someone who can walk with us and be a companion for the journey is a profound source of comfort and strength. We are fortunate if we also have someone who can gently point us toward the deeper spiritual invitation. My emphasis here is on the *transformative* power of this kind of work: there is the possibility that we may not only "heal" and recover our ability to live in the world, but that our way of living may radically shift. This is where the literature on posttraumatic growth and the transformative power of grief becomes so compelling.

We do not need to have known deep depression ourselves in order to be of help to those who are well acquainted with this experience. But the more we can approach the dark without fear, and appreciate the potential power of a spiritual perspective, the more useful we may be as companions and guides. The more our own countertransference is at play in our avoidance of darkness, the less likely we are to be able to serve our clients' needs. And again, the transformative potential of depression may not materialize in particular instances. All we can do is point to possibilities and offer perspectives. For some clients, drawing on spirituality as a resource is more than enough as a powerful way of supporting our clients through suffering.

## Reflecting on Enneagram Style Variations: Depression and Spirituality

Typifying the Enneagram Four pattern, Janice has always been emotionally sensitive and felt out of place in her more practical and intellectually oriented family of origin. As you may recall, the message was: "Why can't you be different?" Not feeling seen or appreciated, she began early in her life to feel shame and question her own worth. Depression was a familiar companion.

Because she finds the search for deeper spiritual meaning to be a guiding motivation (this has been true off and on since college), and because she is at home with imagery and imagination, we have talked about how she draws sustenance from her dreams and reveries, especially during times of depression. With the support of a nurturing presence, someone who *sees* and appreciates her, she is moving forward, exploring a new creative career and dealing with self-doubts.

There are two elements in the work, however, which feel relatively new to her. The first is the idea that the depression itself might be a doorway to a deeper spiritual journey, rather than simply an obstacle to be overcome. She is open to the possibility, so we explore her history from this perspective and return to imagery and themes having to do with her experiences of darkness, loneliness, abandonment, and feeling as if she is adrift in space. We mine for the treasure there, and she begins to see the gifts that have come out of these painful experiences. Of particular note is that she starts not only to value the ways in which her being has been "carved deeper" (which lends support to the feeling of uniqueness and specialness that is often found in the Four pattern), but along the way she also glimpses the possibility that this is the *human condition*. In other words, she is not so unique after all.

What seems to shift her experience even further is turning attention to the body. Imagination is a well-known and comfortable companion for Janice, but when she is invited into direct experience and exploration in her body, something unfamiliar emerges. The sensations that accompany her feelings and images are somehow simpler and more direct. They simply *are*. In some way they are not even "hers," even though they appear in her body. They are human sensations of heaviness, but also emptiness, floating. She finds, to her surprise, that when she simply pays attention and "tracks" them with a kind of detached curiosity, something opens into a space that is not *hers* but which totally embraces her. Perhaps for the first time in her life, she tastes true belonging to what she has called the Mystery. (If her orientation were Christian, she might have experienced and described this as being in the arms of Christ or in the heart of God.) She tastes *home*. This taste will come and go, but the spiritual journey has taken a new turn.

At twenty-two, Kyle (Five) is exploring what it feels like to be on his own. We know that he is introverted and intellectually oriented. He likes having a lot of knowledge, but sometimes this gets him into trouble with his peers. As a child he was most comfortable talking to adults, and he still feels awkward around those his own age. He displays a typical Enneagram Five pattern of being disconnected from his feelings, but when he talks about his relationships with peers, I hear a real desire to be accepted and liked.

He is not someone who wants to share much about his childhood experiences, and apart from some basic factual history, he does not talk much about his early life. It seems that his parents are liberal and well educated, but are trying to support his postponement of higher education and his experiments with job hunting and relationships. Still, he senses hidden expectations and pressure from them.

What he struggles with is loneliness and an anxious kind of despair (depression), which he treats as familiar companions. He wants very much to find a partner (identifying as bisexual), but finds himself overwhelmed by the demands and lifestyle of the urban gay culture around him. His avid interest in technology affords him many opportunities to spend time alone on his computer, but he has not put much energy into developing those skills in order to find stable work. He makes do financially with odd jobs, minimizing his boredom. What "brings him down" is also his astute awareness of the state of the world. From where he stands, there is no point in planning or working for a future, because the global situation is so dire. He knows too much to pretend it is all OK.[24]

Kyle is still young, and not really receptive to "deep inner work." Opening the door by meeting him in the mental sphere is a start. Talking about some of the areas in which he is knowledgeable, and then about the trouble in the world at large, is one way to connect with him in his place of lonely withdrawal and self-protection. An important part of the work is mirroring how hard it is to know a lot, especially among peers, and how challenging it has been to grow up bisexual. From time to time his eyes fill up, and he just sits quietly. There is clearly pain here, despite his efforts to conceal it. He knows there may be biochemical aspects to his depression, but he does not want his experience to be "reduced" to that, and he rejects medication.

His worldview includes a sense that there is *something more* than the physical world, and he has done some reading about various spiritual traditions. As we begin to explore this territory, he realizes quite quickly that he is at the outer limits of his knowledge, and probably at the outer limits of intellectual knowledge in general. This is an interesting crossroads as he considers the possibility, for the first time, that there may be *other ways of knowing*. As a Five, he is drawn to big perspectives, large views: he sees that the first step toward that horizon is cultivating another way of knowing, so he decides to learn meditation. Introduced to some basics in our work together, Kyle takes off on his own, not at this point in community (a class, for instance), but through books and audio sources. Together we frame his despair and depression as a call to his own spiritual journey. He finds that meditation helps him to be more aware of his own internal states, to follow the breath when he feels overwhelmed, and to open to a way of knowing beyond the intellect. These are valuable steps that also create openness to some coaching in social and emotional skills.

## Subpersonalities or Ego States

Many of us frequently say something like, "Well, part of me wants to do this, but part of me is leaning toward that." We find ourselves divided, of two minds, or more! This is not about dissociative personality disorder: this is simply the experience of having distinct traits, inner voices, and energetic impulses, which may correspond to neural networks or somatic patterns (upper right quadrant). Let's explore the potential relevance of having multiple facets of the self in the context of obstacles and openings.

This perspective is not new in psychology. Freud's map of id, ego, and superego is one version. Fritz Perls recognized this inner multiplicity in Gestalt therapy. "Ego state" is a psychodynamic term that refers to organized clusters of perceptions, cognitions, and emotions; when they are too highly differentiated, problems can arise. The psychological work is to bring these into consciousness and establish greater integration. Jung's notion of complexes is relevant here, as is Stan Grof's concept of COEX systems (short for *system of condensed experience*). Grof's definition is as follows:

> A COEX system consists of emotionally charged memories from different periods of our life that resemble each other in the quality of emotion or physical sensation that they share. Each COEX has a basic theme . . . and represents their common denominator. . . . The unconscious of a particular individual can contain several COEX constellations.[25]

A COEX system may be embodied in one or more subpersonalities. We can picture COEX systems, complexes, or major subpersonalities as threads that run through our unfolding life spiral.

*Figure 7.2 Life Spiral with Threads*

When clients complain that they have already done so much work on particular issues ("Why am I still dealing with this?"), I like to share this image with them. The threads (themes, patterns, parts) may run through our expanding lives, but we grow in perspective and in the skillfulness with which we relate to them.

In the theoretical framework of psychosynthesis, the therapeutic approach created by Robert Assagioli, subpersonalities are understood as unconscious patterns or aspects of the self. As long as they remain outside of conscious awareness, they may run our lives in various ways, even as we continue to think of ourselves as unitary selves. But clients can bring attention to this inner cast of characters through active imagination, hypnosis, somatic awareness, and simply by responding spontaneously to inquiries from a therapist. There is then an opportunity to bring about greater integration and to make more conscious choices.

In the Internal Family Systems approach, we are also invited to recognize that there is something in us (the Observer) that can be aware of these various subpersonalities but is not identified with them.[26] This Observer is sometimes described simply as the Self. From a psychospiritual perspective, experience of this Awareness (like the awareness that is cultivated in mindfulness meditation) can be very powerful. When identification with the fragmented parts of self is the norm, each part is experienced as the "self" for the duration of its energetic and cognitive dominance. Each is in charge of an aspect of the personal theater; each has a job to perform. Bringing the Self (Observer or Awareness) into focus shifts the parts into the place of "me" rather than "I." I am aware of *having* these parts; they are not what I *am*.[27]

Some subpersonalities are quite common: the Judge or Inner Critic, the Controller, Skeptic, Victim, Rescuer, Inner Child (which may be wounded, playful, or innocent), Rebel, Warrior, Good Girl or Boy, Achiever, Seeker. Some are quite unique in their focus and in the names that people give them: the Pope, the Giver, the Shark, the Clown, the Volcano, the Ghost, the Dead Tree, the Scared Rabbit. Becoming familiar with the Enneagram can even help people recognize and identify parts in the wings on either side of their primary point, or the points they move toward along the lines of the diagram.

What does all this have to do with obstacles and openings? Individually, any given part may prove to be an obstacle to peace of mind, healthy relationships, and life satisfaction. A repetitive acting out of a certain subpersonality pattern may keep someone stuck in a painful loop. Likewise, parts may serve as barriers to spiritual growth since they engender persistent reactions to life situations and act as blinders to new possibilities and deeper insights. This is not only the case for so-called "negative" subpersonalities, such as the Victim or Critic. Any subpersonality limits our seeing and being in some way. The Good Girl struggles to remain within strict boundaries of behavior, and the Playful Child refuses to acknowledge the importance of responsibility. On a deeper level, when we identify with such an aspect of the self (which is often linked to a particular developmental stage as well as to a particular issue), our access to deeper perspectives is constrained.

On the other hand, when our awareness of these ego states expands and deepens, we can see the whole "play" on the stage of the Self. We are gradually freed from the grip of particular patterns and perspectives. Liberated from identification with parts, we can allow them to play out healthier versions of themselves and contribute to our lives. They show up when they show up, and participate in the intricate dance of life. We have access to a more fluid way of living as well as to the experience of being "something more" than this play, even if we don't know exactly what that is. If we are already on a particular spiritual path, our way forward may become clearer. Seeing the cast of characters and how they have run our lives may even serve as an opening to the spiritual journey: If these characters are not what I am, then who am I?

## Reflecting on Enneagram Style Variations: Subpersonalities

As Devin (Nine) reviews her life and searches for the direction she wants to follow in her remaining years, she has a difficult time finding a focus. Many paths are appealing, and she can relate to a variety of different perspectives. There can also be a kind of internal "laziness" in the Nine, in terms of attending to inner experience and taking action, so it is helpful for her to *enact* these various perspectives as interior characters or parts.

In our work we sometimes use active imagination in a relaxed state, allowing different parts to present themselves to her awareness. She enjoys this process of discovery, and often finds herself surprised by what emerges. We also use the practice of Voice Dialogue with some variations: Devin assumes a place in the room, a posture and voice which capture the essence of a particular part, and speaks from that character as we have a conversation.[28] She then embodies a different or competing part in another place, and we explore that perspective. Finally she settles into a centered place and point of view which she identifies as Aware Devin, and reflects on what she has observed and experienced. Sometimes I simply ask to interview a particular part: "I would like to speak to the Good Girl. Who am I speaking to now?" We explore how that part feels about its role in Devin's life, when it first showed up, and what it finds challenging about its job. Unexpected memories and perspectives emerge. One realization that is often surprising is that even the most challenging part has its origin in an attempt to keep the person safe in some way: its original purpose was to be helpful, even if things don't turn out as envisioned.

For Devin, the most unforeseen part that emerges is one that is really angry. At first, she is very uncomfortable feeling this energy in her body, but as we explore its origins and muted expressions, she begins to recognize its potential value and contribution. Anger was never safe in her family of origin. Her early experiences of her father's unpredictable rage come back into conscious awareness, and she is gradually able to allow herself to feel into her terror as a child. Her own anger manifested in adolescence, when she remembered standing up to him in one particularly violent confrontation. The whole territory of anger and rage has been walled off in her life ever since. When she is willing to allow herself to really experience her feet, legs, pelvic bowl, and abdomen, she begins to find it easier to sit with the surprisingly powerful energy in her gut. She is then able to embody the angry adolescent (whom she calls Vivian the Volcano) in our dialogues. Anger gradually becomes less terrifying, and she even begins to sense the energy itself as an expression of Spirit or the creative Divine. Over time she is able to draw on this interior source of power (which she experiences as emerging from a deeper source) to commit to a path. She chooses to move more deeply into Sufism, as well as to continue these kinds of self-awareness practices.

At fifty-two, Gabriela (Six) is in the midst of a major life transition, torn between her Catholic family roots and her current exposure to new ideas and people. Her recognition of the Loyal Skeptic flavor offers her some perspective. As we continue to look more deeply into all aspects of her experience, we come up with the idea that she has a whole inner committee of parts that make alliances with each other, fight with each other, and generally create mental havoc. Because Six is a head type, this is an entry point she can relate to. But something more embodied is called for, so I encourage her to act out some of the points of view and arguments.

She begins to realize that what is at stake is her sense of belonging and safety. She finds a part that she calls Little Girl, who is very attached to her mother and older sister in particular. As we get to know this subpersonality, she is able to *feel* into what was so comforting in their embrace. Her father was more authoritarian. To move further away from the Catholic faith is to risk the love and acceptance of the people she loves, and the disapproval of the men in her family (father and husband). The part that feels herself pulled in that direction (the Rebel) was active in her life in late adolescence, so she finds herself exploring that younger perspective when she was "questioning everything." She then realizes that the questioning part that is contemporary is not exactly the same as the adolescent Rebel, but more of a mature Explorer. As these perspectives emerge and differentiate, she is more able to feel the feelings that go along with the thoughts and ideas, a shift which allows her anxiety to settle in a way that feels unfamiliar. New, more differentiated feelings emerge: sadness, excitement, resentment.

A lot of new ideas are coming her way: Should she trust the authority of the Church (and her family), her graduate school, or the women in her women's group? Her challenge is to sort through these perspectives and evaluate what feels right to her at this time in her life. Here, too, there are subtle distinctions that emerge in the form of parts. The part of her that always wants to belong, she simply calls the Belonger. That's her job and her sole interest in life. She will do whatever it takes to belong, including wholeheartedly embracing the point of view of the group. Related to this pattern is the Follower, who finds safety in trusting strong authority figures. The Neatnik is not about neatness in the environment, but in the mind: felt as a "he," this part is intolerant of ambivalence and attached to neat, precise, black-or-white formulas. The Skeptic (not the same as the Rebel) is motivated by the need to stand back, stand apart, in order to evaluate the truth value of what is being said and believed. And the Tryer is doing her hardest to succeed in school. When I point out how much courage it took for her to go back to graduate school in midlife, it takes her a while to let that in. Eventually she is able to claim a Braveheart as another part of herself.

As long as I support Gabriela in feeling (emotionally and somatically) as well as thinking, this discovery process offers her valuable self-understanding. In the process she develops greater compassion for herself as she navigates these challenging waters. What later emerges spontaneously is the kind of question that I could not have planned for: "So who's the *real me*?!" Sometimes this kind of question just appears. Sometimes it doesn't. When it does, I see it as a gift. We can take our time unwrapping it.

From there we move into a new phase of our work together in which she begins to revisit her Catholic roots from a different perspective. She is discovering what she finds valuable in the tradition and what she wants to keep in her life. She will eventually build on those discoveries to begin following her own spiritual path and to negotiate her relationships with her family of origin, her husband, her grown children, and her new friends. She also begins to recognize that she has an intuitive ability (a Knower) that probably originated in fear of her father: she used her intuitive skills to avoid his anger and keep herself safe. This is something she values, and she commits to cultivating and trusting more in her life. Here is another obstacle that evolves into an opening.

## The Body

Finally, let's turn our attention to an area that has long been a subject of controversy in the history of religion and spirituality: the body. In the interplay of psychology and spirituality, where does the body fit? The body has received relatively little attention in psychology. The legacy of the controversial figure Wilhelm Reich has been carried forward in Alexander Lowen's Bioenergetics approach, and there are numerous other somatic healing traditions. Somatic psychology, however, has remained a somewhat marginalized field. It is only recently, with the emergence of neuroscience as a major player on the psychological stage, that somatic approaches have gained more attention and respect.[29] The growing popularity of mindfulness and mindfulness-based stress reduction has also brought body awareness into the therapeutic spotlight.

As for the religious traditions, the body has often been viewed as an obstacle to spiritual realization, a source of temptation and distraction. Christianity, for instance, has struggled with this legacy. Other traditions have embraced the body as part of the spiritual path, even as a potential vehicle of deeper spiritual openings. At one extreme is pure materialism: we are nothing but our physical bodies. At the other is a kind of spiritual materialism: we are only pure spirit, and our bodies are our burden to bear until we are released back into the realm of Spirit. Some non-Western cultures are more likely to view mind, spirit, and body as inherently interconnected, and to express their "psychological" difficulties somatically. It is imperative for Western therapists "to be aware that physical complaints for which medical causes cannot be found may have a number of symbolic meanings, or emotional or spiritual explanations."[30]

Clearly the body can be a major obstacle to spiritual growth if it is a source of intense pain or handicap. It is extremely difficult to focus on higher concerns when significant pain is present. There are, of course, many different approaches to pain management, from narcotic medications to breathing techniques. Sometimes bodily pain can open us and carve out space for an unexpected spiritual deepening. The common thread has to do with developing the capacity to be *present with the pain*: "When people in pain learn to shift from the avoidance of body experience in order to avoid the hurt of the pain, they begin to trust and befriend the wisdom of the body." Peter Levine and Maggie Phillips continue:

> The connection between pain, trauma, and spirituality is an important one. Over many years of practice, we have been privileged to witness profound and authentic transformations during the process of healing with many clients. As these individuals have mastered the traumas that have haunted them emotionally, physically, and psychologically, amazing surprise benefits occur, including the release from pain and the opening to joy, exquisite clarity, effortless focus, and sometimes an

> all-embracing sense of peace and oneness. In addition, many of these individuals describe deep and abiding experiences of wholeness and compassion, especially self-compassion.[31]

Let's be very clear and careful here: the risk is that this possibility becomes a "should" for the person in pain, and may become another experience of failure. There are many kinds of pain, many causes, and many different journeys.

Regardless of spiritual expectations, the kinds of exercises and practices that Levine and Phillips offer can be invaluable and liberating. They begin with exercises that use the breath, grounding, and mindful attention to nonpainful parts of the body, as well as managing emotional reactions to the pain. They introduce the experience of the "felt sense," which is a wonderfully gentle way to introduce body awareness.[32] Mindfulness, pendulation, and journaling all have a part to play. A significant factor may just be the awareness that even a painful body *can* serve as an opening to spiritual growth and transformation.

We need perspectives that open up possibilities and allow us to consider mind-body complexities in a more nuanced, *fluid* way. In that spirit, let's explore an idea that embraces both subjective experience and neurobiological research, both psychology and spirituality: the existence of three major centers in the body. Many people are familiar with the idea of the seven chakras that has its origin in ancient India. Knowledge of the chakras came to the West primarily through the tradition and practice of yoga. As centers of energy located in the body, the chakras are understood to be a bridge between mind and body.[33] The three centers of intelligence, on the other hand, are often mentioned these days in neurobiology and in Enneagram literature. The three are typically described as head, heart, and gut. While not directly connected to the chakras, they serve a somewhat similar function in terms of bringing our attention to different ways of knowing and experiencing.

When we explored the Enneagram in chapter 2, we talked about the Thinking Triad (the head center) as including points 5, 6, and 7, the Feeling Triad (heart center) as including points 2, 3, and 4, and the Instinctive

Triad (gut center) as including points 8, 9, and 1. Knowing with the "head" is most familiar to us in the modern world, where the head center represents primarily rational processes and mental problem solving. "Use your head!" "My head tells me to . . ." The "head" points in the Enneagram are oriented toward thinking, questioning, and strategizing about how to stay safe. As therapists we are very aware of how beliefs and stories in our clients' heads can keep them trapped in painful patterns. Fives and Sevens are also drawn to big-picture philosophies, and have contributed a lot to our cultural systems of meaning-making.

However, if we consult the chakra system, we find that the sixth chakra, located in the brow, is also associated with intuition and imagination. In Greek philosophy the word *nous* was associated with intellect or intelligence, pointing to the faculty of the human mind which is capable of understanding what is true or real.[34] Let's consider the possibility that there are different aspects of knowing, ranging from purely rational to more intuitive and imaginal. We might even speculate that there is a developmental aspect here: as consciousness evolves, access to the intuitive dimension of knowing increases.

The heart center is familiar to us in everyday language: "What does your heart tell you?" "In my heart I know that . . ." Often we experience the head and the heart as being in conflict. This is a fascinating area from a neurobiological perspective, as we are discovering that there is indeed "a brain in the heart." The notion of the "heart brain" was introduced in 1991 by J. Andrew Armour. In his text *Neurocardiology*, co-edited with Jeffrey Ardell, he describes the heart's intrinsic nervous system which allows it to act independently of the brain. In the words of cardiologist Mimi Guarneri, "These scientific advances illuminate the fact that while we may believe the brain is our decision maker and ruler, the ten-ounce heart is more powerful than we ever imagined—functioning as a sensory organ, hormone-producing gland, and information processing center."[35] The HeartMath Institute is becoming increasingly well known as a center of research, but it also offers helpful tools and techniques for drawing on the heart's intelligence. Its mission is "to help people bring their physical, mental and emotional systems into balanced alignment with their heart's intuitive guidance."[36]

As Guarneri reminds us, the debate over whether the heart or the head is the seat of the soul (cardiocentrists versus cerebrocentrists) is an ancient one. In terms of our emotional experience, does the brain tell the heart what to feel, or does the heart inform the rest of the body? As you might imagine, my inclination would be to answer "yes." Clearly we have a lot more to learn, but for now we can acknowledge that the heart has a central role to play in our physical, emotional, and spiritual health.

Some cultures place more emphasis on heart-knowing than head-knowing, and indicate this in language and gesture. The heart's way of knowing is associated with feeling, depth, longing, love, and compassion, and the heart has its own kind of intuition.

The heart has long held an important place in spiritual traditions, especially where love plays a central role. In his letter to the Ephesians (1:18), Saint Paul prays that "the eyes of your heart may be enlightened" (flooded with light, illuminated). The eye of the heart is given special significance in Sufism.[37] Some spiritual teachings also refer to the existence of a subtle heart, located in the center of the chest or even a little to the right. In Eastern traditions, the heart chakra plays a pivotal role in bridging from the lower chakras to the higher ones.

From an Enneagram perspective, points 2, 3, and 4 constitute the heart center, where there is a particular sensitivity to mood and feeling, to relating and connecting with others. We can speak of lower and higher octaves of heart intelligence. At one end of the spectrum, we find the more egocentric emphasis on wanting to be loved, appreciated, and seen as special; these are aspects of the heart chakra that can cause suffering and need healing. At the other, there may be an exquisite attunement to the mysterious Heart of the Beloved, to the Divine Longing, and to the Love that surpasses human understanding. In the middle, we find healthy emotional intelligence, which Cindy Wigglesworth considers to be an essential component of spiritual intelligence.

Finally we come to the lowly gut. Again, we find an emerging scientific perspective: the discipline of neurogastroenterology. Michael Gershon proposes that we think of the gut or the bowel as "the second brain."[38] The enteric nervous system can control the gut on its own, but needs to cooperate with the brain. Familiar phrases such as "gut instinct" and "knowing something in the gut" may point to the validity of this perspective.

Some cultures emphasize the importance of the gut as the location of real knowing. Malidoma Somé, a West African teacher and writer, speaks of this as the traditional source of knowing in his Dagara tribe.[39] The lower three chakras, closer to the earth, are related to practical issues in our lives: survival, movement, action. Japanese martial arts emphasize the importance of the *hara*, an energy center in the belly below the navel (generally encompassing the lower three chakras). Connecting with the *hara* gives us a sense of groundedness or stability. This area also has to do with a focus on survival and primary identification with both the physical body and our earthly ancestors. Whether or not we locate this center of intelligence in the actual gut, we can feel that grounded weightiness when we pay attention to the lower part of the torso.

In the Enneagram system, the three points that make up the gut center (8, 9, and 1) share a kinesthetic orientation, paying attention to physical sensation and instinct. The gut can also be the seat of anger and self-centeredness. This is the center that is particularly focused on *doing*, which can be productive but can also become a way of going numb in the comfort of routine. When awake and alert, the gut center gives us an ability to be fully present in the moment, available to another kind of intuitive knowing.

Each of these three centers of intelligence in the body can manifest in challenging ways: they can be, in a sense, obstacles to psychospiritual health and growth if their less healthy aspects are in charge. But they can also serve as valuable openings. Since in mainstream Western culture we tend to be at home in the head, the invitation is to cultivate greater awareness of the heart and the gut. This awareness deepens as we bring our attention to our bodies, to the sensations that are present in different centers, and how they may communicate and interact with each other.

The skill of attuning to the interior of the body in this way is called *interoception*, and it can definitely be cultivated. It is possible to sense inner walls from long ago and to follow threads of connection. Even when clients expect to feel something solid and stuck, movement may appear. Gently and slowly, old wounds and protective barriers can be explored. I have observed a client encountering an inner sense of a "hole," often in the heart or belly. This can be frightening, but if, with the reassuring presence and encouragement of another, one is able to explore it and go deeper, one may feel an unexpected quality such as profound love or peace. Surprising treasures may be uncovered. Where the initial experience is of a gulf between heart and belly, gradually a subtle thread of connection may emerge, bringing unanticipated insights. Sometimes the body becomes a bridge or opening into nonrational ways of knowing, with rich images, connections, and insights. Sometimes there is a surprising awareness that "Oh! These are just sensations! I can simply notice them and not create meaning out of them!" This too may be liberating.

It is not necessary for counselors to think or talk in terms of "energies," particularly with those who follow a more orthodox or mainstream religious tradition. In those contexts, simply noticing body sensations, becoming more at home in the body, may be more than enough. If someone's religious view is that the body is a source of delusion or temptation, then this may not be a useful direction at all. On the other hand, for those who are drawn to a more "spiritual but not religious" path, it may be refreshing to find an openness to these ways of knowing in a therapeutic context.

For those who feel a strong pull toward cultivating a deeper sense of inner knowing, there are helpful resources available. One of my favorites is a book by John Prendergast called *In Touch*.[40] Incorporating perspectives from attachment theory, neurobiology, focusing, and mindfulness literature, Prendergast offers stories from his therapy practice as well as a variety of experiments or exercises. These are designed to help us overcome challenges and distractions and move toward an experience of "relaxed groundedness" and inner alignment. Sometimes it is also important to question our core limiting beliefs while paying close attention to the body sensations that go along with them. One source of this practice, which is becoming more widely used in psychotherapy, is Byron Katie's The Work.[41] We can invite clients to sense into the spaciousness that is always present in the body.

Prendergast offers an intriguing developmental perspective in the form of a four-stage continuum of groundedness. The initial stage is described as "no ground": we feel ungrounded, and we are barely aware of our bodies at all. Often this cutoff stems from early trauma, abuse, or neglect, but it is also a tendency in modern (rational) Western culture. The second stage is "foreground." Here we are more in touch with our bodies. We can drop down from the head into the heart and gut, and even begin to experience subtle qualities such as love and joy. There can be a temptation to pursue these desirable states for themselves, and this is often where the psychospiritual journey comes to a stop instead of continuing to unfold.

In what Prendergast calls the "background stage," it becomes possible to shift awareness from the foreground of experience to the background *context* within which the contents of all experience arise. This sometimes emerges through a profound inquiry into "What is this that perceives? Who am I really?" The figure-ground shift can happen spontaneously when we simply rest in silence, and the mind quietly drops into the heart. We recognize that this "infinite, open, empty, awake awareness" is what we essentially are.[42]

Prendergast calls the final stage "homeground." This is when any remaining distinction between foreground and background dissolves, and we come to realize that the world *is* our body. Everything is known and felt *as awareness*, "not-two." We are home—not we are *at* home, but we are home itself. This is beyond where many of us can even glimpse, so we may seek out direct descriptions from highly evolved individuals. Perhaps surprisingly, there are quite a few contemporary writers and teachers who point us in this direction. The way *through* the body becomes the way *beyond* the duality of mind and body—beyond duality altogether.

## Reflecting on Enneagram Style Variations: The Body

Marissa (Seven) feels frightened and alone as she faces melanoma. As a Seven, she is accustomed to staying busy and excited with new visions and new plans, which are now in question. In addition, her cancer treatments leave her tired and depleted. At first the therapeutic focus is naturally on support and validation.

A little at a time, in each session, she is also invited to focus on her breath, to breathe gently into her belly, and to emphasize longer exhales than inhales (which helps with anxiety). She takes to this eagerly, which suggests that she may be receptive to more body-awareness work. We do a body scan from the feet up, and she recognizes increasing agitation as her attention approaches her upper left arm, the site of the melanoma. When encouraged to pay close attention to where she senses the agitation in her body, she finds it in her head and upper chest, describing it as sharp points jumping around. She then becomes aware of heaviness in her lower belly. With encouragement, she is able to sit with these sensations. In a little while she finds her attention drawn more and more to the belly, where she experiences the heaviness as dark, sort of round, and "thick," solid. She cannot penetrate it, but is able to let her attention rest with it. The words that capture the experience for her are "stubborn, not moving." To her surprise, she finds herself laughing a little. "There is something in me that's holding on and just *not going to die*!" Finding this deep nonverbal will to live is encouraging for her.

Marissa's curiosity about new experiences can serve as a resource. She spends more time being aware of her body over the coming weeks. I suggest to her that this is a kind of surprising gift her body is offering her, because she has felt betrayed by her body. She has wondered if God is punishing her for some failure or transgression, such as turning away from her family's church. Has she been too self-centered, not good enough? Thinking of the melanoma, she recalls the line from psalm 10:15: "Break the arm of the wicked and the evildoer." We agree that she may not be able to see the underlying themes that are at work, and we will continue to explore and pay attention.

As our work unfolds during her treatment (when she feels up to it), we continue to work with breath and body awareness, moving through pain, discomfort, and fatigue. Finding herself increasingly able to approach her body with kindness and compassion as well as curiosity, she gratefully receives the support of her family. She receives more learning about her Native American roots as her grandmother remembers and passes on traditional stories about healing as well as actual practices. These in turn seem to deepen Marissa's connection with the wisdom of her body. Despite all the physical challenges, she finds herself more and more at home in her somatic experience and her interior world.

As she begins to feel stronger, she spends more time in nature, just sitting in a field or under a tree. There is a felt sense of affinity between the natural world "outside" and the natural world "inside." In session she describes the belly sensation as softer but still strong, a source of vibrant energy. There is often a flow from her belly up to her heart area, which was like a "blank, dark space" in earlier explorations. Now her heart feels as if it has "come alive" with radiating warmth and softness.

Marissa begins to relate to her cancer, not as a punishment, but rather as a doorway, a kind of shamanic initiation into a new landscape, an invitation to a new path. Striking out on her own exploration will not be easy, but she brings to the challenge a new sense of groundedness as well as a compassionate heart. While she felt at times that her body had become her enemy, it turns out to be a source of profound learning and joy. Connecting with her body leads her to a healing connection with the natural world and a whole spiritual tradition. Receptivity to the body's teachings may or may not be present in every moment, but the potential gifts are significant.

## Reflecting on Obstacles and Openings in Your Life

As this chapter comes to a close, take some time to reflect on your own experience. What have you experienced as obstacles in your life? Choose one for your initial focus, and reflect on the role it has played in your life. Explore it from all angles. How has it affected your relationships? Your social and work life? What external systems may have increased its negative impact on you? Has it affected your body or your physical life in any way? What has been your subjective experience of this obstacle? Your thoughts, feelings, dreams? How might it have affected your psychological development? Your spiritual journey? You might try drawing an image of this obstacle. Feel its presence or resonance in your body.

Now see if you can also sense how this obstacle has served as an opening in your life, or might still do so. You might glimpse its role in opening you to new perspectives or to some kind of growth you never anticipated. Go slowly here, and be kind to yourself as you explore. There is no right or wrong way to do this. Just consider what you have read in this chapter, and consider the possibilities.

## Chapter Eight

# Glimpsing Beyond the Personal

Having looked into some of the experiences that might offer unexpected openings for psychospiritual growth and transformation, we turn now to a topic that is fascinating for some and simply incomprehensible or uninteresting for others. If we take the possibility of growth and transformation seriously, then what are they pointing to? What are the further reaches of human development? What might lie beyond the realm of the ordinary and the everyday territory of the personal self? This is territory that is familiar in transpersonal and integral psychology, but omitted in most professional discussions of the relationship between psychology and spirituality.

A primary reason for this omission is psychology's long battle to be considered scientific, a project situated within the rational framework of modern Western culture. As we have noted, the scientific commitment has been to reason and empirical data. To make space for what lies "beyond the personal" is to risk entering murky waters, and this may evoke fears of getting lost in "woo-woo" terrain or New Age irrationality. With the increasing emphasis on evidence-based clinical modalities in psychotherapy, the growing interest in mindfulness offers a possible bridge between the commitment to scientific methods and the domain of meditation. But the deeper potential of spiritual growth is often overlooked.

We are going to widen our lens to consider the perspectives, paths, and practices that point to the further reaches of human development. Whether we ourselves are drawn to this journey or interact with others who take it seriously, we will be better informed about the experiences and choices that are involved. We will be better prepared to respond appropriately to experiences that may appear, often unexpectedly, in clients' lives.

The exploration begins with an overview of the possible trajectory of transpersonal development through several stages. Then the focus will shift to the territory of nonordinary (or "altered") *states of consciousness* and the distinction between stages and states. We will also discuss neurotheology, state-inducing spiritual practices (technologies of the sacred), and the role of the ego.

## Transpersonal Development

The essential premise is that the overall direction of human growth and development is toward transcendence of the ego or personal self. We have the potential to realize that the essence of *who we are* extends far beyond the "me, myself, and I" that is our familiar source of identity. This theme figures prominently in numerous religious and spiritual traditions: there is some Mystery (God, Goddess, Allah, Ein Sof, Brahman, the Tao, the Holy, the Beloved, the Light) in which we have our true being or, from a theistic perspective, to which we belong. We are not simply separate individuals floating in a meaningless cosmos; that view is ultimately an illusion, the product of conditioning. The transpersonal journey is toward a deeper truth. When we are able to surrender the sense of a small "me" to the transcendent Being or Reality, we experience reunion with the Mystery, not just as a passing state but as the enduring Reality. In other words, we can realize directly (some say *remember*) that our essential being is far deeper and vaster than the personal image and story with which we usually identify.

From the transpersonal perspective, what we view as "normal" is actually "a form of arrested development," a "psychopathology of the average." Cultures often play a role in defending against development beyond the personal, operating as "collective conspiracies to constrict consciousness."[1] So yes, development beyond the personal is uncommon. But this potential has been the focus of religious/spiritual paths for centuries. In particular, contemplative and mystical traditions have left us with roadmaps that point to a process of liberation from the separate-self identity. Their experience suggests that the human journey takes us from prerational stages to rational stages, and then beyond, to *transrational* or *postrational* stages. This growth process has been carefully documented in terms of practices, evidence, and confirmation by those who have traveled the path.[2]

Each stage offers a deeper and wider perspective. When we move beyond the limits of the rational mind, we encounter realms that extend beyond the physical world whose reality we take for granted, sometimes called *consensus reality*. Transpersonal knowing is no longer exclusively reliant on the five senses but expands to include subtle intuitive abilities. With each new transpersonal stage, the description of the experience becomes more and more elusive, and less believable from the mind's everyday viewpoint. Possibilities expand. Paradox becomes the norm: "reality" is experienced as having a particular characteristic (oneness, for instance) and also the opposite (multiplicity).

A simplified map consists of four broad stages: the psychic, the subtle, the causal, and the nondual (although some do not consider the latter a stage).[3] While many people may have temporary experiences at these levels—tastes, states, or peak experiences—few inhabit these stages on a stable, enduring basis. (In Maslow's terms, the peaks rarely become plateaus.) Hence there is little research. After briefly describing these four stages, we will take a look at the early research that *is* available.

## *Psychic Level*

The psychic level is sometimes called the domain of the soul, which observes and shines through the self. Soul is viewed as being deep within but also as extending beyond the self. It is uniquely individual while also reaching into luminous realms that transcend the personal. Ralph Waldo Emerson's Over-Soul is one version, pointing to the human capacity to bridge between the material and the subtle worlds. The Over-Soul involves a "conscious union, with all of manifestation itself: not just with all humans, but with all nature, and with the physical cosmos, with all beings 'great and small.'"[4] This opening often takes the form of nature mysticism—the direct experience that the natural world is infused with, and is an expression of, Spirit.

Another aspect of this stage is the ability to *observe* the mind's cognitive and perceptual activities and therefore transcend them. Also called the "illumined mind," the psychic level of consciousness lies at the border between the material world and the subtle (nonphysical), bringing a growing capacity for intuitive vision that transcends the thinking mind.[5] It is sometimes referred to as the lower subtle stage.

We are not speaking here of a philosophy: this is a matter of direct experience and knowing. Nor is this simply a temporary ecstatic experience, although the psychic stage may introduce itself through such experiences. The psychic stage is an enduring, more or less stable level of consciousness.

While it's not easy to find accounts of this as an established stage, it is not difficult to find descriptions of *temporary* psychic-level experiences. In physician Yvonne Kason's book *Farther Shores,* which explores transformative spiritual experiences, we find one woman's account of such a temporary glimpse. At the age of twelve or thirteen, she was going for a country walk and was overcome with the breathtaking beauty of the scene.

> I gasped, and in my heart spontaneously cried out an inner prayer: "Oh! Thank you God!" With this prayer I suddenly noticed a change begin in me. The colors started to become brighter and more luminous. Overcome with the beauty, tears of awe rolled down my cheeks. Then, I began to feel as if I was expanding until, suddenly I felt as if I'd merged with and filled the whole scene. I was one with the trees, one with the hills, and one with the sky. I felt totally connected with it all and

> with the love behind the Universe. I have no idea how long I stood there, riveted to the spot, merged into the beauty of God's creation.[6]

Initially we can hear her deep openness to natural beauty as a reflection of the Divine. Then, no longer a witness, she begins to experience a profound oneness with the world around her.

## *Subtle Level*

In this next stage we find a perspective and way of life that are more consistently open to realms beyond the physical world. Someone who inhabits this stage has a permeable consciousness that is naturally open to the direct experience of what are called subtle forms, including visions, illuminations, music, and voices. The subtle realm has been described as "the seat of actual archetypes."[7] In some traditions this is where deities appear to the inner eye, so "deity mysticism" is another description of this developmental stage. The individual whose center of gravity is in the subtle stage also has a sense of self that expands beyond the physical: "I" am more than my body.

From the rational vantage point, it is irrational to believe there are realities beyond the physical, so subtle experiences are viewed as hallucinations. But the evidence suggests there are indeed healthy versions of this capacity. Someone who inhabits the subtle stage in a healthy way has grown beyond most of us. Their development is postrational, not prerational.

Following is a brief account of a (temporary) subtle state experience from Suhrawardi, a twelfth-century Persian philosopher:

> Suddenly I was wrapped in gentleness; there was a blinding flash, then a diaphanous light in the likeness of a human being. I watched attentively and there he was. . . . He came towards me, greeting me so kindly that my bewilderment faded and my alarm gave way to a feeling of familiarity. And then I began

> to complain to him of the trouble I had with the problem of knowledge: "Awaken to yourself," he said to me, "and your problem will be solved."[8]

In subtle experience the reality of Spirit is revealed as lying both within and beyond the physical universe. Ideally, however, such subtle experiences are not valued or pursued in themselves. They are no longer an object of fascination or sought out as they might be earlier in the journey. Some spiritual disciplines (Zen Buddhism, for instance) explicitly discourage the pursuit of such subtle experiences as irrelevant or misleading, since it is too easy to become addicted to the "highs" and to the sense of power and control that they often evoke, thereby missing the deeper spiritual unfolding that is possible.

The mind that is consistently open to the subtle realms has taken up residence in an intuitive reality: ordinary time and space are no longer constraints, and knowing becomes possible through multiple nonlinear avenues. We use the term "intuitive" simply because we lack adequate language to describe this access to direct knowing that does not depend on physical sources of information, linear time, or spatial constraints. The knowing that emerges is often wordless, and many have alluded to the huge challenge of translating these insights into words. Poetry, music, and artistic expression often serve the purpose of communication, although still inadequately.

At the subtle level the journey has, in a sense, led so deeply inward that the inner reality has mysteriously opened to the vastness beyond. The boundaries have begun to dissolve. Inner and outer are known as one. This may also be described as the Soul's union with God or the Beloved.

## *Causal Level*

The causal realm is the unmanifest source of all physical and subtle forms: the Void, the Abyss, the Formless, the Unborn. This stage has different names in different traditions, but each word points to the direct recognition of the Emptiness that is the Ground of Being. The Indian philosopher Aurobindo calls this the Overmind:

> When the Overmind descends, the predominance of the centralizing ego-sense is entirely subordinated, lost in largeness of being and finally abolished; a wide cosmic perception and feeling of boundless universal self replaces it . . . an unlimited consciousness of unity which pervades everywhere . . . a being who is in essence one with the Supreme Self.[9]

The drop of water has dissolved back into the Ocean. There is simply silent awareness, consciousness without consciousness *of* anything. If there is any content at all, one can only describe it as "extremely subtle." We find hints of the causal in the writings of Christian mystic Dionysius the Areopagite, who describes the "mysteries of theology" as "veiled in the dazzling obscurity or the secret Silence, outshining all brilliance with the intensity of their Darkness."[10] Meister Eckhart, another Christian mystic, points to the causal in his distinction between God and Godhead: in the Godhead, both self and God are transcended in pure formless Spirit.

## *Nondual Level*

Again, words fail us here. The nondual points to a return, a re-embracing of form. According to some, this only becomes truly possible *after* passing through absorption into the unmanifest/emptiness. Other accounts suggest that access to nondual realization is always available. Either way, there is an awakening to the non-separateness of form and formlessness, to the ultimate identity of knower and known, this and That. Nondual is not-two, in which all is embraced:

> No objects, no subjects, only this. No entering this state, no leaving it; it is absolutely and eternally and always already the case: the simple feeling of being, the basic and simple immediacy of any and all states, prior to the four quadrants, prior to the split between inside and outside, prior to seer and seen, prior to the rise of worlds, ever-present as pure Presence, the simple feeling of being: empty awareness as the opening or

> clearing in which all worlds arise, ceaselessly: I-I is the box the universe comes in.[11]

From a nondual perspective, even the distinction between "spiritual" and "not spiritual" loses its significance. There is a contemporary literature on nondual consciousness in which people speak of opening to this realization of their "True Nature." For some people, in a variety of traditions, this "awakening" has come after long spiritual study and practice. For others it has emerged almost spontaneously, creating unique kinds of shock waves. The opening may begin as a temporary glimpse, but then evolves into an enduring way of being. There is even current conversation about the possible intersections of nondual wisdom and psychotherapy, with important consideration given to the ongoing work of psychospiritual integration following an initial awakening to nondual reality.[12] Eckhart Tolle is probably the most well-known of those who speak publicly about this perspective.

This map of the higher states favors a view of the nondual as the ultimate reality or truth, a view which has an Eastern flavor to it, although it is also found in some Western mystical traditions. For those who place supreme value on a theistic understanding of the Divine and a personal relationship with God, development through these stages would culminate in union with the Divine, in the unitive life.[13] As we consider a wide range of perspectives on psychology and spirituality, we need to remain flexible in relation to these kinds of models. The Ultimate is beyond our capacity to understand: Is it possible that both nonduality and relationship with the Divine may be "true"?[14] On a more mundane level, we have to keep taking into account the ways in which culture influences spiritual experience.[15]

## *The Pre/Trans Fallacy*

Some interpreters compare transpersonal stages to the experience of the infant prior to the development of ego. Since both involve nonpersonal, nonegoic, nonrational qualities, it is an easy confusion to make. This is known as a "pre/trans fallacy."[16] One form is the reduction of the transpersonal to the prepersonal; that is, everything described as transpersonal is said to be just a regression to primitive pre-egoic consciousness (to the womb, in Freud's view). The other form of the fallacy is the elevation of the prepersonal to the transpersonal, suggesting that we begin life "in heaven" and that everything after early childhood is a downward slide. In other words, we are born pure and enlightened (in a state of oceanic undifferentiation, "trailing clouds of glory," in Wordsworth's words) and just get confused as we grow up.

For those who view infants as little Buddhas or Christs, we can point to a counterargument from Jenny Wade. As noted in chapter 7, she draws on some unusual research that suggests the existence of a "mature, physically transcendent source of consciousness that coexists with the immature consciousness originating from the fetal body."[17] However, she goes on to distinguish the transcendent consciousness in infancy from the "pure consciousness" of enlightenment: the former remains *dualistic* (there is me, and there is other), and generally seems egoically "attached" to particular preferences.

In short, there is a crucial difference between prerational functioning that comes without understanding (without the ability to apply essential rational principles) and transrational functioning that understands but goes beyond rationality. The difference has much more to do with the person's level of subjective awareness than with his or her objective behavior.[18] The individual who is enlightened, awake, in unitive consciousness, is definitely not like an infant, despite the appearance of a kind of innocence. He or she has incorporated and learned from reason and personal perspective, but is no longer bound by or identified with them.

## *Contemporary Research on Transpersonal Stages*

The most substantial body of research on transpersonal stages comes from the work of Susanne Cook-Greuter, with more recent contributions from Terri O'Fallon.[19] In the chapter on the development of consciousness (chapter 6), we considered Cook-Greuter's findings on the first stage beyond integral, known as "ego-aware, paradoxical." Let's now look beyond that transitional phase.

## ABSORPTIVE-WITNESSING STAGE

This research category includes three of the transpersonal stages: psychic, subtle, and causal. Combining them makes sense for several reasons. First, these stages are very rare, and we simply lack data. Second, the experience at these levels is very difficult to express in language, which is the research tool. Finally, therapists are unlikely to see people at these stages. (Cook-Greuter guesses that they comprise no more than 1 percent of the population.)

We can discern three central characteristics of this broad stage: ready access to nonordinary states of consciousness, a more stable witnessing mode, and a widening of concern for others.[20] First, access to nonordinary states is now fluid and no longer requires techniques and practices. We might say that these states become almost ordinary, offering a consistent spiritual lens on "reality." Lucid dreams and causal (formless) awareness in sleep may become familiar experiences. Second, the capacity to witness the mind (glimpsed in the transitional ego-aware stage) now becomes more stable. Mental processes are no longer the source of decisions or actions. As identification with the ego or personality fades, there is now openness to the immediate, present flow of experience which is not bound to "I/me/mine" or even to a conventional time frame. Self-transcendence is no longer the goal of the spiritual search, but the living reality. And finally, because they no longer recognize any real separation between themselves and others (or the physical world), those who are at home in this stage naturally embrace all life in their compassion. Fowler describes this as the universalizing of moral concern.

## NONDUALITY

Integral psychotherapist Mark Forman argues that nonduality is not actually a development stage, a perspective which finds wide agreement.

Strictly speaking, it is not "tied to development," and may be "realized before completion of the absorptive-witnessing stage."[21] In nondual realization, we know directly that self and other, spirit and the material world, are not-two. Further untangling of egoic identification continues to unfold in a gradual process of living and embodying the truth of the initial realization.

## Some Therapeutic Implications

Why do these higher stages matter to those of us who largely inhabit personal realms? Although these stages of development beyond the personal are rare in the general population, having a "feel" for their characteristics gives us a glimpse of the overall direction of human growth. We may then be able to recognize features of these later stages without pathologizing them. It is also valuable to recognize that if our sense of self-and-world is in the more typical range, we may not be able to offer much substantial help to a client who primarily functions from a transpersonal perspective. We may find it useful to address specific issues and challenges, but the overall frame may remain beyond our grasp. Indeed, it can be very challenging for those whose center of gravity lies in a transpersonal stage to find direct support and help. One resource is the internet, of course, enabling access to teachers or therapists via phone, Skype, Zoom, and YouTube.

From a broader perspective, the fields of transpersonal and integral psychotherapy are vital sources of therapeutic approaches. For example, in chapter 6 we encountered the perspective of Michael Washburn, a transpersonal theorist with a Jungian orientation. He describes a spiral path in which regression in the service of transcendence gives way to regeneration in Spirit, and finally to the integration of ego and Dynamic Ground, now present as the sacred void, transparent Spirit.[22] Transpersonal psychotherapist Brant Cortright discusses this and other theoretical perspectives, such as those of Assagioli (who posits not only the Higher Unconscious, but also the Self, which is the unmoving, "enduring, immortal essence" of the spiritual "I") and the Diamond Approach.[23] Let's take a closer look at the latter.

The Diamond Approach is unique in presenting itself as a spiritual path rather than a psychotherapy approach, but the psychological dimension plays a vital role. Hameed Ali (writing under the pen name of A. H. Almaas) offers a valuable integration of object relations theory and body sensing with a spiritual perspective. Central to this work is the term *essence*, which has an elusive but centrally important meaning. Essence is an actual presence, which can be experienced directly. It has something in common with energy, and something to do with "true nature." Development moves us toward the realization of essence as our basic nature. The path to this reconnection draws on the insights of depth psychology as well as spiritual wisdom, helping us to soften the defenses created by early wounds. We are then able to experience these "holes" or wounds directly, and rediscover the essence that was blocked. Beyond this process lies the possibility of full Self-Realization, as Being or Presence that is no longer personal.[24]

Psychotherapists are more likely to encounter transpersonal dimensions in relation to temporary *states* of consciousness, since these may appear at any stage. When clients have state experiences as part of an intentional spiritual practice, we need a nonpathologizing framework of meaning for them. If nonordinary states appear without any preparation or expectation, it is especially important to understand what is happening since the experience can be frightening and destabilizing.

## Nonordinary States of Consciousness

Many people are curious about "highs" or temporary tastes of something unusual. What are they? What is their significance? We call these *altered* or *nonordinary states*, indicating that they represent a radical shift from the norm of everyday experience. In our exploration of developmental stages in chapter 6, we took an outside perspective on the structural unfolding of a person's worldview. It is now time to clarify the distinction between structural stages and *states of consciousness*, which are subjective experiences.

Human beings experience a wide range of states, from normal and "ordinary" to "nonordinary" or "altered." What counts as ordinary and normal varies from culture to culture. Charles Tart, a transpersonal psychologist who has made a lifelong study of states, suggests that our ordinary state of consciousness "is not something natural or given, but a highly complex construction, a specialized tool for coping with our environment and the people in it, a tool that is useful for doing some things but not very useful, and even dangerous, for doing other things."[25] Here is a simple taxonomy of states of consciousness:

**Phenomenal States.** These include fluctuating moods, emotional states such as anger or joy, states of depression, lethargy, excitement, and so on. They are ordinary experiences that have particular flavors. Phenomenal states come and go, although some may last longer than we would like (depression, for instance), while others leave too soon (ecstatic joy). All subjective experiences belong to the upper left quadrant, and also have physiological or biochemical correlates in the upper right quadrant: this is a both/and situation, not an either/or. Finding biochemical or neurological correlates of states does not invalidate the experiences.

**Nonordinary States.** Sometimes called altered states, these are distinctly different from what we recognize as ordinary waking consciousness. They may be *endogenously* induced (through natural means such as running, lovemaking, dancing, fasting, and meditating) or *exogenously* induced (by substances introduced into the body). Nonordinary states may appear spontaneously, but the likelihood of their occurrence may be heightened through intentional cultivation or *training*. Shamanic journeying and meditation are two such means of creating trained states through specific practices.

**Natural States.** A different lens is offered by some Eastern traditions (Vedanta in Hinduism and Vajrayana in Tibetan Buddhism, for example), suggesting that all human beings have access to five *natural* states of consciousness:

- *Gross waking states:* these appear in what we would call ordinary consciousness.
- *Subtle dream states:* experiences in vivid dreams (which we all have, whether we remember them or not), or daydreams, visions, meditations.
- *Causal formless states:* states of deep dreamless sleep, which we do not typically recall, but which some people with advanced state-training can experience directly. Vast, empty spaciousness can be experienced in meditation.
- *Witnessing states:* the capacity to witness or be aware of state experiences. We all have this capacity in ordinary life, but it is particularly striking in lucid dreaming and can be cultivated.
- *Nondual awareness:* "is not so much a state as the ever-present ground of all states."[26]

While there are more refined, trainable aspects to these natural states, the point is that *all* human beings have access to them regardless of their developmental stage. (I harbor an unconfirmed intuition that some people are highly sensitive and naturally more open to psychic and subtle states.) On the whole, natural states do not develop. Young children can be awake and dream. Enlightened sages sleep and dream. But as we have noted, some states are *amenable to training*, and can therefore show "state-stages" of developing capacity and subtlety. These are very different from the developmental stages described earlier.

A client may spontaneously experience a nonordinary state that defies labels. I was sitting with a client who was struggling with early childhood pain, loss, and fear, and the ongoing echoes of belittling, derogatory words from others. As she felt into her heart with compassion for her younger self, she suddenly had an experience of her heart "breaking open" beyond anything she had ever imagined. She described feeling the freedom she had always been searching for—especially in her flying dreams—in her own heart. Tears fell as she laughed in wonder and amazement: "Home has always been here!" I sat quietly, reflecting her joy and giving her all the space she needed.

In the following session (two months later, due to a surgery) she mused over a significant shift. Despite physical challenges, she was now feeling more peaceful, sleeping well, and having no more nightmares. She also reflected on a sudden change in her troubled relationship with her adult daughter, who had—right after our previous session—become loving and appreciative. As the client shared these experiences, she initially expressed puzzlement, and then we simply laughed in wonderment. Neither of us had a rational explanation, but there was a lot of gratitude in the room.

State-stages are very fluid, unlike developmental structure-stages. Still, anyone who has meditated for years can easily relate to the idea that access to states improves with practice. There is evidence from both Eastern and Western traditions that at least in many forms of meditation and contemplation, training leads to a typical sequence of unfolding capacity, from gross to subtle to causal to nondual states.[27] But even a beginner can have a "peak" experience of a much higher (subtle, causal) state of consciousness, although this is only a temporary "peek" or glimpse. It may serve as motivation to continue practice, as a gift of grace, or less usefully, as a shiny thing to pursue for its own sake.

In transpersonal psychology any discussion of states of consciousness must include the significant contributions of Stanislav Grof, Czech psychiatrist and one of the founders of the field. Beginning with his psychedelic research in the 1960s, Grof has spent his career exploring and developing a map of the human psyche. He focuses on the category of nonordinary states which he calls *holotropic*, meaning "turning toward wholeness."

The mainstay of his work since the 1960s has been research with Holotropic Breathwork (mentioned in chapter 7), using breathing techniques, music, and bodywork to plumb the depths of nonordinary states. Beginning with archetypal experiences at the perinatal level of the unconscious, which he sees as an important gateway to the collective unconscious, he goes on to map a variety of transpersonal state experiences.

These include states in which there is an expansion of awareness *within* space-time and consensual reality, those in which there is experience *beyond* space-time and consensual reality, and actual transpersonal experiences. He considers the latter to provide supportive evidence for Wilber's scheme of low subtle, higher subtle, causal, and nondual states.[28]

## States versus Stages

Having differentiated between states and stages, let's consider an intriguing perspective on their relationship. Ken Wilber and Allan Combs, director of the Center for Consciousness Studies at the California Institute of Integral Studies, have collaborated on a diagram known as the Wilber-Combs Lattice. (shown on next page).

The diagram tells us that a person at any developmental stage can have a peak experience of any gross, subtle, causal, or nondual state of consciousness, but will *interpret* that experience through the lens of the developmental stage that is their center of gravity. This idea has profound implications for understanding the interplay of psychology and spirituality.

Let's imagine that someone has a subtle state experience of intense light and love. If he is Western and predominantly influenced by Christianity, he will likely interpret this as an encounter with some aspect of the Christian tradition. With a center of gravity in the Magic stage of development, he may see this as Jesus and relate to him primarily as the "magician," who could turn loaves into fish, transform water into wine, and still the stormy seas. In this egocentric frame, he may interpret this appearance as an indication that Jesus is going to intervene magically in his life to bring about a desired goal. In the mythic stage, he may feel his experience to be an encounter with the Absolute Truth-Giver, affirming the truth of his beliefs and the importance of adhering to his faith community. At the rational level, Jesus may be experienced as both Divine and human, a teacher of universal love, accepting of other religions, representing a call to a reasonable spiritual path. From the Pluralistic perspective,

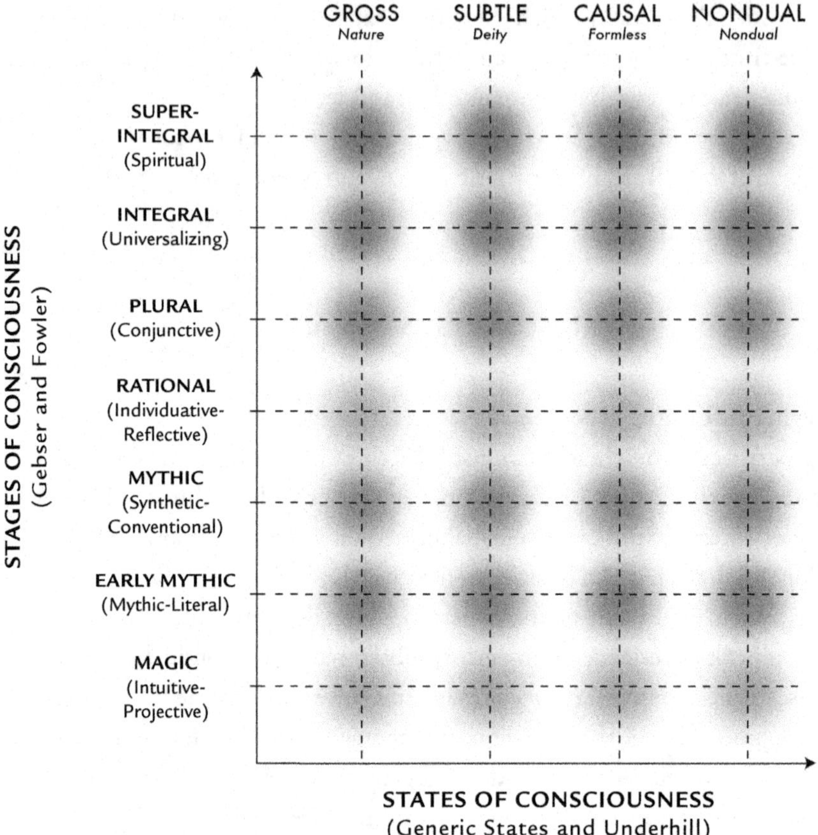


*Figure 8.1 The Wilber-Combs Lattice of States and Stages*

he may be deeply touched by this profound experience, feeling the depth and also the universality of the appearance. *The experience and its interpretation unfold* as development unfolds. So "a spiritual experience" or an "altered state of consciousness" is not just one thing to all people: there are important differences in interpretation. This would apply to all kinds of states, from near-death to substance-induced experiences.

For those who are particularly interested in states of consciousness, here is another valuable distinction. When we are talking about a nonordinary state, we are usually referring to an experience *of particular phenomena*. A nonordinary state experience at the psychic level, for instance, may be a mystical vision of the beauty of a natural scene. At the subtle level, a person may hear celestial music or have a vision of a spiritual being. The focus is on the object of experience, or *what is experienced*. But of even more significance is the source or subject of awareness (rather than the object): the point of observation, the knower, who or what is experiencing.[29] This is called the *vantage point*, and it turns out that this, too, evolves through state-stages that correlate with subtle, causal, and nondual levels. Like the structural stages of development, each new vantage point transcends, includes, and *vivifies* the preceding one. All lower vantage points are still available, but now shine in their transparency to the Reality that transcends them.

Repeated experiences of transpersonal states may help open the way to a stage shift.

## *States of Consciousness: Dimensions of Reality?*

At some point questions may surface regarding the meaning of both states and stages: Do they point to something "real"? Is Reality actually multidimensional? Is it true that there are planes or dimensions beyond the physical? On the one hand, contemporary physics and cosmologies point to complexities beyond what we can even imagine: quantum physics, string theory, unified-field theory, multiple universes. These all raise questions that are unanswerable within the Newtonian worldview that we take for granted in our daily lives. Obviously, we can't attempt answers. But *how we relate to the questions* influences how we will respond to clients who have unusual experiences.

Let's return for a moment to Wilber's four quadrants, representing the inside and the outside of the individual and collective dimensions of human experience. State experiences, as we have noted, belong in the upper left quadrant of individual subjective experience. Since every subjective experience has an objective correlate in the upper right quadrant, the intriguing implication is that every state of consciousness has a corresponding brain state, *but cannot be reduced to the latter.*

A less obvious possibility is that for every subtle state experience there is a corresponding "subtle body." This is something that is taken for granted in various spiritual traditions, from esoteric to New Age to Eastern to Catholic. (Saint Theresa of Avila described out-of-body experiences.) We take for granted that in the waking state, we are aware of the gross physical body. But when we are dreaming, no longer operating with the physical body, we are having fluid subtle body experiences, of feelings, images, and energy. One way to put this is that nonphysical experiences (in the upper left quadrant) have energetic vehicles (in the upper right).[30] The possibility of subtle bodies is, of course, rejected by the modern scientific mind, which is committed to the material aspect of the upper right quadrant as the only reality.

This brings us face-to-face with the question of whether nonordinary states of consciousness are basically delusions (even if brain-based) or experiences of actual realities. Clients may wonder: "Is this *real*?" Huston Smith, the well-known religious studies scholar, has taken a clear position on this question. He maintains that levels of experiences-of-the-self correspond to levels of actual reality. His diagram of the Great Chain of Being in various wisdom traditions depicts this worldview.

From this perspective, we have physical bodies that operate on the physical plane, and subtle (energetic/nonphysical) bodies that move on the subtle plane. Out-of-body and near-death experiences, and even some very vivid dream experiences, all suggest this level of reality. If a client shares a significant experience of seeing (in a dream or while awake) a loved one who has died, how are we going to respond to that? Do we dismiss it as a delusion, whether or not we describe it as such to a client? It depends on our worldview, our developmental center of gravity, and our experience with nonordinary states. But our response *matters*.

Aldous Huxley's popularization, *The Perennial Philosophy,* includes "the metaphysic that recognizes a divine Reality substantial to the world of things and lives and minds; the psychology that finds in the soul something similar to, or even identical with, divine Reality; the ethic that places man's final end in the knowledge of the immanent and transcendent Ground of all being."[31] But in today's postmodern world, such a metaphysical interpretation is highly suspect. Critics call this a "naïve"

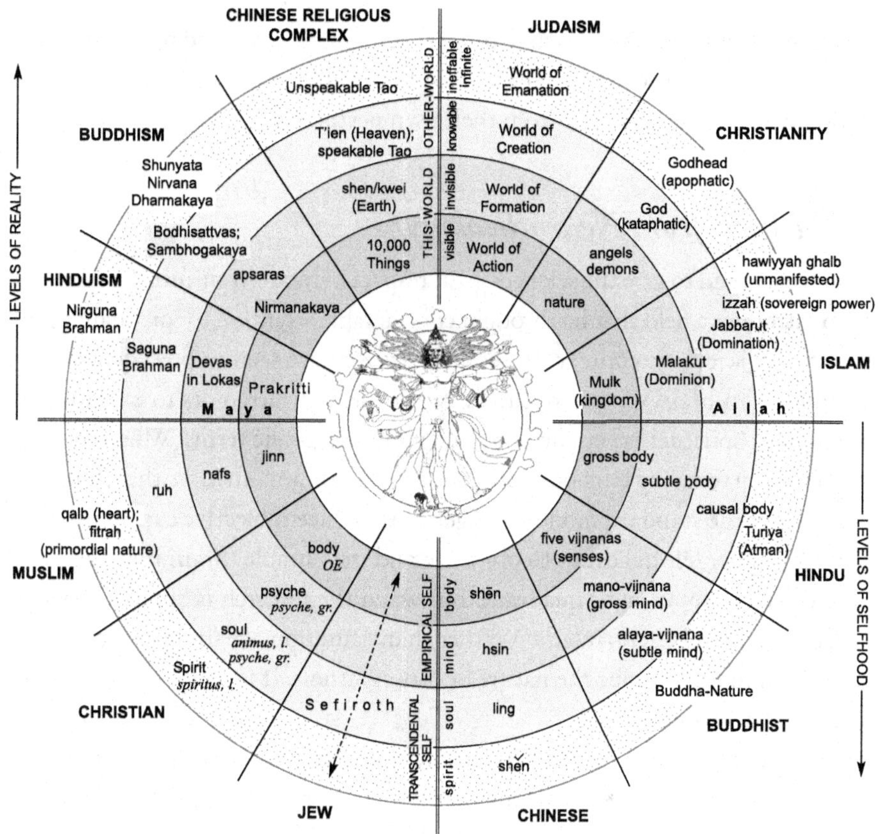


*Figure 8.2 Huston Smith's Great Chain of Being*

view, the "myth of the given," arguing that in our "postmetaphysical" world we have to question whether these preexisting structures are "real." Instead, we are urged to view them as "structures of consciousness" that have "developed in time, evolution, and history."[32] The nature of Reality *cannot be known for certain*.

On a practical level, I lean toward accepting what people believe and experience as real for them (barring psychosis, a discernment to be considered in chapter 9). We have explored ideas that make room for complexity, such as developmental stage, cultural meaning, and personality type. We do not need an absolute truth in order to remain receptive and respectful. I encourage counselors to remain open to possibility, and to be aware of dogmatism that may arise from their own perspective.

## *The View from Neurotheology*

Since we tend to give the sciences great respect in modern culture, I'd like to introduce a field that has brought considerable attention to spirituality within a scientific context. In recent years we have seen unprecedented progress in brain science research. Neurotheology attempts to explain religious/spiritual experience and behavior in scientific terms. When the focus is on reducing religious state experiences to brain function, the effort is part of the standard modernist agenda to reduce subjective experience in the upper left quadrant to objective and measurable (brain imaging) data in the upper right quadrant. But when the research is approached with an interest in *correlations* rather than causation, we find that there is much to learn about the nature of consciousness. It is an invitation to expand horizons.

In the 1980s, Michael Persinger focused on what came to be called the "God spot," a spontaneous firing in the brain's temporoparietal region, which leads to enhanced communication between the right and left temporoparietal areas. This in turn produces confusion between the sense of self and others, which he describes as a sense of unboundaried "presence."[33] While this is now viewed as an oversimplification, new technology has opened the way for new complexities. Functional imaging technologies—single-photon emission computed tomography (SPECT), positron emission tomography (PET), and functional magnetic resonance imaging (fMRI)—give us a glimpse of actual brain activity during spiritual/religious experiences.

Andrew Newberg is a neuroscientist who has authored and coauthored numerous books on the brain and spiritual/religious experience. Using SPECT imagery, his research found that Tibetan Buddhist meditators had increased flow of activity through the frontal cortex and thalamus (indicating focused attention), and decreased activity in the posterior superior parietal lobes. Similar results were obtained in a study of Franciscan nuns at prayer. Translation: with an enhanced ability to focus attention, there was a lessening of activity in areas that have to do with defining the body and its orientation in space (an aspect of "self").[34]

This pattern holds up with a range of contemplative practices. However, Newberg has gone on to explore brain scans during other kinds of practices such as chanting, speaking in tongues, and channeling. Here he finds a slightly different pattern: there is still a decrease in parietal lobe activity—correlated with the disappearance or fading of sense of self and an emerging "neurological sense of 'unity'"—but now a *decrease* in frontal lobe activity. If frontal lobe activity suggests a sense of control, then this decrease may accompany a feeling of surrender.[35]

A broader perspective emerges from the research of cognitive neuroscientist Mario Beauregard. He worked with Carmelite nuns, using brain scans under several conditions: recalling mystical experience, during actual contemplation, and in "control" restful states.[36] He found increased theta activity during actual mystical experience, and overall involvement of many brain regions (not just the temporal lobes, which were a focus of early research). After examining numerous arguments and explanations, Beauregard argues for the *nonmaterial origin of spiritual/religious experiences.*

When I find myself at a loss as to how to make a place for spiritual dimensions in our rational scientific age, I turn to an appealing perspective in the work of William James. In *The Varieties of Religious Experience,* he suggests that like a prism, the brain may have a *transmissive* function: our brains might serve as "thin and translucent places" in the material universe, allowing access to a richer and "more real" reality.[37] We may think that the notion of the brain as a prism or lens is just a foolish metaphor. However, neuroscientists have tremendous difficulty explaining consciousness as a function or product of the brain, and as we have seen in this brief discussion, some neuroscientists do hold a view similar to the prism metaphor. What if, as they suggest, the brain is a function of and a *transmitter* of Consciousness?

## Technologies of the Sacred

The phrase "technology of the sacred" points to practices capable of inducing holotropic (oriented toward wholeness) states for spiritual purposes. In ancient and aboriginal cultures these practices included particular kinds of drumming, dance, music, and breath practices, as well as isolation, fasting, sleep deprivation, and more. The ritual use of psychedelic plants was familiar in many ancient cultures. Such substances are known as *entheogens*, which literally means "generating the divine within." More formally, the *Oxford English Dictionary* defines *entheogen* as "a psychedelic substance (typically a plant or fungal extract) or drug, esp. when used in a religious ritual or to bring about a spiritual experience."[38]

We can understand all these practices as forms of state training in which we learn to access nonordinary states of consciousness and thereby gain knowledge, healing, guidance, and a larger perspective. Let's take a closer look at a few of these "technologies."

### *Somatic Practices*

Holotropic techniques frequently focus on the body in order to bypass the power of the mental realm, which tends to keep us harnessed to familiar constructs of everyday reality. Rhythmic practices that "entrain" (cause to fall into synchrony, or sweep along in its flow) the body and mind, such as drumming and chanting, are included in this category. Ecstatic dance involves the whole body in moving freely and rhythmically, which can also create new openings: the dance of the whirling dervishes in the Sufi tradition is an example. Various neo-pagan approaches seek ecstatic states through active embodied rituals. Breathwork (which may be included in any of these other practices) typically introduces breathing rhythms that shift the accustomed pattern and induce biological changes. Native American rituals include drumming and chanting, but some also use sweat lodges. These don't typically involve movement, but may involve chanting as well as the somatic experience of heat and smoke in a confined space: the mind is induced to surrender, and subtle state experiences may emerge.

These are all active techniques. More passive approaches like fasting and sleep deprivation (keeping a vigil, for instance) also have a clear impact on the body-mind. Again, when we shift from the customary physiological channels and bypass mental control, openings become possible.

## *Meditation and Prayer Practices*

We briefly considered meditation when we were exploring spirituality as a resource in chapter 3, but now let's focus specifically on the creation of state changes.

Concentration practices focus the attention on a single object, such as the breath. Focus itself (not a typical mode for many of us) can induce a nonordinary state: the lens of ordinary awareness narrows. Many meditation practices eventually emphasize opening up the lens to focus on awareness itself. All content (body sensations, emotions, thoughts) arises in consciousness and passes away, like leaves on a stream or clouds in the sky. When we learn to loosen identification with the *contents* of awareness, we may not only suffer less from our thoughts, but eventually come to rest *as* awareness itself. This is not just a state, but the awareness of all states.

There are also devotional practices in which the Divine is seen or experienced, not as vast impersonal consciousness, but as a supreme Being or Presence with whom one can develop an I-Thou relationship. The relationship unfolds and deepens in the heart or soul, inducing experiences of deep bliss or ecstatic absorption. This emphasis flowers in the Abrahamic traditions (Christian, Islamic, and Jewish prayer and contemplation) as well as in Hindu bhakti (devotional) practices, although devotional aspects certainly exist in Buddhism as well (especially Tibetan Buddhism).

One example of a Christian practice that blends meditation and devotion is Thomas Merton's version of contemplative prayer in Catholicism. Father Thomas Keating has brought this approach to more mainstream attention in the contemporary form known as Centering Prayer. The practice of contemplation elaborated by theologian Martin Laird draws from early Christian traditions and invites the reader into the mystery of Silence.[39] I would also include the highly ritualized liturgies of traditional

Catholicism and the ecstatic visions that may be experienced in deep prayer. A focus on states is an intentional aspect of the charismatic movement in the Catholic Church. Members participate in prayer and song together, seeking out and welcoming the gifts of the Holy Spirit, such as speaking in tongues, healing, and prophecy. Evangelical Christians may experience nonordinary states through personal experience of God's grace, especially in a conversion or born-again experience. Pentecostal Christians practice speaking in tongues. Worshippers in many African American churches experience public ecstasies in the form of shouting out and singing. So practices to train nonordinary states are more common than we may realize.

## *Entheogens*

The use of entheogens is largely prohibited these days. What was once an arena of exploration and discovery in the 1960s has become suspect in many circles. We do, however, see evidence of a resurgence in such organizations as the Multidisciplinary Association for Psychedelic Studies (MAPS), which is, for example, conducting current research with ayahuasca and MDMA. Use of cannabis (with varying amounts of psychoactive THC) is becoming more common, for medical as well as recreational purposes. The synthetic substance known as LSD, which fueled a great deal of research at one time, is now illegal, although small research projects continue.

What we know about the use of entheogens is that "set and setting" are very important. This phrase refers to the physical, mental, social, and environmental context in which the substance is used. Such a context includes intentional preparation of the participants, establishment of a sacred purpose, and the security and comfort of the body and physical setting. Meditation and/or ritual may have a role to play. These are all features of the experience that highlight the spiritual context and intention and heighten the possibility of a positive nonordinary state experience.[40]

As counselors we may well encounter cannabis users, although they often have no spiritual intention in mind. As for the more powerful substances, who knows? A client may or may not reveal the use of an entheogen, and their intent may focus on "the high" without any spiritual orientation. However, it is important to know that the Native American Church has explicitly embraced the sacramental use of peyote and has had the legal right to do so since the American Indian Religious Freedom Act of 1978.

### Reflecting on Personal Experiences of Nonordinary States

Have you ever had an experience that seemed to be a taste of something beyond ordinary reality? If so, did it come spontaneously? Sometimes these tastes come in moments of joy—watching an extraordinary sunset or witnessing a baby's birth. Sometimes a moment may be deeply painful, and yet a kind of opening occurs. Whatever the context, take a few moments to reflect on the memory, focusing on images, thoughts, and body sensations.

If the nonordinary state seemed to present itself as the result of some intentional action or practice, reflect on that. Was it a surprise? Did you want to repeat it, or was it frightening? How did you feel about its temporary nature?

If you have never experienced such a state, notice if you have set a very high bar. Such states do not have to be transcendent or otherworldly. They can simply feel like openings to perceiving the world in new and unexpected ways.

## *Validating the Growth Focus of Spiritual Practices*

In chapter 4, we considered some ways in which spiritual practices can serve as resources. We can see how the pursuit of altered states may be an attempt to escape from an unhappy life, through drugs, alcohol, or sex. But beneath these escape strategies, we need to remember that there is often a longing, a thirst for wholeness, not just a running-from. Bringing this perspective to bear on addiction patterns may uncover some overlooked therapeutic territory.

Other clients may engage in spiritual practices for the explicit purpose of deepening and growing. We have an opportunity to integrate their experience into our work together and explore its meanings and possibilities more deeply. The Griffiths give the subject of spiritual practice serious consideration:

> A spiritual practice is a method for transforming one's being—mind and body—to expand its openness to spiritual experiences. What is important is not the symbolic meaning of the enacted behaviors but the change in consciousness that ensues. Examples of spiritual practices involve dietary disciplines, physical exertion, quieting of body arousal, or chanting, which religions throughout the world have employed to facilitate a desired state of consciousness.[41]

It is important to listen carefully for nuances of meaning when such practices are described. The therapist's curiosity and openness can serve to deepen the conversation, which in turn may enrich the client's own experience.

Along the path of spiritual development, the purpose of spiritual practice continues to evolve. As one moves into the ego-aware, paradoxical stage, one becomes less interested in experiencing nonordinary states and more interested in realizing the nature of the experiencer. One way of expressing this shift is that spiritual practice is often the search for something, for an *addition* to experience, but at some point it becomes more about *subtraction*, self-emptying and surrender of the personal self. We will consider this possibility next, as we focus on the role of ego in transpersonal development.

## What about the Ego?

This is the natural question that arises from a psychological point of view: How can we do without the ego? Surely it's the essential core of the healthy person, without which there is all kinds of trouble. We need ego strength to withstand the subjective and objective storms of life. Freud sees the ego as the stabilizing force, the reality principle that is needed to mediate between the forces of id and superego. Jung tells us that we need a strong and healthy ego to meet the unconscious without crumpling. While too much ego can be a problem, it is feared that *not enough ego* will render us virtually helpless to navigate the demands of adult life and subject us to a variety of mental health problems. The challenge here is that we are often using the term "ego" in different ways.

Here are some clarifications from Wilber:

> Most transpersonal researchers refer to the higher stages as being "beyond ego" or "transegoic," which seems to imply the ego is lost. But this confusion is almost entirely semantic. If by ego you mean an *exclusive* identification with the personal self, then that *exclusiveness* is mostly lost or dissolved in higher development. . . . But if by ego you mean a functional self that relates to the conventional world, then that ego is definitely retained (and often strengthened). Likewise, if you mean—as psychoanalysis does—that an important part of the ego is its capacity for detached witnessing, then that ego is definitely retained (and almost always strengthened). . . . Also, if by ego you mean—as ego psychology does—the psyche's capacity for integrating, then that ego is also retained and strengthened.[42]

In other words, the *functional capacities* of ego remain and are often enhanced. In the course of healthy development, we grow our capacities for integration, regulation, impulse control, organization, anticipation, decision making, and so forth. Under "good enough" circumstances, we develop the "capacity to organize and manage both internal functioning of the psyche as well as external functioning in the world."[43] These are useful for survival and protection and navigation in our world. But the key is this: these capacities are not the property of a *thing* that we can actually point to. The term "ego" here is a theoretical construct that describes an organizing principle in human life.

The other domain of ego is *self-representation*: the "capacity to synthesize a consistent self-concept out of various images of itself."[44] In other words, the ego becomes our identity. In the course of growing up in a particular culture, we come to believe that this "manager" is *who we are,* the composite of all the things that an individual identifies with: my name, my birthday, my body, my family, my possessions, my job or role, my country, my beliefs and values, my God. *Who I am* is also made up of memories, and in particular, we assume that we are our thoughts.

This self-image construction, which develops through childhood and adolescence, serves us in many ways. It gives us immediate access to a repertoire of specific responses and strategies, and a sense of grounding and confidence that is useful for navigating life. However, identification comes with some costs.[45] For one thing, it tends to be static: we assume the things we identify with are permanent (bodies, roles, relationships, successes, and memories, for example). And yet life is always changing, so we struggle with insecurity and loss.

From a larger perspective, the course of human development is a story of shifting identification. As the days pass, we find ourselves constantly grasping to hold onto "the center," the core of what we take ourselves to be. (Mindfulness practice loosens our identification with thoughts, emotions, and sensations, which is why it is so useful for stress reduction.)

Another liability is that we did not choose most of what we automatically identify with. The inner sense of *who I am* (upper left quadrant) interacts with many factors in the other quadrants: genetics, our physiological characteristics, culture, family relationships, socioeconomic status, geography, and much more. In other words, ego identity is largely constructed as a product of *conditioning*. Most people have ready, automatic answers to the question: "Who are you?"

In the course of development we may come to recognize this to varying degrees. We may experience an "identity crisis," a questioning of everything we thought we were. If we keep going, we may realize that *we don't really know who we are*. We set out on a journey, a search, for our essential deeper self. This is a process of psychospiritual growth. Some may eventually experience "coming home" to the mystery of Being, the Silence, direct experience of belonging to the Divine, or union with All That Is. The sense of being a separate self dissolves to varying degrees. Beyond the personal, identification fades or falls away.

It is primarily the lack of a healthy *functional* ego that can create difficulties for those on a spiritual path. But even a basic developmental ego-identification may be useful. John Engler, a psychologist and Buddhist teacher, is well known for his pithy statement that "one has to be somebody before one can be nobody." Spiritual practices that may be described as "uncovering" techniques can, he argues, be risky for those with poorly differentiated, weakly integrated object relations: "with faulty self-object differentiation the observing ego cannot take distance from what it observes."[46] Without this developmental foundation, there is a potential that the fragile, vulnerable sense of self can be fragmented further.

> Both a sense of self and insight into the ultimate illusoriness of its apparent continuity and substantiality are necessary achievements. . . . The attempt to bypass the developmental tasks of identity formation and object constancy through a misguided attempt to "annihilate the ego" has fateful and pathological consequences.[47]

Development beyond the ego is decidedly *not* a matter of returning to an imagined state of infantile merging: that would be a problematic regression. In Engler's terms, it is a matter of both self *and* no-self. We can have a provisional sense of self *and* "insight into the ultimate illusoriness of its apparent continuity and substantiality."[48]

This both/and formulation points beyond a developmental view into the Buddhist perspective that the separate self has always been an illusion, and *never did actually exist.*[49] Paradox reigns in these deeper realms. But it is also essential to remember that the Buddhist tenet of no-self is only one view. Other traditions do posit the spiritual reality of a soul, individual spark, or essence. From this perspective, healthy development involves temporary identification with the relative reality of a personal, earthly ego-self. In the process of further spiritual growth, disidentification may unfold as a deeper soul essence is revealed.

Finally, I offer a reminder that most of us are also aware of multiple "selves." While we may be aware of an essential identification, especially when asked who we are, in daily life we often operate from a variety of ego states or subpersonalities. So the preceding chapter's discussion of subpersonality dynamics remains a relevant aspect of this whole question. As a rule, we do find it easier to become aware of these partial identifications and to disidentify from them, at least temporarily. But they tend to have quite a hold on us.

## Reflecting on Enneagram Style Variations: Temporary Ventures Beyond the Personal

In Rob's early experiments with psychoactive drugs, including LSD, we may see an attempt to escape from his traumatic growing-up experiences. But these explorations also point to a longing for a deeper truth, a hunger for something beyond ordinary reality. When they are given interested attention in the therapeutic conversation, it becomes clear that he did actually have some nonordinary state experiences that were significant pointers for him. He glimpsed the insubstantiality of his separate existence and identity. Something that he felt was rock solid (and often painful) seemed to dissolve temporarily. These openings set the stage for his interest in a Buddhist path.

It is useful for him to recognize aspects that are often part of the Eight pattern: with a strong energetic core, he acknowledges that he tends to seek out stimulation, experiences that are vibrant and "alive." This love of intensity can create an addictive tendency: "more" nonordinary states are better than "fewer." But his early twelve-step work helped him establish some healthy principles, and he chooses to channel his energies toward meditation practice for a deeper purpose.

Devin (Nine) illustrates a different dynamic. In the attempt to avoid conflict, Nines often find themselves merging with other people and points of view, and have to work to differentiate their own perspective. At one level her African American identity, along with all its gifts and challenges, is very clear. And yet her inner core (or the possibility of having one) remains a mystery to her. The prospect of being a separate self who can assert herself is frightening to her. She wants to focus on what is peaceful and harmonious, and avoid what may be conflictual. Spiritual paths that emphasize "up and out," "transcending the ego," hold a natural appeal for her.

As we saw in the preceding chapter, her therapeutic work leads her into the somatic experience of her own anger. Contact with this instinctual core turns out to hold a key for her ongoing psychospiritual development: to avoid this would be spiritual bypassing. She gradually becomes more awake to her own alive being, more grounded and present. She begins to invest more deeply in the Sufi path, which embraces both body practices and the mystical longing of the heart. The realization that "the way out is the way through" turns out to hold great importance for her, and she is able to appreciate the importance of a both/and perspective.

Let's take a brief look at some of the other characters. Linn (Three) did not seek out a nonordinary state. It appeared suddenly in the form of her near-death experience, which runs counter to everything she takes for granted and terrifies her. Our work includes listening to her, educating her, and establishing a context for the NDE so that eventually she may find some meaning in it. Janice (Four) is at home with imaginal experiences. These may not all be nonordinary states of consciousness, but some of them probably reflect subtle state openings. She welcomes them and allows them to offer her guidance. Kyle (Five) has had some nonordinary experiences, which he keeps secret for the most part. We don't know very much about them, but they may be glimpses of deeper realities. Acknowledging their meaning sets the stage for deeper trust and potential exploration. Finally, as Marissa (Seven) begins to explore Native American traditions, she has her grandmother to guide her into state-altering rituals and new ways of seeing.

## Chapter Nine

# Potential Psychospiritual Challenges

We turn our attention now to some of the challenges and pitfalls that can arise as part of the spiritual journey itself. I have saved this topic for last because it is too easy in our modern world, and especially in the context of counseling, to focus immediately on the problematic aspects of spirituality and religion. But recognition of the challenges is essential if we are to understand the interplay of psychology and spirituality, and also develop skillfulness in anticipating and responding to the challenges themselves.

This chapter will take a few different perspectives on this complex topic. First we will make use of descriptive categories drawn from transpersonal and spiritual literature. The category boundaries are not always clear, but it is important to consider distinct origins, issues, and contexts. We will begin with a broad range of experiences known as "spiritual emergencies," a concept that is one of the most valuable contributions from the field of transpersonal psychology. Our focus will then shift to potential problems associated with spiritual practice. We will also consider unhealthy forms of spirituality/religion in which unresolved psychological dynamics play a key role, including extremist forms of religion. Finally, we will turn our attention to territory that is specific to the context of therapy: fundamental ethical considerations and current diagnostic categories related to spirituality and religion.

## Spiritual Emergencies

In earlier chapters we explored the idea of life as a spiritual journey (chapter 5) and the idea of psychospiritual development (chapter 6). This movement toward a deeper and expanded way of being is a natural process which, despite ups and downs, is usually gradual. This may be called *spiritual emergence*. While it is by no means a universal experience, spiritual emergence is natural because human beings have an innate capacity for this kind of growth, depending on their life circumstances.

However, some people suddenly find themselves in a period of such rapid and dramatic change that their coping capacities are overwhelmed. They find themselves in a crisis, a *spiritual emergency*, in which they are overwhelmed by inner experiences (nonordinary states) that challenge their relationship to "reality" and to other people who take that reality for granted. Such experiences have been recognized for centuries in a variety of different religious traditions, but in the modern medical model, they are routinely pathologized and medicated. Here it is appropriate to emphasize the crucial importance of cultural context: to some extent, the suffering involved in these emergencies has a lot to do with the discrepancy between the conditioned cultural worldview and the individual's nonordinary experience.

The transpersonal view, on the other hand, emphasizes the healing and transformative potential of such experiences when they are received with understanding and guidance. Such "growth-producing disturbances" have been called by many names: "positive disintegrations," "creative illnesses," "regenerative processes," "and "renewals." When the spiritual aspect is paramount, they have also been called "divine illnesses," "mystical experiences with psychotic features," "metanoiac voyages," and "visionary states."[1]

Stan and Christina Grof have done much of the pioneering work on spiritual emergencies—a term that they coined. In their view,

> The common denominator of all crises of transformation is the manifestation of various aspects of the psyche that were previously unconscious. However, each spiritual emergency

> represents a unique selection and combination of unconscious elements—some of them biographical, others perinatal, and still others transpersonal.[2]

While these exteriorizations of the unconscious and superconscious (higher and lower unconscious) fall along a continuum, the Grofs have found it useful to distinguish a number of significant patterns. Their list of spiritual emergencies varies slightly in different publications, but we will consider the most prominent patterns. This is a general introduction. I encourage those interested in more specific therapeutic questions to consult the resources suggested in the endnotes.

## *The Awakening of Kundalini*

Clearly recognized in Hindu and Buddhist traditions, this is an activation or awakening of a form of subtle energy sometimes known as serpent power. In the human body it "sleeps" at the base of the spine. When aroused, it rises in the form of active energy (*shakti*) up the spine, through the chakras, to the top of the head. But along the way it encounters stress points or blocks (associated with the chakras), the clearing of which can produce dramatic physiological and psychological experiences: powerful sensations of heat and energy, violent shaking, as well as involuntary movements, gestures, postures, laughing, crying, and various noises. Visual and auditory experiences can be intense, and emotions may range from ecstasy to terror and despair. Many of these manifestations may be interpreted as psychotic symptoms, and the challenge of distinguishing between kundalini and psychosis is discussed in a number of sources.[3] From the spiritual perspective, the entire process is one of purification or balancing.

## *Near-Death Experiences*

The literature on near-death experiences has grown rapidly, particularly in popular culture. Raymond Moody's early work *Life After Life* was published in 1975 and is still widely read. With technical advances in medicine, more people have survived clinical death and returned to report what they went through. A cursory internet search will quickly affirm the frequency of these experiences. Frequently, people describe passing through a kind of dark tunnel toward a brilliant and indescribable light. There may be a life review, encounters along the way with deceased loved ones or other spiritual beings, as well as music and scenes of ineffable beauty. There is less discussion of experiences that are negative or frightening, but they certainly exist. Scientific literature debates the objective reality of such experiences. For instance, critics debate the definition of clinical death, and consider possible medical explanations for the experiences described.

Of particular interest to us here are the after-effects. While some people may smoothly integrate the experience into their lives, especially if they live in a sociocultural context which is accepting, others find themselves facing a dramatic and profound shift in their sense of identity and reality. They may doubt their own sanity, fear ridicule, and struggle with readjusting to their everyday lives and relationships. Long-held values and beliefs may suddenly come into question, and customary patterns of behavior may no longer feel viable. They may keep the experience a secret for fear of being ridiculed or called crazy, and the resulting separation from loved ones can leave them with a profound sense of loneliness. Sometimes the reaction to having to return to this life is one of anger and depression: "I don't want to be here!"

Bruce Greyson, now professor emeritus of psychiatry and neurobehavioral sciences at the University of Virginia, co-edited a volume entitled *The Handbook of Near-Death Experiences* and has written many journal articles on the subject. He emphasizes the crucial importance of creating a safe space for the near-death experiencer, listening attentively and open-mindedly, appreciating the powerful impact of the experience, and over the long term, supporting the exploration of deep questions about existence and purpose.[4]

## Reflecting on Enneagram Style Variations

We have discussed Linn's NDE within the context of trauma, but it is also a spiritual emergency. Linn's style (Three) is practical and rational, so the impact of this experience has been deeply upsetting to her worldview and coping strategies. Since she has not had any prior interest in spirituality, she has no context within which to hold either her NDE or the intuitive abilities (psychic openings) which have come in its wake. In addition to supportive listening, some psychoeducation about the phenomenon is valuable in order to provide some normalization based on research. Support for her personal journey of meaning-making is essential.

While personality style may or may not play a significant role in the response to an NDE, we can consider some broad possibilities. For instance, someone with a Seven pattern might conceivably be excited by the novelty of a positive experience, but be thrown into a panic by a negative NDE. An Enneagram Four might be inclined to embrace the depth of feelings associated with the powerful experience, but might also be susceptible to some degree of ego-inflation in terms of feeling "special." An Enneagram Five might be particularly drawn to the noetic aspects of the experience: the term refers to the intellect, but in this context connotes a sense of revelation or deep knowing of the truth.[5] An Enneagram Nine might love the feeling of peace associated with the experience, and perhaps feel enriched by the sense of some kind of core identity, no matter how difficult to describe. These are just some possibilities to alert us to possible individual variations.

## *Psychological Renewal through Return to the Center*

This term comes from the work of John Weir Perry, a Jungian-trained psychiatrist who explored the visionary experiences of young adults going through their first psychotic break.[6] They typically found themselves in the midst of an archetypal conflict between forces of good and evil, light and darkness, preoccupied with the theme of death and the historical journey of the human being in the cosmos. Fascination with opposites often played out with sexual themes, and resolved in the mythological union of the Sacred Marriage. The process typically culminated in an experience of being raised to an exalted status (like a world savior) and undergoing an experience of birth or rebirth for the individual and the world. Perry saw this theme of renewal as a movement toward individuation.

In the 1970s, Perry founded an experimental residential treatment center in San Francisco called Diabasis House. (The Greek word *diabasis* means "crossing over.") There young adults in their first acute schizophrenic break, instead of encountering medication and shock treatment, were given a comfortable, safe residence where they could go through the experience over a three-month period with the support of painting, dance, massage, meditation, and supportive conversation. Perry found that the acute schizophrenic phase usually lasted no more than six weeks. Patients emerged with the realization that they had undergone a profound transformational crisis and reentered the world with new insights and capacities—"weller than well," in Perry's words. Perry also suggested that there were striking parallels between these experiences and those of prophets and reformers throughout history, reflecting mythic themes and images of humankind as a whole.

## *Awakening of Extrasensory Perception (Psychic Opening)*

While the appearance of paranormal abilities may accompany a variety of spiritual emergencies—either temporarily or as more permanent openings—these are usually subordinate to the central experience. Psychic openings can be intriguing and exciting, but in many spiritual/religious traditions are considered secondary to the primary goal of spiritual growth. The pursuit of such experiences for their own sake can lead to what Jung calls ego inflation, and is generally discouraged. At times, however, there can be a sudden and overwhelming influx of information from "nonordinary sources." The individual is left frightened, reeling, confused, and unable to screen out the input.[7]

Out-of-body experiences are considered to be in this category.[8] These may happen out of the blue: someone suddenly finds herself looking down on her body from the ceiling, or traveling to other locations and perceiving (accurately, it may turn out) what is taking place there. If there is no familiarity with the phenomenon through reading or media sources, the OBE traveler may fear she is going insane. Friends and family may support this latter view, and mental health professionals will probably use the term "dissociation."

Others describe a sudden influx of unwanted telepathic ability: knowing what others are thinking, correctly predicting future events, or accurately perceiving what is happening in a remote location. Again, these experiences are disturbing not only because they are unfamiliar, but also because they clash with our modern Western view of reality. Such abilities are taken for granted by shamanic healers, but in contemporary society, people question the sanity of the perceiver and/or may be truly frightened by such trespass across the taken-for-granted boundaries of time, space, and the body.

Again, it is important to recognize that a gradual emergence of intuitive capacities does not constitute an emergency. Gabriela (Enneagram Six), for instance, finds herself growing increasingly intuitive, but this unfolding is gradual. She is even able to appreciate this "knower" aspect of herself, especially when she realizes that it has had a useful role since childhood.

## *Past-Life Memories and Experiences*

This is another kind of violation of common beliefs and practices. While polls suggest that 20 to 25 percent of Americans believe in some form of reincarnation, this number leaves a lot of people who are very skeptical about spontaneous experiences of other historical periods and places.[9] On the other hand, in many parts of Asia a past-life experience might well be met with interest rather than skepticism.

Such experiences typically arouse powerful emotions as well as serious questions about identity and reality. Such an opening may occur spontaneously in the midst of everyday life, in childbirth, or even in sexual experience.[10] There are likely to be conflicts with others who cannot accept the validity or meaning of such "memories." Complications in present-day relationships may result from the perception of past karmic patterns. When this kind of information is met with acceptance and interest, however, difficult relationships as well as a variety of psychosomatic ailments have been known to resolve themselves.[11]

## *Unitive (Mystical) Consciousness*

Here we find experiences that are not always thought of as problematic: mystical experiences which involve the dissolution of the self's boundaries. We have looked at psychic-level experiences which involve a sense of merging with nature, for instance, as well as subtle- and causal-level experiences which may entail union with a spiritual being or with the "dazzling dark." While sought after by many, when such an experience comes unbidden it may well become a crisis. Our ordinary perception of ourselves and the world naturally contains boundaries and separations. If plunged into this kind of unitive consciousness, the response may be one of terror. And if others learn of it, they may pathologize the reluctant mystic.

### *Reflecting on Enneagram Style Variations*

Marissa, the twenty-eight-year-old facing a life-threatening illness, brings her Seven pattern to her journey. As she explores her Native American roots and comes to feel more at home in her body, she is also drawn to being in nature. She becomes more and more attuned to the joy of existence, open spaciousness, and freedom. If she were to have a mystical experience of oneness with nature, chances are that she would be able to integrate this experience relatively smoothly *because* she has a spiritual context for it as well as her grandmother's support. This is not to say that it would be trivial—the power of such an opening is immense and sometimes life changing—but it probably would not constitute a spiritual emergency for her.

## *Dark Night of the Soul*

We briefly considered this category when we talked about the spiritual journey in chapter 5. The individual who encounters this kind of spiritual emergency plunges into an experience of desolation, hopelessness, fear, meaninglessness, and abandonment by the Divine. While any of the other spiritual emergencies can lead to a dark night, this category traditionally refers to the loss of connection with the Divine. Practices that used to have meaning, such as prayer and meditation, become dry and empty; life is desert-like. For some this may feel like depression, and medication may be suggested. But for others, the way out is the way through: what is being enacted is a shedding of an outworn skin, a mask, or identification with the personality. Support for this journey can make all the difference, but may also need to be sustained over a long period of time.

### Reflecting on Enneagram Style Variations

Charles (One) goes through his own kind of dark night following his wife's death. The loss of meaning, loneliness, and lack of spiritual connection combine to create an experience of profound desolation. Janice (Four) is familiar with the depths of depression which might evolve into a dark night of the soul. We can think of this along a spectrum: there are no objective criteria in terms of severity. Rather, the framing of such an experience as a spiritual emergency has a lot to do with the intensity of subjective suffering, duration, or inability to function in daily life.

## *Assistance in Spiritual Emergencies*

If we encounter something along the lines of a spiritual emergency, either personally or professionally, what do we do? What follows is a brief discussion of the kinds of strategies that may be helpful, as well as potentially useful resources.

The first instinct may be to tamp down or contain the experience. While this grounding approach is perhaps not the ideal response from a spiritual point of view, we need to acknowledge that people often have responsibilities and commitments to meet. They may not have the kind of support they really need, and they may simply be too frightened or overwhelmed to consider the prospect of deeper exploration. Here are some curtailment strategies:

- Temporarily suspend (or cut back on) spiritual practice and inner exploration (experiential therapy, dreamwork, meditation, chanting, Tai Chi, spiritual reading, etc.).
- Adjust diet. There are various approaches offered in this category, but basically the recommendation is to eat smaller, more frequent meals. Some sources recommend avoiding caffeine, refined sugar, and alcohol, while others suggest that limited, temporary use of these may be helpful for some people. (Glucose, for example, is a brain nutrient.) Eating protein daily is useful, and for more grounding, red meat, cheese, grains, and root vegetables (any heavy foods) are sometimes suggested.
- Increase sleep and rest time if possible. Some people experience an unusual sleepiness or heaviness, while others can barely sleep at all. A warm bath can help.
- Get regular exercise. Simple manual work in the house or garden is a good start (washing floors, stacking wood, weeding), but moving the body is important (jogging, walking, bicycling, swimming, dancing).
- Ground the body and energy, especially in nature. This is a general category that includes such activities as gardening, lying on the ground, feeling roots going from the bottom of the feet deep into the earth. Some people find that longer outbreaths are helpful in reducing a sense of anxiety or agitation.

When there is capacity and time for opening to the experience, creative expression can help to channel the physical and emotional energies—drawing, painting, or sculpting. Dreamwork can give deeper access to the process in the inner world. Some people find great value in listening to evocative music and allowing spontaneous movement (shaking, stretching) and sound (crying, singing) to flow; the focus is on the inner experience, not on the form of the expression. Bodywork may help open up tight and contracted places in the body. Certain kinds of breathwork are also powerful openers, but this exploration should be undertaken with an experienced guide. And, of course, various forms of spiritual practice play an important role, although again, guidance under these circumstances is recommended.

There are clearly significant challenges in distinguishing a true spiritual emergency from psychosis, clinical depression, or a manic episode. Diagnostic issues will be considered at the end of the chapter.

## Difficulties and Pitfalls Associated with Spiritual Practice

Many spiritual traditions acknowledge the possibility of serious psychological or physical complications in the course of committed spiritual practice, particularly meditation. Any kind of intense and/or prolonged spiritual focus has the potential to lead to challenging experiences. For instance, fasting can result in significant problems, some of which may be similar to those I am about to describe. There are numerous ancient stories of visions and hearing voices that, in the modern world, would be considered psychotic; the Buddha, Muhammad, and Jesus are just three of the best-known examples.

While these kinds of experiences may be rare, the potential hazards of meditation are beginning to be more widely acknowledged as the practice becomes more popular. Learning about the nature of such pitfalls is important. And of course, appreciating the dynamics of such challenges helps us to deepen our understanding of the interplay of psychology and spirituality.

In this brief exploration I draw on the work of Jack Kornfield, a well-known American Buddhist teacher. Although he focuses on Buddhist practice, his treatment of this subject is illuminating for anyone who practices systematic meditation.[12]

## *Physical and Emotional Pain*

This is a common challenge that many meditators experience. Kornfield suggests that there are three kinds: the pain that indicates you are sitting incorrectly, the pain that comes from an unaccustomed posture, and the pain that emerges from the release of various kinds of chronic tension. The latter points to the existence of deep patterns of psychological blocking due to accumulated stress and trauma. The experience of increasing intensity and eventual release of such somatic patterns is not uncommon for participants on meditation retreats: patterns of anger, terror, and (less obviously) sleepiness or restlessness may present themselves. If the meditator can allow these experiences to arise and observe them with mindful awareness, that may be enough to move through them. Sometimes expert support and facilitation are required. Kornfield suggests that for those who become skilled at closely observing such "hindrances," "we find that no state of mind, no feeling, no emotion actually lasts more than fifteen or thirty seconds before it is replaced by some other one."[13] In other words, close attention reveals that sensations and feelings tend to *move and shift.*

## *Mental Challenges*

Another challenge that may surface is an inability to think clearly, remember things, or make decisions. While some of this may occur because of the seclusion and disorientation that are part of an extended practice time, there is another possible source: spiritual retreat tends to weaken our "worldly motivation." The thinking process slows way down or stops during meditation, and we find it virtually impossible to participate in active comparisons and decision making. Returning to everyday life can be very disorienting. Kornfield suggests that grounding practices are important, particularly in bridging between extended periods of practice and everyday life. (Grounding includes reconnecting with the body and literally with the pelvis, the legs, the feet, and the earth.)

## *The Temptation to Escape*

This category points to the possibility of using practice as a means of escaping the challenges of living in the world. If we are afraid of our emotional pain, relationships, work, responsibility, and the world, then intense practice can be used as a way to retreat and hide. In Jungian terms, we turn to practice as a way to bolster our ego and avoid our shadow. These kinds of patterns will be considered in more detail shortly.

## *Raptures*

There is a second level of challenges as practice deepens. These energetic experiences may include trembling and "powerful, spontaneous releases of physical energies in the body, called *kriyas*, that can be scary to people."[14] Some of these patterns of release can unfold over months or years. Other kinds of rapture sensations include vibrations, tingling, prickles, temperature fluctuations, a sense of floating above the body or the body changing shape, hypersensitivity of smell, touch, or hearing, and intense visions of gold or white light (nonordinary states). In ordinary Western life we would call these delusions, and pathological labels are not far behind. The practitioner may experience intense emotional fluctuations, visions of past lives, or archetypal apparitions. A variety of spiritual emergencies can appear in the midst of intense, prolonged spiritual practice. The problem is not that these experiences occur, but that people are afraid of them, resist them, and judge them. In other words, the difficulty arises out of our own reactions. What we resist, traps us—and prolongs the struggle. Alternatively, we get attached to the blissful experiences, and get stuck trying to hold on to or repeat them. This is a grasping response which, in addition to stopping the spiritual unfolding, can lead to ego-inflation and escapism. The true challenge, from this perspective, is to practice observing and *letting go.*

## *The Awakening of Kundalini*

We have already considered this category through the lens of spiritual emergency. Kornfield describes the feelings of heat, vibrations, and tingling that may be part of this awakening, and the specific challenges associated with blockages in the various chakras: tension and coughing in the throat, for instance, or nausea and vomiting in the lower chakras. While the opening of the heart chakra may involve sweetness, there is usually also pain, because we tend to be constricted in this area. People are afraid they are having a heart attack. Kornfield's response, which comes from long experience, may sound humorous but also challenges us to the core:

> I usually say to them, "What better place to die than a retreat? Don't you think so?" We have not lost anybody yet, although some day it may happen. Still, it is important to have one's heart opened. So I say: "Go back and sit. Either your heart will open in your body or out of your body."[15]

## *Meditation-Induced Psychotic Episode*

Sustained spiritual practice can loosen our defenses and bring difficult material to the surface in both mind and body. In rare cases, the intensity of such experiences may reach such an extreme that a psychotic episode is triggered. In Kornfield's many years of experience he has found this to be very rare, usually occurring in meditators who have previously been hospitalized for mental illness. They may experience intense auditory and visual hallucinations, sleeplessness, or paranoia. It is crucial to try and help slow the process down and encourage grounding: activities that literally bring the energy down into the body and toward the earth; jogging; walking (especially in bare feet); digging in the garden; showers; a diet of heavier foods such as grains and meat. Others have recommended wrapping the individual in a thick, heavy blanket. In extreme circumstances a small dose of a tranquilizer has been used.

### Reflecting on Enneagram Style Variations

While none of our Enneagram characters offer these kinds of extreme examples, I want to draw attention to Rob (Eight) as a possible candidate for complications. For one thing, he is drawn to a Buddhist path, which focuses on meditation practice. His Eight pattern is characterized by intensity, and he might well decide to approach his practice as a challenge to master. Applying willpower to long retreats, challenging himself to overcome physical or mental pain, could result in some kind of crisis. Helping him to be aware of these tendencies, and of the egoic roots of such a "desire to conquer," might support him in learning to approach his practice with more moderation. He has something valuable to learn about Buddhism as the Middle Way.

## The Persistent Power of Ego

As we have discussed, we need a *functional, executive ego* to navigate the world. For those who consciously undertake a spiritual journey, there are some particular ego-related pitfalls that have been noted in many traditions. These usually involve attempts by the *self-representational ego* to grab onto spiritual "accomplishments" to bolster the sense of identity: "Look at who I am now!" "Look how far I have come!" But there can also be an opposite movement, in which the ego shames and punishes another part, turning the attack inward. We will explore these ego-related distortions under some contemporary labels.

## *Spiritual Materialism/Spiritual Narcissism*

The likelihood of egoic temptation is clearly recognized in the stories of Jesus in the wilderness and the Buddha under the bodhi tree: enticements related to power, fame, riches, and fulfillment of all desires. When there is evidence of spiritual "progress," it is all too easy for the individual to identify as *the one who is advanced*, to take ownership of spiritual accomplishment. Tibetan teacher Chögyam Trungpa Rinpoche described this as spiritual materialism. One becomes more egocentric, not less, but in "higher" and "better" ways! This is sometimes described as being trapped in "golden chains." They may be dazzling in their beauty, but they are chains nonetheless.[16]

Some of the manifestations of spiritual materialism include using accomplishments to make money, flaunting the spiritual pedigree, and constantly recounting one's spiritual experiences and insights. The essence of the pattern is pride, whether subtle or not so subtle. We might also describe this as a problem of attachment to one's spiritual identity. When the spiritualized ego parades itself as special, as king or queen of the mountain, we can see the psychological dynamic of narcissism at work. This is similar to Jung's concept of *ego-inflation*, in which the ego identifies with a powerful archetype.

## *Spiritual Bypassing*

We owe this term to contemporary psychologist John Welwood, who wanted to help Westerners understand "how the ego can coopt spiritual ideas and practices by attempting to bypass, rather than work through, the wounded, confused, and even damaged aspects of our psyches."[17] He emphasizes the necessity of dealing with what he calls our "basic human needs, feelings, and developmental tasks."[18] The spiritual bypassing pitfall is a particularly common one, at least in Western culture. Many people who are struggling with basic life challenges find themselves drawn to a spiritual path as a kind of escape. They envision spiritual life as helping them rise above such difficulties. In the process they become involved in the project of creating a new spiritual persona, free from shadow and all their unresolved psychological issues.

It is not difficult to see how this may overlap with spiritual materialism and spiritual narcissism. "What, me? I don't have to deal with those problems anymore," or "I'm on a higher path, I don't need to pay attention to those issues." Personal difficulties are ultimately only "illusions." Taking a larger, "impersonal" view is claimed to be the higher road, since painful feelings are unimportant remnants of limited personal perspectives. Anything is preferable to basic human vulnerability. Psychological defenses are shored up, and shadow is free to do its work.

An in-depth exploration of spiritual bypassing suggests these common manifestations:

> Exaggerated detachment, emotional numbing and repression, overemphasis on the positive, anger-phobia, blind or overly tolerant compassion, weak or too porous boundaries, lopsided development (cognitive intelligence often being far ahead of emotional and moral intelligence), debilitating judgment about one's negativity or shadow side, devaluation of the personal relative to the spiritual, and delusions of having arrived at a higher level of being.[19]

While it may sound simple to recognize and address the more blatant forms of spiritual bypassing, most people are caught in more subtle patterns.

Here it may be helpful to revisit the distinction between ascending and descending spirituality. The former path emphasizes transcendence of the earthly realm (seeking "wings"), viewing this world as limited, untrustworthy, and illusory. The descending perspective is more "rooted" in this world, emphasizing the immanence of Spirit in nature, relationships, embodiment, service, and compassion. The ascending path is especially vulnerable to spiritual bypassing, but each has its gifts and limitations. Here is a succinct comparison:

> An ascending approach has the potential upside of encouraging greater freedom and less fear in the adherent—that one's soul or ultimate destiny transcends this world and death—but also risks repression of the body and negative detachment from daily life. A descending approach, which encourages engagement in life and seeing the sacred in the mundane, may result in greater emotional connection and embodiment in the day to day, but may also result in a limited perspective.[20]

This distinction also offers a lens for understanding differences in personality style. An individual with an Enneagram Five pattern may lean toward an ascending, "up and out" spirituality, while someone with an Enneagram Two pattern may be more inclined to prefer a descending, embracing approach. Extremes of both can be problematic. On the other hand, we may shift orientations in the course of a life journey. Someone in his early twenties may feel passionately called to an ascending perspective, move to a descending path in the process of raising a family and working, and then return to more of an ascending view in later life.

When we are considering our own susceptibility to spiritual bypassing, it can be helpful to seek out relationships with others who not only have some spiritual wisdom but also some psychological astuteness. If we are counseling others on a spiritual path, then it is important to validate both the spiritual and psychological points of view. Because it is usually counterproductive to challenge someone's spiritual beliefs directly, the more productive approach is a gentle exploration of the difficult experiences that arise in life and an empathic consideration of the challenges that are present. Ongoing therapeutic exploration of defenses and personality dynamics may then be the route to more direct encounters with shadow material, repressed emotions, and neurotic patterns. *Awareness* of this territory is the key.

The client's openness to confronting shadow material and deep defenses depends on many complex factors. This may be partly a matter of developmental stage. For instance, someone whose center of gravity is at the conformist or conventional stage might not be a good candidate for in-depth psychological introspection. Loyalty to an external authority might be the primary dynamic, overriding self-exploration; the counselor can play the role of a healthy authority figure. On the other hand, it would be a mistake to assume that someone at a postmodern or integral stage is open to excavating unconscious material and facing painful shadow material. As we know, even "advanced" spiritual teachers can fall prey to temptations of power and sexuality without acknowledging their own susceptibility. Psychological defenses can be very firmly entrenched.

As professional helpers, our training has probably prioritized the psychological perspective. In this context, the commitment to honor the client's spiritual view can be highly challenging. There really is no objective standard by which to evaluate the importance of spiritual versus psychological health. When is it valid for clients to forgo sexual involvement for an extended period if this feels like part of their spiritual journey? How can we discern whether a client's desire to leave a relationship is essentially an escape from crucial issues or surrendering to a spiritual call? If our own leaning is toward a descending spirituality perspective, are we more likely to assess an ascending-oriented client as displaying pathological symptoms? These and other questions point to the murky territory of ethical considerations, which we will explore shortly.

## *Defensive Spirituality*

The concepts of defensive and offensive spirituality offer another useful lens through which to view unhealthy psychospiritual dynamics.[21] The first of these, the defensive pattern, focuses on the ways in which spirituality can be used to deny or devalue the psychological self. As with spiritual bypassing, the individual may use spiritual or religious rules and practices in a defensive mode to disengage from common human challenges such as anger, sexuality, or the desire for power or money. The problem with such a pattern from a psychological perspective is that the repressive efforts may not be sustainable and may even backfire in ways that are difficult to control. The rigidity of such a pattern defines its nature, and also paves the way for its implosion. Courting "punishment" for a self that is judged as "evil" is an extreme version of defensive spirituality, manifesting a masochistic pattern.

A therapist discerning such a pattern can simply listen and witness for a time, without supporting the pattern. Sometimes it is appropriate to challenge more directly, by asking questions that invite a deeper conversation. For instance, "When might it be important to ask for a raise or recognition of valuable work done?" Such action might be considered more acceptable in the context of family financial needs. Exploration may also be encouraged through a focus on metaphors that occur in the client's language. Together, counselor and client might imagine new conversations or alternative life stories. Sometimes it can be productive to consider subpersonalities when the client has access to rational and relativistic stage resources. For instance, "So, there's a part of you that really wants to be good and obey this rule because it seems that this is what God wants. How does that part show up in your life? Is there another part that sometimes feels differently? How does that part speak up?"

If the client's center of gravity is in the conformist or conventional stage, the therapist can often use rule replacement as an effective strategy, directly suggesting an alternative guideline.[22] A more direct challenge of a defensive belief may be warranted if the client's suffering is intense, or if the therapist comes from the same religious/spiritual tradition as the client.

Again, there may be times when abstinence from ordinary pleasures and rewards may be appropriate on the spiritual journey, when ascending spirituality has its place. There is no easy formula.

## Reflecting on Enneagram Style Variations

Let's consider two possibilities. First, this defensive pattern might be associated with an Enneagram One pattern. Although we do not see strong evidence of it in Charles, he does wonder if he is weak, selfish, or a rule breaker. The One pattern is often focused on right and wrong, improvement, and ideals. When those preoccupations are intensely focused inward on the self, they can become harsh and controlling. The client may exhibit a tendency toward self-punishment and self-deprivation in an attempt to repress unacceptable impulses and desires.

Sienna (Two) has a tendency to focus on other people's needs in order to be loved. While Twos often take great pride in being such a source of love and value in other people's needs, beneath this pride lies an unrecognized but deep hole of shame and need (as well as anger). An unhealthy version of this pattern might take the form of self-deprecation and self-abasement. Trying hard to please her pastor and focus on the needs of her faith community could begin to constitute a form of defensive spirituality.

## *Offensive Spirituality*

This pattern has a narcissistic flavor, like ego inflation. Spirituality is used to make one feel special, immune to ordinary temptations or pitfalls, even infallible. Sometimes it is one's tradition or teacher that is invested with superiority, rather than the personal self. But in either case, it is not an easy defense mechanism to confront, because it feels good!

When there is some openness, pointing out contradictions can begin to penetrate the shield: "It's curious that you have reached such an advanced spiritual stage and yet have such painful experiences in relationships. How do you make sense of that?" Such a question may lead to a deeper look at the fallible human that is still present. In situations where the stance is more rigid, integral psychotherapist Mark Forman suggests that it usually runs its course, since life has a way of providing ample opportunities for reality checks. If the offensive pattern is entrenched, it is unlikely that the individual will seek therapy.[23]

## *Religious Extremism and Authoritarianism*

Counselors often experience understandable trepidation about encountering this pattern, given the visibility of religious extremism in our world. All the depth and beauty, mystery and comfort that spirituality can offer are weighed against the terror, oppression, and manipulation that are also associated with religion. The outcome is often professional rejection of the whole territory. In spiritual circles, religion becomes the enemy and all its potential gifts are overlooked. Perhaps we can take an approach that has softer edges, acknowledging that extremism and authoritarianism are more associated with religions in general, but that human fallibility can generate extremes in any context. There is always the possibility of a dark side, and shadow can be collective as well as individual.

So how do we discern what is "extreme"? The Griffiths take a post-modern perspective: "Expressions of religious or spiritual experience are harmful when they violate the relatedness on which spirituality is based."[24] For them the principle of relatedness—to the Divine, other people, the natural world, one's body—is the core source of guidance for their therapeutic work. Harm to relatedness is enacted whenever there is exclusion, disempowerment, exploitation, or destruction. This usually begins with the familiar human tendency to establish some kind of rigid boundary (me vs. you, us vs. them), and the valuing of one side over the other.

Authoritarian religious/spiritual leaders are seen as one manifestation of the violation of the principle of relatedness or interdependence. When a leader's pathological narcissism (ego inflation) requires that followers worship and obey without question, such power and control clearly has a destructive impact, not only in terms of the actions taken or demanded but also in terms of psychological harm. We see this pattern in cults and in violent religious extremism.

On the other hand, it would be unwise to throw out all forms of spiritual leadership in reaction to the worst kinds. Welwood suggests that groups with the greatest potential for destructive behavior share the following characteristics:

- ***"The leader assumes total power to validate or negate the self-worth of the devotees, and uses his power extensively."*** Such leaders display enormous self-confidence and arrogant disregard for the opinions of others. Followers identify with the leaders, thereby gaining a sense of security and worth.
- ***"The central focus of the group is a cause, a mission, an ideology that is not subject to question."*** This is the one and only Truth,

never subject to doubt or question. Followers are vigilant and suspicious of their fellows, on the lookout for disloyalty or betrayal.

- ***"The leader keeps his followers in line by manipulating emotions of hope and fear."*** The leader offers promises of rewards—salvation, heaven, earthly benefits—and also threatens "doom, vengeance, or damnation" if followers do not strictly adhere to the rules.
- ***"There is a strict, rigid boundary drawn between the group and the world outside."*** Outsiders are often seen as evil, whether they are family members or strangers. This kind of extreme entitlement at the group level can, as we know, be very dangerous.
- ***"Corrupt cult leaders are usually self-styled prophets who have not undergone lengthy training or discipline under the guidance of great teachers."*** Here Welwood makes a crucial distinction between pathological leadership and spiritual leaders who have followed a recognized and long-standing tradition, mentored by recognized teachers—an apprenticeship path. Such a journey is well-recognized within Buddhism and other Asian traditions, and to some extent within Catholic religious orders.[25]

We need subtle discernment: rather than throwing the proverbial baby (leader) out with the bathwater, it is vital to make distinctions. There is obviously a huge gray area to consider, and there are many leaders who fall short, have sex with their followers, or become addicts. But despite our Western suspicion of gurus, there is such a thing as healthy, "relative" spiritual authority. There may be much to learn from someone who has traveled further on the path. "The role of effective teachers is to instruct, encourage, and correct the student, as well as to provide an example of what is possible."[26] This kind of leadership is based on a *relationship* in which teacher and student are acknowledged to have distinct roles, but ideally are recognized as both serving spiritual growth. Ego surrender may be invaluable at times. Submission to absolute power is another response entirely.

Let's consider these issues from a developmental perspective. Recalling the mythic-literal, conformist level in terms of faith development, some traditions exhibit a black-and-white perspective, clear boundaries between in-group and out-group, and reliance on the membership group (religion) as a primary source of identity. At this stage, an ethnoentric viewpoint is the norm. However, it is important to recognize that there may be both an extreme and a moderate version of such a worldview.[27]

An extremist version may be more likely to carry remnants from the former transitional stage, Opportunistic-Egocentric, in which there is greater emphasis on absolute power and on the need to enlist supernatural forces for protection. Such a perspective would more easily lend itself to the rise of a pathological hierarchy. A heathier, more moderate version, on the other hand, would lean toward the next (transitional) stage, conventional-traditional. Here one is likely to find a focus on the mythic stories of the tradition, such as the miracles of Jesus or the life of Muhammad. There is still an absolute sense of right and wrong, a reliance on external authority as the source of morality, and a strong sense of role-identity, but with a less radical flavor. As we evaluate the possibilities for destructiveness among major religious traditions, it is vital to remember this distinction between more and less healthy versions of the conformist stages.

There are many gray areas where it is challenging to find the kind of clarity we seek. We may not be confronting an obvious cult but encountering religious practices and beliefs which lie outside the accepted mainstream. One of the issues that is often particularly challenging for professionals is a group's dedication to rejecting medical interventions in favor of faith. We can find examples of this with Christian Scientists and Jehovah's Witnesses. These are particularly challenging situations when minors are involved, and medical ethics require intervention.

## Reflecting on Enneagram Style Variations

Vulnerability to religious extremism and authoritarianism may be associated with any personality pattern. There are many factors that could conceivably contribute to this vulnerability, such as childhood history, life crises, trauma, and the influence of close relationships. Someone with an Eight pattern might be more likely to find him- or herself in a position of power and authority than in a position of follower. Similarly, while Sixes are usually wary of authority, some (social subtypes) fear the disapproval of authority and may become compliant, while others (counterphobics) manage their fear by taking on a strong intimidating role themselves.

Devin, as a Nine, could have found herself falling prey to an extremist religious community along the way, although we see no evidence of this actually happening. Some Nines have a tendency to avoid confronting harsh realities and can fall into a dreamy kind of avoidance. If a strong leader wants to take action for them, they may willingly submit since they have difficulty contacting a strong sense of self. In the attempt to avoid conflict, they can "go along to get along." These are tendencies that might contribute to the likelihood of becoming a follower in an extremist spiritual/religious community.

## *Problems of Spiritual Destinations and Pathways*

When might we acknowledge that a spiritual or religious calling may override conventional obligations? In our secular modern world, can we recognize the importance of following a deep summons to turn away from a conventional path (career, marriage, family) in order to pursue a spiritual path? Is it necessarily dangerous to retreat from the material world in order to devote oneself to the nonmaterial? What criteria do we use in our roles as professionals and as persons in families and relationships?

As we have seen, the preservation of relatedness may serve us as a guiding principle for evaluation. Another lens is offered by Kenneth Pargament, who suggests that a well-integrated (healthy) spirituality is defined "by the degree to which the individual's spiritual pathways and destinations work together in synchrony with each other."[28] His framework validates spiritual health on its own terms, not simply in psychological terms.

The concept of spiritual destinations has to do with the person's perception of the sacred. Problems may arise when someone's "god" is "too small" (one-sided, with insufficient depth and range, failing to embrace the complexities of human life), or is a "false god" (an inadequate substitute for the sacred, such as food, alcohol, or drugs). Such forms of the sacred are, in Pargament's words, "not up to the task."

> They fall short in generating the sacred qualities of transcendence, boundlessness, and ultimacy. They are less capable of eliciting spiritual emotions, providing organization and coherence, and serving as a resource to the individual. As a result, the person who pursues a less-than-adequate form of the sacred is likely to be crippled from the start, no matter how proficient he or she may be in spiritual study, spiritual practice, or any of the other spiritual pathways. Without a strong and compelling destination, the search for the sacred can fall apart, with dangerous consequences for the individual and those around him or her.[29]

Another kind of challenge arises when a person holds two very different images of the Divine at the same time. These kinds of internal conflicts are likely to have psychological roots. For instance, from a psychodynamic perspective someone without adequate parenting may not develop a coherent self-structure. The result is a pattern of "splitting." Such an individual may develop representations of the sacred that mirror this internal tension between "good other/bad other," "good me/bad me." There are several possible patterns: ambivalence toward the sacred (oscillating between uncritical worship and bitter disillusionment), self-degradation (splitting off the parents' "badness" and incorporating it into an unworthy or fallen self), and demonization of self or others (an extreme form of self-degradation, or responding to the tension by projecting all evil externally, often onto a group perceived as evil). The result is generally some form of suffering.[30]

While spiritual destinations concern perceptions of the sacred, spiritual pathways have to do with ways of connecting with and following the sacred. Problems in the latter domain include a lack of breadth and depth, problems of fit between destinations and pathways, and problems of continuity and change. When a person's spiritual life is essentially superficial, without commitment or deep exploration (dabbling in the spiritual marketplace, for instance), he or she may lack the resources to cope with life's most challenging spiritual questions. If someone with an Enneagram Three pattern is drawn to spirituality because it offers opportunities for achievement and goal-oriented action, he may find himself unable to sustain interest when life presents experiences of failure or invalidation.

The problem of fit applies to such situations as spiritual extremism and spiritual hypocrisy. In more extreme cases of the latter, we see the appropriation of a spiritual pathway for antispiritual goals, as in the sexual abuse of children and women in some Catholic and Evangelical churches. There may also be a lack of fit between an individual and his or her social context. Such a clash occurs quite frequently, and often results in painful struggles. Many LGBTQ individuals experience profound conflicts between their sexual orientation and their religion, or the religion of their families of origin. Couples from different faith backgrounds face their own versions of this challenge. Sometimes such tensions can lead to transformative dialogue and change in both individuals and groups, but there are often outright relational ruptures or uncomfortable, fragile compromises.

Finally, there are problems of continuity and change. One example is a pattern of rigidity, an inability to bend with the winds of change on the spiritual path. Because identification with a particular group or perspective is burdened with psychological and emotional baggage, people may lock themselves into a particular set of beliefs or practices. This lack of flexibility or failure to evolve creates its own kind of suffering, particularly when life presents significant changes and challenges.

The other side of the coin is the inability to maintain commitment, jumping around from one path to another. This is, for example, an area of vulnerability for the Enneagram Seven pattern. With a Six pattern, on the other hand, loyalty may keep one committed, even when change might be wiser. There is an ongoing debate about whether one should commit to a single path instead of exploring a variety of paths. In our times, the second pattern is particularly common because we have access to so many options. But continuous, superficial path-hopping, while good for avoiding boredom and challenge, is less than ideal from a spiritual perspective.

Pargament's definition of well-integrated spirituality offers substantial food for thought:

> At its best, spirituality is defined by pathways that are broad and deep, responsive to life's situations, nurtured by the larger social context, capable of flexibility and continuity, and oriented toward a sacred destination that is large enough to encompass the full range of human potential and luminous enough to provide the individual with a powerful guiding vision. At its worst, spirituality is dis-integrated, defined by pathways that lack scope and depth, fail to meet the challenges and demands of life events, clash and collide with the surrounding social system, change and shift too easily or not at all, and misdirect the individual in the pursuit of spiritual value.[31]

## Ethical Dilemmas

The interplay of psychology and spirituality raises significant ethical issues for those in the helping professions. Being alert to potentially difficult territory and slippery slopes can help us slow down, take time for careful consideration, and seek consultation and supervision if needed. I approach these issues as *dilemmas* because I want to suggest that, despite our own prejudices in this territory, there is often no easy or obvious answer.

### *Dignity and Welfare of the Client*

Respecting and promoting the client's dignity and welfare is our primary responsibility. In this context, our basic obligation is to open space for a client's religious or spiritual experience, perspective, practices, and beliefs. This often means that we need to *invite and welcome* these into our relationship, since clients may well be wary of sharing their deepest questions and values with us. As we have seen, the embrace of religion and spirituality in counseling contexts has been slow to develop, and clients sense this.

Of primary importance is attentive and open-minded listening, in order to catch a phrase or image that suggests a possible spiritual or religious theme. We can then acknowledge hearing it and gently explore its meaning with the client. This opens the way so that the client begins to feel safe sharing what is deeply private and held so close to the heart. If the client's religious orientation is one we recognize but are not very familiar with, it is incumbent upon us to learn more so that we can understand the client's framework of meaning. This requires us to do our own research; it is not the client's job to educate us.

If the client's words point more toward an individual spirituality, we need to explore what particular words or descriptions mean to him or her. "What is that like for you?" "How does that feel?" "How do you experience that in your body?" We have discussed the advisability of beginning with metaphors, inner conversations, stories, and somatic experience, skirting around beliefs as much as possible. If it becomes evident that the client's perspective is in direct conflict with ours, then we have our own work to do, including consultation or supervision.

## *Informed Consent and Counselor Self-Disclosure*

Clients have a right to know what to expect in the counseling process so that they can make their own decisions about participating in the work. One form that this takes is a document. We open the door and offer safe space by including a statement that exploration of religious and spiritual concerns is welcomed in the work, at the client's discretion. Of course, this statement could potentially be a negative for some clients, which is also a reaction worth exploring.

However, there are more subtle issues. If the therapist has a particular spiritual/religious path, is it necessary to disclose that? Is it inappropriate to display books or works of art which have spiritual/religious meaning? These are questions that have a lot to do with the therapist's explicit professional focus. Working in an openly Christian agency makes such overt disclosure quite easy, for example. A therapist may choose to focus on a Buddhist approach and to concentrate on clients for whom that path is meaningful. On the other hand, if the practice is more open-ended, then caution around exhibiting such information is appropriate.

What are therapists to do if asked directly about their religious or spiritual orientation? The answer to this question may depend partly on how much emphasis the therapist puts on the role of transference in the therapeutic relationship. Some professional texts advocate turning the question back on the client: "I'm wondering why that is important to you?" This question may prove useful, but if the client pursues the inquiry, the query is likely to come across as evasive and ultimately undermine the relationship. In my own practice the question has rarely been asked. My open-ended responses have usually been satisfactory. In one instance my reply about my love of the Christian path was unsatisfactory to the client, who really wanted to work in a more scripture-based way. Although we had already done some good work around her grief, she decided to seek explicitly Christian counseling elsewhere. We both felt this was entirely appropriate.

## *Competence and Training*

Beyond a basic understanding of the territory, I advocate more in-depth study in areas that are of particular interest. For instance, some may want to pursue studies in transpersonal, Jungian or integral psychology, in Buddhist approaches to mindfulness and compassion in therapy, or in the Enneagram. In addition, learning more about particular traditions or orientations is invaluable, even if not officially considered to be professional training. Consulting with others who are familiar with a specific path is a very important aspect of professional competence.

And as we have noted, professional counseling/psychotherapy organizations are now coming out with official lists of competencies (even training programs) for practitioners. Following these guidelines will add breadth and depth to one's preparation.

## *Self-Knowledge*

Unpacking one's own history is essential, so writing a spiritual autobiography (as suggested in chapter 5) can be a significant step; exploration of the material in dialogue with others or with a therapist is ideal. Childhood prejudices and wounds around religion can enter into work with clients in subtle ways: a therapist's facial expression or turn of the head may be enough to signal judgment. Likewise, exploration may be derailed by a failure to pick up on a client's tentative cue because of personal discomfort. For many professionals, unease simply results in total avoidance of this highly charged territory. The role of countertransference in this domain may be much more substantial than is often recognized.

## *Dilemmas Related to Conflicting Values*

Honoring diverse points of view is central to the ethical code: we are trained not to impose our own values on our clients. This respect for individual rights and opinions is an essential aspect of the Modern and Postmodern developmental stages, and has been given a rightful place of importance in terms of multiculturalism. However, these perspectives also have their limitations. For instance, at the Rational/Modern stage, while there is respect for individual rights, there also tends to be a rejection of earlier points of view (such as the Mythic/Literal) that are considered "irrational." For a counselor whose center of gravity is in the Modern stage, many spiritual or religious values and beliefs would fall into this pre-rational category. For counselors whose center of gravity is in the Relativistic/Postmodern stage, negative attitudes toward both Conventional and Rational perspectives may infuse their work. At each new stage there tends to be an initial rejection of the perspective of the prior stage, until some of that perspective is included or integrated.[32]

The Integral/Multiperspectival stage is often characterized as the first stage in which we are truly able to embrace different perspectives, in both a cognitive and affective sense. We need to remember, however, that this stage is only beginning to emerge in the world. And development, as we have acknowledged, tends to be uneven and messy. Even for those whose line of cognitive intelligence reaches into Integral, the affective or moral lines of intelligence may center in prior stages (strongly influenced on this issue, I suggest, by family-of-origin experiences).

If clients have the courage to share their deepest spiritual experiences, hopes, and fears with us, how we respond is crucial. No matter how collaborative and open-minded we may attempt to be, it is simply the norm that when clients seek our help, they project a certain amount of authority onto us, and if this is accompanied by the development of a caring relationship or alliance, our opinions and values carry a lot of weight. We must do our best to keep our personal perspective in the background. This necessitates dealing with our own existential questions and emotional struggles elsewhere.

There are some specific questions that counselors often raise. Let's revisit the question of prayer. Asking clients to pray with us is not appropriate unless we have clearly identified ourselves as counseling within a specific religious tradition. If clients ask us to pray with them, it may be enough to respond by respectfully honoring clients' verbal or silent prayer with our attention and body language. There tends to be less concern about the role of meditation in therapy, in part, I think, because counselors in mainstream American culture do not typically have old "baggage" about meditation. In addition, mindfulness has become more part of the mainstream in psychotherapy, backed by a growing body of research. But as I have pointed out, for some more traditional or fundamentalist Christians, meditation is suspect because it is open to influence from unknown or dangerous sources. For these clients, staying close to scripture is the wiser path.

Other obvious examples of conflicting values have to do with opposing opinions about subjects such as abortion or same-sex relationships. Here, too, we are asked to be present with the client's experience and perspective, bringing as much openness and caring to the conversation as we can. We may explore the origins of such values and their impact on current life, as well as any internal or external conflicts that they may engender. I am partial to the suggestion that "we meet a person in a manner that is easy to forgive."[33] Again, when we have strong feelings about certain issues, consultation or supervision is in order.

Still, there are times when there is no clear path. An ethical dilemma is described as such because there is typically no one right answer. We are already bringing our psychological perspectives and values to bear on the client's spiritual journey when we discern spiritual bypassing, defensive or offensive spirituality, or spiritual practices that seem too extreme. If an adult client believes his or her faith is sufficient to deal with an illness, we may, despite our own misgivings about forgoing medical treatment, be able to find a way to accompany them on this exploratory journey, even as we encourage facing profoundly difficult existential questions. If, however, a client is keeping his child or elderly parent from receiving critical medical treatment for reasons of faith, that is a different ethical issue that requires intervention.

A client's participation in an extremist religious group is cause for real concern and grounds for deeper exploration and questioning in the counseling work, as well as for self-education and supervision on the therapist's part. Along the therapeutic spectrum of support and challenge, more challenge may be appropriate. But again, what the counselor might classify as an extremist group or even a cult may not be viewed that way by everyone; hence the need for self-education and supervision, as well as consultation with those who have pertinent religious background and expertise.

A related question has to do with how much counselors should take on or avoid a teaching role. We may introduce a variety of spiritual or religious perspectives if such exposure is seen as helping clients expand their horizons, particularly if the individuals seem curious. But again, unless a specific orientation is disclosed in a written description of one's professional practice, we need to avoid taking on the role of spiritual teacher. We often do psychoeducation of various kinds in our practice: a Jungian therapist, for example, introduces new concepts to clients in the course of their work together. But specifically assuming the role of spiritual teacher is problematic. We may offer guidance if our paths are similar, but it may also be valuable to share resources and point clients elsewhere for further exploration.

Just as we each draw on particular theoretical frameworks in our practices, we may also benefit from a thoughtful probing into our own ethical principles to supplement the professional guidelines by which we are bound. We have seen that the Griffiths draw on the criterion of relatedness. Pargament has developed his own approach in terms of what constitutes a well-integrated spirituality. This is a matter for substantial reflection over time as we mature in our work. My bias is also toward exploring such principles within the context of professional conversation, connecting the "di-" in "dilemma" and "dialogue": it can take "two" (or more than two) to find a pathway through such difficult territory.

## Reflecting on Personal Resources and Biases

Did you write a spiritual autobiography when invited to do so in chapter 5? If not, consider revisiting those questions and exploring your own story. We also investigated triggering "velcro" scenarios earlier, but we have traveled through a lot of territory since then. They are worth revisiting now, particularly in an ethical context. These can be explored through personal reflection, but sharing these in dialogue with a supportive partner can be very helpful.

- What religious/spiritual words or phrases trigger a negative reaction in you? What attitudes? Notice your emotional responses, but also remember what that feels like in your body, what images or memories may be evoked, as well as what thoughts are set in motion.
- Explore any similar reactions to visual images, music, smells.
- Recall whether you have ever been able—or see if you are able now—to be fully *present* with these kinds of reactions. This might depend on the intensity of the memories or present experience, so it is wise to approach this exploration with compassion and support. What inner or outer resources might help you to be present with your experience in this way?

- If you are able to summon at least some ability to be present with your own experience, then you may have space to explore options. For instance, could you imagine yourself in the other person's shoes, temporarily stepping inside their world and their worldview? What matters most within that worldview? What is frightening, threatening, comforting, empowering? Can you find some curiosity in yourself? What questions might you want to ask someone whose point of view triggers you? Can you imagine asking those questions in a way that is easy to forgive, caring and respectful? Even if you can't condone or support the words or actions that might flow from this other point of view, can you find any common ground as a fallible, vulnerable human being?
- If these explorations are particularly challenging, there are choices available. As a counselor or psychotherapist, you may decide you cannot ethically work with certain clients. You may want to delve further into your own religious/spiritual history in the context of professional conversations, supervision, and/or personal therapy. Most importantly, I invite you to bring compassion to your own experience as one of many who may have suffered hurt in the context of religion/spirituality. You are not alone.

## Diagnostic Considerations

We come now to the specific question of how psychospiritual challenges are viewed from the perspective of professionals faced with the task of diagnosis. The DSM—*Diagnostic and Statistical Manual of Mental Disorders*, now in its fifth edition (2013)—is the standard reference for those in the mental health field (despite ongoing controversy and criticism). It should not come as a surprise in the context of this inquiry that mental health experts were slow to give specific attention to the territory of religion and spirituality, even in relation to psychopathology.

The introduction of a specific diagnostic category related to religion and spirituality came with the DSM-IV, published in 1994. David Lukoff (a clinical psychologist), Francis G. Lu, and Robert Turner (both psychiatrists) proposed the inclusion of a category called "psychoreligious or psychospiritual problem" in 1991.The proposal was accepted with a title change: "Religious or Spiritual Problem." Here is the definition:

> **V62.89:** This category can be used when the focus of clinical attention is a religious or spiritual problem. Examples include distressing experiences that involve loss or questioning of faith, problems associated with conversion to a new faith, or questioning of spiritual values that may not necessarily be related to an organized church or religious institution.[34]

The V code addresses problems related to "other psychosocial, personal, and environmental circumstances," and this one has been carried over into the DSM-V. V codes identify conditions other than a disease or injury as well as significant factors that may influence present or future care. A V code may be included in the official diagnosis if it is a focus of treatment.

The original proposal had included four types of *religious* problems. The two omitted in the final version were "change in denominational membership" and "intensification of adherence to religious practices and orthodoxy." Lukoff has advocated for the inclusion of an additional category, despite its omission from the DSM-V: involvement in new religious movements and cults.

Scant attention has been given to *spiritual* problems in the DSM. In the original proposal, the guiding definitions of religion and spirituality were as follows:

> **Religion:** "adherence to the beliefs and practices of an organized religious institution."

> **Spirituality:** "the relationship between a person and a transcendent reality, not involving a specific religious affiliation."[35]

Lukoff, Lu, and Turner advocated for the inclusion of two specific spiritual issues, mystical experiences and near-death experiences, but these were replaced by the very general phrasing, "questioning of other spiritual values which may not necessarily be related to an organized church or religious institution."

Let's look at the present V code categories more closely.

## *Loss of Faith*

From a developmental perspective, some loss of faith may be experienced in the natural course of transitioning from one meaning-making stage to another. This may or may not involve a crisis. More intense forms of loss of faith may occur, for example, in the wake of a significant loss or trauma, as we saw with Charles, or in the aftermath of a betrayal, as Sienna went through with her pastor. If a therapist authoritatively challenges a client's religious beliefs, this could also result in a devastating loss of faith because of the power of the transference relationship. Someone who leaves a religious path or is ostracized for disobeying fundamental tenets might go through such a crisis of meaning. An example would be someone who becomes disillusioned with Jehovah's Witnesses and separates from the community. Such a decision is not undertaken lightly since it typically results in shunning by family and community. As with other kinds of loss, there may be subsequent struggles with anger, despair, sadness, isolation, and emptiness. The sense of loneliness is typically exacerbated by the lack of support, since loss of faith fits within the category of disenfranchised grief (when the loss is typically not recognized by others).

A powerful example of the potential impact of loss of faith comes from research conducted by Pargament and some colleagues.[36] In their study, elderly patients who felt alienated from God, felt they were being punished, or felt abandoned by their church community, were at greater risk of dying (a 19–28 percent increase) within the next two years, compared with those who had no such religious doubts. Most hospice programs recognize the crucial importance of the patient's spiritual or religious orientation, and provide support services for helping patient and family cope with challenges and draw on resources.

Walking through this kind of profound existential loss is a challenge to both client and therapist. It is important for the therapist to realize that the crisis may eventually lead to growth and opening, but the darkness cannot be minimized or sugar-coated. There is no timetable for the healing journey. What can be offered is a steadfast accompaniment, support for exploring the depths, possible revisiting of earlier experiences of trauma or abandonment, and consistent attention both to internal resources (breath, body, memories, dreams, images, religious/spiritual figures) and to external ones (friends, mentors, nature, animals, music, creative expression).

## *Problems Associated with Conversion to a New Faith*

Any significant change in meaning-making orientation can be problematic and difficult. Conversion to a new faith may follow a prior loss of faith (or departure from a prior religious community), and there may be a bypassing of the psychological challenges involved in the earlier loss. Uncertainty about the new framework of belief may be present for some time. "What do I actually believe? How much can I surrender to this new framework?" There may be new practices to learn and follow, as well as potential self-doubt about one's ability to "do it right." In addition, there is the whole issue of finding one's way into a significant new community, along with a possible history of social anxiety, self-criticism, or co-dependence. "Will I be accepted? Will I make mistakes? Do I really belong?" When conversion to a new faith comes in the context of marriage or committed partnership, relational dynamics and difficulties may be involved.

As we can see, spiritual emergencies have been omitted from the V code: for instance, there is no recognition of the potential impact of a mystical or near-death experience. The variety of challenges that we explored earlier in this chapter are not explicitly named within the framework of the DSM. However, the V code may be used as an additional factor when, for instance, meditation has exacerbated or precipitated psychological difficulties. Since the V code allows for consideration of "other conditions that may be a focus of clinical attention," this leaves room for the occurrence of a religious or spiritual problem *concurrent* with a mental disorder.

## *Concurrent Conditions and Differential Diagnosis*

Co-occurring difficulties are a very real possibility. Bipolar disorder is a good example: it is not unusual for a manic episode to involve a spiritual dimension.[37] Someone with a diagnosis of obsessive-compulsive disorder may present with particular symptoms in the area of religious rituals. What makes intense relationship to a religious practice shade over into an obsessive-compulsive category? Perhaps there is an exclusive and excessive focus on a particular ritual rather than on the overall religious life, and the specific area of focus is often typical of the disorder (cleanliness, for instance, or obsessive thoughts about a punitive God). It is, of course, essential to consider cultural variations as well as contextual circumstances in terms of the client's broader religious practice.

The possible co-occurrence of a psychotic disorder with a religious or spiritual problem is a huge and complex topic, one that is explored within transpersonal psychology/psychiatry circles. Joseph Campbell is often quoted as saying in his lectures that "the psychotic drowns in the same waters in which the mystic swims with delight."[38] But the boundaries are usually unclear. Lukoff, for example, has proposed a new category of "psychotic episode with mystical features," but it has not found acceptance. John Nelson, a transpersonal psychiatrist, integrates medical and neuroscientific research with transpersonal (Eastern) perspectives.[39] With a rich foundation of clinical examples, he explores the "many faces of madness" in spiritual emergencies and nonordinary states of consciousness, and brings an unusual perspective to the understanding of schizophrenic and borderline conditions. Such sources lie outside the normal range of clinical training, but they deserve more attention.

Even if we acknowledge the potential significance of religious-spiritual dimensions, there are enormous challenges in making a differential diagnosis between psychopathology and religious-spiritual problems. We know enough now to take cultural differences into account, but there is much more to consider. Lukoff suggests, at a minimum, that when considering a spiritual emergency that has psychotic aspects, we look for the following indicators of a positive outcome: 1) good pre-episode functioning, 2) acute onset of symptoms within the previous three months or less, 3) stressful precipitating factors for the psychotic episode, and 4) a positive exploratory attitude toward the experience.[40]

Psychiatrist James Griffith offers an invaluable discussion of what can happen when "mental illness infiltrates religious life." Acknowledging the challenge of clinical discernment, he offers this perspective:

> Intense religious experiences, particularly in group contexts, can produce within a normal person literally any symptom of psychiatric illness, including hallucinations, delusional fears, dissociative trance states, or panic anxiety. Such a person is badly served by a label of mental illness. Moreover, a person with a bonafide mental illness may yet be able to elaborate a rich, complex spiritual life, in which personal spirituality helps provide resilience against the illness.[41]

He goes on to consider the potential interplay of religion and mood disorders (dark night/major depressive disorder, religious passion/mania), religion "disorganized" by psychosis, and religion "shrunken" by an anxiety disorder, suggesting approaches and questions which can help to distinguish psychiatric symptoms from "troubling but normal" religious behaviors. His suggestions for assessment reflect professional humility and genuine respect for both religious experience and clinical expertise (which may save a patient's life).

## Closing Thoughts

The interplay of psychology and spirituality: this is clearly a vast and multifaceted territory. We have explored a variety of perspectives: practical, theoretical, professional, and personal. Other lenses, of course, lead to different emphases and therapeutic approaches. My hope is that the *questions themselves* have become more compelling and will invite further exploration.

As we cultivate curiosity and compassion, we are more likely to be open to the meaning of spirituality and religion in our clients' lives as well as in our personal interactions with others in our communities. We can then make more room for diverse perspectives, experiences, and flavors, and remain "related," in dialogue. We are able to appreciate the supportive role of spirituality and religion in the lives of those who are struggling or in pain. We have an understanding of how spirituality may influence human growth and development, and how psychological and spiritual aspects of life can influence each other. And we also recognize the potential challenges that may arise as psychology and spirituality interact in this interweaving we have described as *psychospiritual*.

Human beings have the potential to grow up (from a developmental perspective), wake up (to state experiences of deeper realities), clean up (by owning our shadow aspects), and show up (in all areas or quadrants of life).[42] From a global perspective, these dimensions of human possibility feel vital as we face the challenges of the twenty-first century. The deeper our self-awareness and capacity for plumbing the depths of the psyche, and the wider our embrace of all dimensions of life, the more we have to contribute to our clients and perhaps to our world.

# Afterimages: Roots and Wings

What if we were to welcome interplay, not just as a tool for cognitive understanding, but as a way of imagining, sensing, listening, and seeing? Instead of concluding with an intellectual perspective on the relationship between psychology and spirituality—terms which may even have lost their freshness at this point—let's take a leap into the landscape of metaphor and see what emerges.

Our guiding images are roots and wings. How might these images reflect the themes and perspectives we have been exploring? Let yourself explore the possibilities.

## *As human beings:*

***We have roots,*** acknowledging what we begin with: childhood experiences, intergenerational influences, cultural patterns, genetic predispositions.

We are invited to feel these more consciously, acknowledging how they feed us, tie us down, and shape our experience.

***We can grow wings,*** freeing us from the constraints of the story, from habits of mind, from patterns of feeling and action, from ego and conditioning.

We can develop the liberating capacity for presence and awareness and may engage in spiritual or religious explorations.

## *As helpers and professionals:*

***We have roots,*** grounded in understanding of human psychology *and* of spirituality and religion.

We can take the time to learn about human growth and development from multiple perspectives, about the larger context of spirituality and religion in our world, about traditions and practices, and about approaches that honor both psychology and spirituality.

***We can grow wings,*** feeling free to listen, explore new landscapes and perspectives, reaching farther afield.

We can risk new questions, accompanying clients in their quests, going beyond familiar territory, and sharing new insights with colleagues unacquainted with these perspectives.

***We have roots,*** allowing us to dig deep into the psyche, into the dark and hidden places, into soul, and into the body.

We can become familiar with the inner pathways, going by feel, by the Braille method, being willing to accompany others into the places that may be feared.

***We can grow wings,*** becoming open to the farther reaches of human experience, to unfamiliar landscapes, to new ways of seeing and knowing.

We can learn to suspend doubts for the sake of new insights, becoming willing to rise above habitual worldviews and to allow for possibilities.

***We have roots,*** reaching for profound insights and intuitions about potential challenges and intricate intertwining of the human psyche and spiritual longings.

We can keep digging and searching for wisdom in psychology, in the spiritual traditions, and in personal accounts. If we have our own spiritual or religious path, we can ground and deepen our work by beginning the day with a private meditation, prayer, or ritual.

***We can grow wings***, daring to travel new and unfamiliar pathways.

We can seek freedom from traditional categories and remain open to new discoveries.

In all these versions of roots and wings, we find an invitation to be rooted in understanding and in the compassionate embrace of ourselves and others, and are encouraged to reach for wings in the search for more expansive wisdom and insight.

In the end, roots and wings may not be as separate as we think.

# Selected Bibliography

## Enneagram Perspectives

Chestnut, Beatrice. *The Complete Enneagram: 27 Paths to Greater Self-Knowledge*. Berkeley: She Writes Press, 2013.

Cron, Ian M., and Suzanne Stabile. *The Road Back to You: An Enneagram Journey to Self-Discovery*. Downers Grove, IL: Inter Varsity Press, 2016.

Daniels, David. *The Essential Enneagram: The Definitive Personality Test and Self-Discovery Guide – Revised and Updated*. New York: HarperOne, 2009.

Maitri, Sandra. *The Spiritual Dimension of the Enneagram: Nine Faces of the Soul*. New York: Jeremy P. Tarcher/Putnam, 2000.

Riso, Don and Russ Hudson. *The Wisdom of the Enneagram: The Complete Guide to Psychological and Spiritual Growth for the Nine Personality Types*. New York: Bantam, 1999.

Riso, Don and Russ Hudson. *Discovering Your Personality Type: The Essential Introduction to the Enneagram, Revised and Expanded*. New York: Houghton Mifflin, 2003.

Rohr, Richard and Andreas Ebert. *The Enneagram: A Christian Perspective.* New York: Crossroad Publishing Co., 2001.

Wagele, Elizabeth and Renee Baron. *The Enneagram Made Easy: Discover the 9 Types of People.* New York: HarperCollins, 1994.

## Therapeutic Perspectives on Integrating Spirituality

Davis, John. *The Diamond Approach: An Introduction to the Teaching of A.H. Almaas.* Boston: Shambhala, 1999.

Griffith, James and Melissa Griffith. *Encountering the Sacred in Psychotherapy: How to Talk with People About Their Spiritual Lives.* New York: The Guilford Press, 2002.

Masters, Robert. *Spiritual Bypassing: When Spirituality Disconnects Us from What Really Matters.* Berkeley: North Atlantic Books, 2010.

May, Gerald. *The Dark Night of the Soul: A Psychiatrist Explores the Connection Between Darkness and Spiritual Growth.* New York: HarperOne, 2004.

Pargament, Kenneth. *Spiritually Integrated Psychotherapy: Understanding and Accessing the Sacred.* New York: Guilford Press, 2007.

Schwartz, Richard. *Internal Family Systems Therapy.* New York: Guilford Press, 1997.

Welwood, John. *Toward a Psychology of Awakening: Buddhism, Psychotherapy, and the Path of Personal and Spiritual Transformation.* Boston: Shambhala, 2000.

## Jungian and Soul Perspectives

Aizenstat, Stephen. *Dream Tending: Awakening to the Healing Power of Dreams.* New Orleans: Spring Journal Inc., 2009.

Dunne, Claire. *Carl Jung: Wounded Healer of the Soul.* New York: Parabola Books, 2000.

Hillman, James. *The Soul's Code: In Search of Character and Calling.* New York: Random House, 1996.

Johnson, Robert. *Inner Work: Using Dreams and Active Imagination for Personal Growth.* New York: Harper and Row, 1986.

Jung, C. G. *Memories, Dreams, Reflections.* New York: Vintage Books, 1989.

Mattoon, Mary Ann. *Jung and the Human Psyche: An Understandable Introduction.* New York: Routledge, 2005.

Richardson, Peter Tufts. *Four Spiritualities: Expressions of Self, Expression of Spirit.* Palo Alto, CA: Davies-Black Publishing, 1996.

Stein, Murray. *Jung's Map of the Soul: An Introduction.* Chicago: Open Court, 1998.

Stein, Murray. *Transformation: Emergence of the Self.* College Station: Texas A&M University Press, 1998.

Tarrant, John. *The Light Inside the Dark: Zen, Soul, and the Spiritual Life.* New York: HarperCollins, 1998.

### Transpersonal Perspectives

Cortright, Brant. *Psychotherapy and Spirit: Theory and Practice in Transpersonal Psychotherapy.* Albany: State University of New York Press, 1997.

Grof, Christina and Stanislav Grof. *The Stormy Search for the Self: A Guide to Personal Growth through Transformational Crisis.* New York: Jeremy P. Tarcher/Putnam, 1990.

Grof, Stanislav. *Psychology of the Future*. Albany: State University of New York Press, 2000.

Grof, Stanislav. *Holotropic Breathwork: A New Approach to Self-Exploration and Therapy*. Albany: State University of New York Press, 2010.

Nelson, John. *Healing the Split: Integrating Spirit into Our Understanding of the Mentally Ill*. Albany: State University of New York Press, 1994.

Scotton, Bruce, Allan Chinen, and John Battista, eds. *Textbook of Transpersonal Psychiatry and Psychology*. New York: Basic Books, 1996.

Vaughan, Frances. *Shadows of the Sacred: Seeing Through Spiritual Illusions*. Wheaton, ILL: Quest Books, 1995.

Wade, Jenny. *Changes of Mind: A Holonomic Theory of the Evolution of Consciousness*. Albany: State University of New York Press, 1996.

Walsh, Roger and Francis Vaughan, eds. *Paths Beyond Ego: The Transpersonal Vision*. New York: Jeremy P. Tarcher/Putnam, 1993.

Walsh, Roger. *Essential Spirituality: Exercises from the World's Religions to Cultivate Kindness, Love, Joy, Peace, Vision, Wisdom, and Generosity*. New York: John Wiley, 1999.

Washburn, Michael. *Embodied Spirituality in a Sacred World*. Albany: State University of New York Press, 2003.

## Integral Perspectives

Combs, Allan. *Consciousness Explained Better: Towards an Integral Understanding of the Multifaceted Nature of Consciousness*. St. Paul, MN: Paragon House, 2009.

Di Perna, Dustin. *Streams of Wisdom: An Advanced Guide to Integral*

*Spiritual Development.* Occidental, CA: Integral Publishing House, 2014.

Forman, Mark. *A Guide to Integral Psychotherapy: Complexity, Integration, and Spirituality in Practice.* Albany: State University of New York Press, 2010.

McIntosh, Steve. *Integral Consciousness and the Future of Evolution.* St. Paul, MN: Paragon House, 2007.

Smith, Paul. *Integral Christianity: The Spirit's Call to Evolve.* St. Paul: Paragon House, 2011.

Wilber, Ken. *Sex, Ecology, Spirituality: The Spirit of Evolution.* Boston: Shambhala, 1995.

Wilber, Ken. *Integral Psychology: Consciousness, Spirit, Psychology, Therapy.* Boston: Shambhala, 2000.

Wilber, Ken. *Integral Spirituality: A Startling New Role for Religion in the Modern and Postmodern World.* Boston: Integral Books, 2006.

## Developmental Perspectives

Fowler, James. *Stages of Faith: The Psychology of Human Development and the Quest for Meaning.* San Francisco: Harper and Row, 1981.

Kegan, Robert. *In Over Our Heads: The Mental Demands of Modern Life.* Cambridge: Harvard University Press, 1994.

Liebert, Elizabeth. *Changing Life Patterns: Adult Development in Spiritual Direction.* St. Louis, MO.: Chalice Press, 2000.

### Nonordinary-Experience Perspectives

Bache, Christopher. *Life Cycles: Reincarnation and the Web of Life.* St. Paul, MN: Paragon House, 1998.

Grof, Stanislav and Christina Grof, eds. *Spiritual Emergency: When Personal Transformation Becomes a Crisis.* New York: Jeremy P. Tarcher/Putnam, 1989.

Holden, Janice, Bruce Greyson, and Debbie James, eds. *The Handbook of Near-Death Experiences: Thirty Years of Investigation.* 2nd ed. Westport, CT: Praeger Publishing, 2009.

Kason, Yvonne. *Farther Shores: Exploring How Near-death, Kundalini and Mystical Experiences Can Transform Ordinary Lives.* Toronto, Canada: Harper Collins, 1994.

Perry, John Weir. *Trials of the Visionary Mind: Spiritual Emergency and the Renewal Process.* New York: State University of New York Press, 1998.

### Spiritual, Contemplative, and Nondual Perspectives

Bodian, Stephan. *Wake Up Now: A Guide to the Journey of Spiritual Awakening.* New York: McGraw Hill, 2008.

Bourgeault, Cynthia. *The Heart of Centering Prayer: Nondual Christianity in Theory and Practice.* Boston: Shambhala, 2016.

Caplan, Mariana. *Halfway Up the Mountain: The Error of Premature Claims to Enlightenment.* Chino Valley, AZ: Hohm Press, 1999.

Caplan, Mariana. *Eyes Wide Open: Cultivating Discernment on the Spiritual Path.* Boulder: Sounds True, 2009.

Katie, Byron. *Living With What Is: Four Questions That Can Change Your Life.* New York: Crown Archetype, 2002.

Kornfield, Jack. *After the Ecstasy, the Laundry: How the Heart Grows Wise on the Spiritual Path.* New York: Bantam Books, 2001.

Mijares, Sharon, ed. *Modern Psychology and Ancient Wisdom: Psychological Healing Practices from the World's Religious Traditions.* 2nd ed. New York: Routledge, 2016.

Prendergast, John, Peter Fenner, and Sheila Krystal, eds. *The Sacred Mirror: Nondual Wisdom and Psychotherapy.* St. Paul: Paragon House, 2003.

Prendergast, John, and G. Kenneth Bradford, eds. *Listening From the Heart of Silence: Nondual Wisdom and Psychotherapy, Volume 2.* St. Paul: Paragon House, 2007.

Teasdale, Wayne. *The Mystic Heart: Discovering a Universal Spirituality in the World's Religions.* Novato, CA: New World Library, 2002.

## Religious Diversity/Pluralism Perspectives

Eck, Diana. *A New Religious America: How a "Christian Country" Has Become the World's Most Religiously Diverse Nation.* New York: HarperSanFrancisco, 2002.

Patel, Eboo. *Out of Many Faiths: Religious Diversity and the American Promise.* Princeton, N.J.: Princeton University Press, 2018.

# Notes

## Chapter 1

1. Karen Armstrong, *Fields of Blood: Religion and the History of Violence* (New York: Alfred A. Knopf, 2014), 5.
2. For a provocative discussion of religious extremism, see Neil Kressel, *Bad Faith: The Danger of Religious Extremism* (Amherst, N.Y.: Prometheus Books, 2007). His research leads him to this definition: "Religious extremists can be defined as those persons who—for reasons they themselves deem religious—commit, promote, or support purposefully hurtful, violent, or destructive acts towards those who don't practice their faith," 53. Fundamentalism is *not* equivalent to religious extremism. For more information on fundamentalism, see Karen Armstrong, *The Battle for God: Fundamentalism in Judaism, Christianity and Islam* (New York: Random House, 2000).
3. "A problem is something which I meet, which I find completely before me, but which I can therefore lay siege to and reduce. But a mystery is something in which I am myself involved, and it can therefore only be thought of as a sphere where the distinction between what is in me and what is before me loses its meaning and initial validity." Gabriel Marcel, *Being and Having*, tr. Katharine Farrer (Westminster, UK: Dacre Press, 1949), 117.
4. For this application of the inside-outside notion I am indebted to the work of Ken Wilber on "zones," or "hori-zones," which point to a zone of awareness or a "world" of phenomena. There are eight of them, each calling for its own methodology of study or understanding. The theory is complex and not necessary to our discussion, but I refer interested readers to Ken Wilber, *Integral Spirituality: A Startling New Role for Religion in the Modern and Postmodern World* (Boston: Integral Books, 2006).

## Chapter 2

1. This hyphenated form suggests the inseparability of the two aspects. I also prefer the term "sense" to "view" because visual metaphors imply a certain distancing, and what we are talking about is much more implicit and embodied.

2. See Jerome Kagan and Nancy Snidman, *The Long Shadow of Temperament* (Cambridge, MA: Belknap Press, 2004).

3. The Keirsey-Bates Temperament Sorter is often associated with Myers-Briggs, but there are significant practical and theoretical differences between the two. There are also some differences between Jung's theory and the research findings in Myers-Briggs.

4. See Marti Olsen Laney, *The Introvert Advantage: How Quiet People Can Thrive in an Extrovert World* (New York: Workman Publishing, 2002), and Susan Cain, *Quiet: The Power of Introverts in a World That Can't Stop Talking* (New York: Broadway Books, 2013).

5. C. G. Jung, "Psychological types," in *The Portable Jung*, ed. Joseph Campbell (New York: Penguin, 1971), 245.

6. Peter Tufts Richardson, *Four Spiritualities: Expressions of Self, Expressions of Spirit—A Psychology of Contemporary Spiritual Choice* (Palo Alto, CA: Davies-Black Publishing, 1996), 45.

7. Ken Wilber, *Integral Psychology: Consciousness, Spirit, Psychology, Therapy* (Boston: Shambhala, 2000), 194.

8. Richardson, 108.

9. Richardson, 146.

10. Ichazo, working in South America, synthesized a number of elements from Neoplatonist writings, the Christian concept of the seven deadly sins, and the mystical Jewish teachings of the Kabbalah. In the 1970s Naranjo, born in Chile and trained as a psychiatrist, and designated as one of three successors to Gestalt therapist Fritz Perls, went through Ichazo's Arica training. When Naranjo returned to California he began to teach the Enneagram systems. A number of contemporary Enneagram teachers (Helen Palmer, A. H. Almaas—also known as Hameed Ali—and Robert Ochs, a Jesuit) were among his early students.

11. Susan Rhodes, *The Positive Enneagram: A New Approach to the Nine Personality Types* (Seattle: Geranium Press, 2009).

12. Don Riso and Russ Hudson, *The Wisdom of the Enneagram: The Complete Guide to Psychological and Spiritual Growth for the Nine Personality Types* (New York: Bantam, 1999), 51.

13. Karen Horney's *Neurosis and Human Growth: The Struggle towards Self-realization*, 2nd ed. (New York: W. W. Norton, 1991). For an exploration of connections between the Enneagram and Horney's theory, see Sandra Maitri, *The Spiritual Dimension of the Enneagram: Nine Faces of the Soul* (New York: Jeremy P. Tarcher/Putnam, 2000).

14. For an exploration of the twenty-seven subtypes, see Beatrice Chestnut, *The Complete Enneagram: 27 Paths to Greater Self-Knowledge* (Berkeley: She Writes Press, 2013).
15. See Riso and Hudson, 75–87.
16. Each point is associated with a particular flavor of Essence, like a facet of a diamond. In the words of Sandra Maitri, "Essence is not one static state or experience, but may arise in our consciousness as different qualities such as compassion, peacefulness, clarity, acceptance, impeccability, spaciousness, and intelligence, to name just a few, each with a characteristic feeling tone and quality of presence—even with its own unique taste and smell. These various manifestations or features of our Essence of True Nature are called the Essential Aspects." Maitri, 8. As our personality becomes more transparent, our unique flavor of Being shines through as the Essential Aspect associated with our Enneagram point.
17. See David Daniels, *The Essential Enneagram: The Definitive Personality Test and Self-Discovery Guide* (New York: HarperOne, 2000), and Don Riso and Russ Hudson, *Discovering Your Personality Type* (New York: Houghton Mifflin, 2003).
18. Mark Forman, *A Guide to Integral Psychotherapy: Complexity, Integration, and Spirituality in Practice* (New York: State University of New York Press, 2010), 238. The subsequent summary of research in this section is also drawn from Forman.
19. Ken Wilber, an early contributor to transpersonal psychology, has developed a perspective known as integral theory. He writes about the contrast between agency and communion in a number of his books. See *Sex, Ecology, Spirituality: The Spirit of Evolution* (Boston: Shambhala, 1995), and *The Eye of Spirit: An Integral Vision for a World Gone Slightly Mad* (Boston: Shambhala, 1997).
20. Judith Jordan and Alexandra Kaplan, *Women's Growth in Connection: Writings from the Stone Center* (New York: Guilford Press, 1991).
21. Forman, 242.
22. Wilber, *The Eye of Spirit*, 196.
23. Wilber connects Agape with the Christian idea of God loving humankind (so loving the world that he gave his only begotten Son, John 3:16), and Eros with Plato (in the Symposium, Eros is characterized as a way of ascending to contemplation of the Divine). Plotinus, the Neoplatonist (204–270 CE), advocates for balancing and uniting Ascent and Descent. See Wilber, 1995, 338–344.
24. Forman, 235.
25. Forman, 241.
26. Pamela Hays, *Addressing Cultural Complexities in Practice: Assessment, Diagnosis, and Therapy*, 3rd ed. (Washington D.C.: American Psychological Association, 2016). Other sources include the following: Marsha Wiggins Frame, *Integrating Religion and Spirituality into Counseling: A Guide to Competent Practice* (Pacific Grove, CA: Thomson Learning, 2003); P. Scott Richards and Allen E. Bergin,

eds., *Handbook of Psychotherapy and Religious Diversity*, 2nd ed. (Washington DC: American Psychological Association, 2014); Mary Fukuyama and Todd Sevig, *Integrating Spirituality into Multicultural Counseling* (Thousand Oaks, CA: SAGE, 1999). I also recommend several pertinent chapters in Bruce Scotton, Allen Chinen, and John Battista, eds., *Textbook of Transpersonal Psychiatry and Psychology* (New York: Basic Books, 1996). For a resource dealing with East-West cultural differences without the religious emphasis, see Richard Nisbett, *The Geography of Thought: How Asians and Westerners Think Differently and Why* (New York: Free Press, 2004).
27. These are drawn primarily from Frame, cited above.
28. Celia Falicov, "Religion and Spiritual Traditions in Immigrant Families," in *Spiritual Resources in Family Therapy*, 2nd ed., ed. Froma Walsh (New York: Guilford Press, 2009), 156–173. This volume also includes discussion of spirituality and religion in therapy with African American families, and of family therapy in the context of a variety of religious orientations (Buddhism, Christianity, Judaism, Hinduism, and Islam). For deeper exploration of the growing *religious diversity* in America, I suggest Eboo Patel, *Out of Many Faiths: Religious Diversity and the American Promise* (Princeton, N.J.: Princeton University Press, 2018).
29. Forman, 256.
30. Forman, 254.
31. A good example of evidence against a Western bias comes from a research study in the collectivist-oriented West African country of Mali, where 90 percent of the participants scored at a high level on a test of identity development ("postconformist"), despite their collectivist values (Forman, 255). Is it possible that Westerners who favor individualistic values may simply be conforming to Western social norms?

## Chapter 3

1. "The Changing Global Religious Landscape," Pew Research Center, April 5, 2017, http://www.pewforum.org/2017/04/05/the-changing-global-religious-landscape/
2. "America's Changing Religious Landscape," Pew Research Center, May 12, 2015, http://www.pewforum.org/2015/05/12/americas-changing-religious-landscape/
3. Diana Eck, *A New Religious America: How a "Christian Country" Has Become the World's Most Religiously Diverse Nation* (New York: HarperSanFrancisco, 2002), 2. Another valuable resource is Robert Putnam and David Campbell, *American Grace: How Religion Divides and Unites Us* (New York: Simon and Schuster, 2010).
4. For example, see the Interfaith Amigos (www.interfaithamigos.com). Ted Falcon, Don Mackenzie, and Jamal Rahman, *Getting to the Heart of Interfaith:*

*The Eye-Opening, Hope-Filled Friendship of a Pastor, a Rabbi & a Sheikh* (Nashville: SkyLight Paths Publishing, 2009), and *Religion Gone Astray: What We Found at the Heart of Interfaith* (Nashville: SkyLight Paths Publishing, 2011). Also Eboo Patel, *Interfaith Leadership: A Primer* (Boston: Beacon Press, 2016).

5. See Robert Jones, *The End of White Christian America* (New York: Simon and Schuster, 2016). Jones is the founding CEO of a prominent research group, the Public Religion Research Institute.

6. See "Pledge of Allegiance to the Flag of the United States of America," *Encyclopaedia Britannica*, updated September 1, 2018, https://www.britannica.com/event/Pledge-of-Allegiance-to-the-Flag-of-the-United-States-of-America.

7. "Fundamentalism, Evangelicalism, and Pentecostalism," The Pluralism Project, http://pluralism.org/religions/christianity/christianity-in-america/fundamentalism-evangelicalism-and-pentecostalism/

8. http://www.pewforum.org/2015/05/12/americas-changing-religious-landscape/

9. "When Americans Say They Believe in God, What Do They Mean?" Pew Research Center, April 25, 2018, http://www.pewforum.org/2018/04/25/when-americans-say-they-believe-in-god-what-do-they-mean/

10. "'Nones' on the Rise," Pew Research Center, October 9, 2012, http://www.pewforum.org/2012/10/09/nones-on-the-rise/

11. David Tacey, *The Spirituality Revolution: The Emergence of Contemporary Spirituality* (New York: Brunner-Routledge, 2004), 32.

12. For praise, see Robert Forman, *Grassroots Spirituality: What It Is, Why It Is Here, Where It Is Going* (Charlottesville, VA.: Imprint Academic, 2004). For critique, see Wade Clark Roof, *Spiritual Marketplace: Baby Boomers and the Remaking of American Religion* (Princeton: Princeton University Press, 1999). See also sociologist Robert Wuthnow's informative exploration of the worlds of "spiritual shoppers" and both inclusive and exclusive Christians, in *America and the Challenges of Religious Diversity* (Princeton: Princeton University Press, 2005).

13. Brother Wayne Teasdale coined this term. See his book *The Mystic Heart: Discovering a Universal Spirituality in the World's Religions* (Novato, CA: New World Library, 2002).

14. Roof, *Spiritual Marketplace.*

15. Robert Wuthnow, *After Heaven: Spirituality in America Since the 1950s* (Berkeley: University of California Press, 1998).

16. Christopher Partridge, ed., *New Religions: A Guide. New Religious Movements, Sects, and Alternative Spiritualities* (New York: Oxford University Press, 2004).

17. See Sarah Pike, *New Age and Neopagan Religions* (New York: Columbia University Press, 2004).

18. Stephen Prothero, *Religious Literacy: What Every American Needs to Know—and Doesn't* (New York: HarperCollins, 2007). Unlike Diana Eck, Prothero emphasizes

the *differences* among religions in his book *God is Not One: The Eight Rival Religions that Run the World* (New York: HarperOne, 2001). It is also useful to have an understanding of some basic terms, philosophical as well as religious, including theism/monotheism, polytheism, pantheism, panentheism, transcendence, immanence, nondualism. A quick dictionary consultation will help.

19. "Knowledge Center: Competencies," American Counseling Association, http://www.counseling.org/knowledge-center/competencies. Vieten, C., Scammell, S., Pilato, R., Ammondson, I., Pargament, K. I., & Lukoff, D. (2013). Spiritual and religious competencies for psychologists. *Psychology of Religion and Spirituality,* 5(3), 129-144.

20. Kenneth Pargament, *APA Handbook of Psychology, Religion, and Spirituality, 2 vol. set* (Washington DC: American Psychological Association, 2013).

21. There are other approaches that have explored the relationship between psychology and spirituality. Sufism and the yogic tradition both have sophisticated psychologies, for instance, and there are esoteric traditions (e.g. Rudolf Steiner) that take psychology seriously. Ecopsychology and psychological perspectives influenced by shamanic and indigenous traditions are growing in popularity as well.

22. Informative discussions of this "psychological spirituality" may be found in the work of some sociologists of religion. See Robert Fuller, *Spiritual but not Religious: Understanding Unchurched America* (New York: Oxford University Press, 2001).

23. See Philip Cushman, *Constructing the Self, Constructing America: A Cultural History Of Psychotherapy* (Boston: DaCapo Press, 1995).

24. See "The Psychotherapy and Spirituality Summit Package," Sounds True, https://www.soundstrue.com/store/psychotherapy-and-spirituality-summit?sq=1.

25. Kenneth Pargament reports on this research in *Spiritually Integrated Psychotherapy: Understanding and Addressing the Sacred* (New York: Guilford Press, 2007), 9. We need to approach such surveys with caution, however, as they tend to work from their own premises—in this case, a focus on religion and belief in a personal God—leaving out therapists who might describe themselves as "spiritual but not religious."

26. Pargament, *Spiritually Integrated Psychotherapy*, 11.

27. James Fowler, *Stages of Faith: The Psychology of Human Development and the Quest for Meaning* (San Francisco: Harper and Row, 1981).

## Chapter 4

1. Harold G. Koenig, *Medicine, Religion, and Health: Where Science and Spirituality Meet* (West Conshohocken, PA: Templeton Foundation Press, 2008), 11. For a clinical perspective on how religion can be harmful as well as helpful, see James Griffith, *Religion that Heals, Religion that Harms* (New York: Guilford Press, 2010).

2. Haruki Murakami, *What I Talk About When I Talk About Running: A Memoir* (New York: Vintage Books, 2009).

3: Jamal Rahman, *Spiritual Gems of Islam: Insights and Practices from the Qu'ran, Hadith, Rumi, and Muslim Teaching Stories to Enlighten the Heart and Mind* (Woodstock, VT: Sky Light Paths Publishing, 2013).
4. "Footprints in the Sand," The Official Website for Footprints in the Sand Operated by the Estate of Mary Stevenson, http://www.footprints-inthe-sand.com/index.php?page=Poem/Poem.php.
5. See John Welwood, *Toward a Psychology of Awakening: Buddhism, Psychotherapy, and the Path of Personal and Spiritual Transformation* (Boston: Shambhala, 2000), 164–5.
6. Arnold van Gennep, *The Rites of Passage* (Chicago: University of Chicago Press, 1960).
7. See Louise Mahdi, Steven Foster, and Meredith Little, eds., *Betwixt and Between: Patterns of Masculine and Feminine Initiation* (La Salle, ILL: Open Court, 1998).
8. See the research of the HeartMath Institute at www.heartmath.org.
9. The subject of prayer is covered in many contemporary books on religion and spirituality in psychotherapy/counseling, usually under the heading of interventions or strategies. Topics commonly covered include types of prayer, appropriate use of prayer in the context of treatment, and questions about praying with clients. See, for example, Len Sperry, *Spirituality in Clinical Practice* (New York: Routledge, 2012).
10. John Prendergast, *In Touch: How to Tune In to the Inner Guidance of Your Body and Trust Yourself* (Boulder, CO: Sounds True, 2015), 107.
11. Thomas Merton, *New Seeds of Contemplation* (New York: New Directions Books, 1962), 221.
12. Elias Amidon, *The Open Path: Recognizing Nondual Awareness* (Boulder, CO: Sentient Publications, 2012), 117.
13. See Pargament, 137–8. He draws on the Christian-oriented classic by J. B. Phillips, *Your God Is Too Small* (New York: Touchstone, 2004).
14. There is a growing body of research on the efficacy of prayer—usually intercessory prayer for others—with a focus on measuring the actual medical effects for patients. For a popular source, see Larry Dossey, *Healing Words: The Power of Prayer and the Practice of Medicine* (New York: HarperOne, 2011). Dossey's interpretation of the positive effects of prayer emerges from his own understanding of consciousness and nonlocal mind.
15. For a useful overview of meditation paths in different traditions, see Daniel Goleman, *The Meditative Mind: The Varieties of Meditative Experience* (New York: Jeremy P. Tarcher/Putnam, 1988). For a contemporary exploration of ancient practices of meditation, prayer, and ritual in relation to psychological healing, I recommend Sharon Mijares, ed. *Modern Psychology and Ancient Wisdom:*

*Psychological Healing Practices from the World's Religious Traditions.* 2nd ed. (New York: Routledge, 2016).

16. Rick Hanson, *Buddha's Brain: The Practical Neuroscience of Happiness, Love, and Wisdom* (Oakland, CA: New Harbinger Publications, 2009).

17. Daniel Goleman and Richard Davidson, *Altered Traits: Science Reveals How Meditation Changes Your Mind, Brain, and Body* (New York: Avery, 2017).

18. Roger Walsh, *Essential Spirituality: The 7 Central Practices to Awaken Heart and Mind* (New York: John Wiley & Sons, Inc., 1999).

19. For an informative discussion of various forms of meditation and their relationship to psychotherapy, see Brant Cortright, *Psychotherapy and Spirit: Theory and Practice in Transpersonal Psychotherapy* (Albany: State University of New York Press, 1997).

20. James Griffith and Melissa Griffith, *Encountering the Sacred in Psychotherapy: How to Talk with People About Their Spiritual Lives* (New York: The Guilford Press, 2002), 174.

21. Beyond forgiveness is the act of atonement, a subject explored in a collection of essays edited by Phil Cousineau, *Beyond Forgiveness: Reflections on Atonement* (San Francisco: Jossey-Bass, 2011). The term *atonement* has religious overtones that are challenging for some, but it essentially refers to an act that rights a wrong, makes amends, or offers restitution and compensation. Sometimes described as the missing piece between forgiveness and reconciliation, atonement can be a powerful step in a healing journey.

22. Jeffrey Kauffman, ed., *Loss of the Assumptive World: A Theory of Traumatic Loss* (New York: Brunner-Routledge, 2002), 1.

23. Viktor Frankl, *Man's Search for Meaning* (Boston: Beacon Press, 2006).

24. James Fowler, *Stages of Faith*, 4–5.

25. See Pargament for a deeper discussion of what he calls "problems of spiritual destinations."

26. James Griffith and Melissa Griffith, 139. For more examples of effective existential questions in therapeutic contexts, see James Griffith, *Religion that Heals, Religion that Harms* (New York: Guilford Press, 2010).

27. Langston Hughes, "Island," in *The Collected Poems of Langston Hughes*, ed. Arnold Rampersad (New York: Vintage Books, 1994).

28. Griffith and Griffith, 67.

29. See *The Handbook of Posttraumatic Growth*, ed. Lawrence Calhoun and Richard Tedeschi (New York: Routledge, 2006).

## Chapter 5

1. Positive psychology, which has gained recent attention, has a different meaning. The focus is on the scientific study of what makes life worth living. Proponents call

for the field of psychology to emphasize strength as much as weakness, fulfillment as much as healing, and what is good as much as what is problematic in life.

2. See Esther Hicks and Jerry Hicks, *The Law of Attraction: The Basics of the Teachings of Abraham* (Carlsbad, CA: Hay House, Inc., 2006).

3. See the classic work by Evelyn Underhill, *Mysticism: The Nature and Development of Spiritual Consciousness* (Oxford: Oneworld Publications Ltd., 1993).

4. Frances Vaughan, *Shadows of the Sacred* (Wheaton, ILL: Quest Books, 1995), 7-8. I will be drawing on some of her distinctions in what follows.

5. See "The Ten Oxherding Pictures," Internet Sacred Text Archive, http://www.sacred-texts.com/bud/mzb/oxherd.htm.

6. Dale Cannon, *Six Ways of Being Religious: A Framework for Comparative Studies of Religion* (Belmont, CA: Wadsworth Publishing, 1996).

7. Jack Kornfield, *After the Ecstasy, the Laundry: How the Heart Grows Wise on the Spiritual Path* (New York: Bantam Books, 2001), 5.

8. Kornfield, 28.

9. Kornfield, 39.

10. In an article about psychotherapy and the midlife transition as an initiation experience, Jan and Murray Stein clearly suggest, from a Jungian perspective, that the "psychological purpose of this transition seems to be the transformation of consciousness." Jan Stein and Murray Stein, "Psychotherapy, initiation, and the midlife transition," in *Betwixt and Between: Patterns of Masculine and Feminine Initiation,* L. Mahdi, S. Foster, and M. Little, eds. (La Salle, Ill: Open Court, 1987), 289.

11. Kornfield, 98.

12. A wide range of brief stories about awakening or enlightenment may be found in the collection *Mystics, Masters, Saints, and Sages: Stories of Enlightenment,* ed. Robert Ullman and Judyth Reichenberg-Ullman (Boston, MA: Conari Press, 2001). Another introduction can be found in Les Hixon, *Coming Home: The Experience of Enlightenment in Sacred Traditions* (Los Angeles: Jeremy P. Tarcher, 1989).

13. An intriguing exploration of the subject of premature claims to enlightenment can be found in Mariana Caplan, *Halfway Up the Mountain: The Error of Premature Claims to Enlightenment* (Chino Valley, AZ: Hohm Press, 1999).

14. Of Adyashanti's numerous books, the one that is most pertinent here is *The End of Your World: Uncensored Straight Talk on the Nature of Enlightenment* (Boulder, CO: Sounds True, 2010). His website is www.adyashanti.org.

15. For contemporary resources, see Gerald May, *The Dark Night of the Soul: A Psychiatrist Explores the Connection Between Darkness and Spiritual Growth* (New York: HarperOne, 2004), and Thomas Moore, *Dark Nights of the Soul: A Guide to Finding Your Way Through Life's Ordeals* (New York: Penguin Books, 2004).

16. See Brant Cortright, *Psychotherapy and Spirit: Theory and Practice in Transpersonal Psychotherapy*, 219–220.
17. To indicate the breadth and depth of Metzner's research, here is the territory he explores: "The writings of Eastern and Western spiritual traditions, comparative mythology, literature and poetry, the writing of philosophers and teachers in the esoteric, shamanic, yogic, and hermetic traditions, and the formulations of modern depth psychotherapy, anthropology, and transpersonal psychology." Ralph Metzner, *The Unfolding Self: Varieties of Transformative Experience* (Novato, CA: Origin Press, 1998), xi–xii.
18. The Jungian analyst Murray Stein delves deeply into this natural transformation as a metaphor for the midlife experience. The dissolution of the larva represents the essence of the liminal experience: on the way to its emergence as a butterfly, it undergoes a virtual death. Murray Stein, *Transformation: Emergence of the Self* (College Station: Texas A&M University Press, 1998).
19. See the modern version in Paulo Coelho, *The Alchemist* (New York: Harper Collins, 2006). Earlier versions include a short story written by H. P. Lovecraft in 1908: see *The Complete Fiction of H.P. Lovecraft* (New York: Chartwell Books, 2016). There is also a Hasidic story by Rebbe Nachman of Breslov (1772–1810) called "The Treasure under the Bridge."
20. T.S. Eliot, "Little Gidding," part four of "Four Quartets," in *Collected Poems, 1909–1962* (New York: Harcourt Brace Jovanovich, 1991), 208.
21. Sharon D. Parks, "Home and Pilgrimage: Companion Metaphors for Personal and Social Transformation," *Soundings* 72.2-3 (Summer/Fall 1989): 297– 315, 310.
22. To learn more about the way that taken-for-granted metaphors shape our language and experience, see George Lakoff and Mark Johnson, *Metaphors We Live By*, 2nd ed. (Chicago: University of Chicago Press, 2003).
23. John Tarrant, *The Light Inside the Dark: Zen, Soul, and the Spiritual Life* (New York: HarperCollins, 1998).
24. Cited from his letters in Claire Dunne, *Carl Jung: Wounded Healer of the Soul* (New York: Parabola Books, 2000), 3. The word *numinous* is derived from the Latin *numen*, meaning "deity," "divine will," or "spirit." The numinous has a strong spiritual or religious quality and suggests something mysterious, awe inspiring, and filled with a supernatural presence. The term was popularized by German theologian Rudolf Otto.
25. C. G. Jung, *Memories, Dreams, Reflections* (New York: Vintage Books, 1989), 347.
26. Murray Stein, *Jung's Map of the Soul: An Introduction* (Chicago: Open Court, 1998), 156.
27. Stein, 175.
28. Developing some of Jung's ideas further, James Hillman elaborates on this notion of "calling" in *The Soul's Code: In Search of Character and Calling* (New

York: Random House, 1996). In Hillman's words, "I am answerable to an innate image, which I am filling out in my biography" (4). There is, he argues, a psychological reality to the call of fate: in my inner experience, I am the innate image of my fate. Here we meet again the idea of the "call" to the spiritual journey, but with a more specific and personal interpretation, and with an emphasis on the *ongoing* nature of the call and its role as guide.

29. Jung, 318.

30. Jung, 343.

31. See Connie Zweig, *The Holy Longing: The Hidden Power of Spiritual Yearning* (New York: Jeremy P. Tarcher/Putnam, 2003), 10.

32. Jung, 181.

33. James Hillman, "Peaks and Vales: The Soul/Spirit Distinction as Basis for the Differences between Psychotherapy and Spiritual Discipline," in *Puer Papers* (New York: Spring Publications, 1979), 64.

34. Hillman, 64.

35. Tarrant, *The Light Inside the Dark*, 13.

36. Tarrant, 18.

37. Tarrant, 19.

38. Drawing on the ideas of St. Bonaventure, Wilber proposes that we have three "eyes of knowing": the eye of the flesh (through our senses), the eye of mind (reason), and the eye of contemplation. Each has its own valid territory, and one cannot be reduced to another. See Ken Wilber, *The Eye of Spirit* (Boston Shambhala, 1997). I suggest that there are also variations within the eye of contemplation: the eye associated with mindful awareness, the eye of the heart (devotional), and the eye of imagination, which offers access to the realm of "soul" and the subtle realm.

39. Henry Corbin, "*Mundus Imaginalis,* or the Imaginary and the Imaginal," in *Swedenborg and Esoteric Islam,* tr. L. Fox (West Chester, PA: Swedenborg Foundation, 1995), 1–34. There is an important distinction between this imaginal realm as described in Islamic spiritual literature and the realm of the unconscious as put forth by Jung and Hillman. The Jungian view remains confined to the limits of the psyche versus opening to multiple (subtle) dimensions of reality. The latter is what is of passionate interest to Islamic philosophy.

40. Jung, 183.

41. See, for instance, Janet Dallet, "Active Imagination in Practice," in *Inner Knowing: Consciousness, Creativity, Insight, and Intuition*, ed. Helen Palmer (New York: Jeremy P. Tarcher /Putnam, 1998), 103–109, and Robert Johnson, *Inner Work: Using Dreams and Active Imagination for Personal Growth* (New York: Harper and Row, 1986).

42. I am indebted to Stephen Aizenstat, *Dream Tending: Awakening to the Healing Power of Dreams* (New Orleans: Spring Journal Inc., 2009).

43. *Lectio Divina* is an ancient Christian practice, from the Benedictine monastic order, which traditionally has four movements: reading a scripture passage, meditating on its meaning, praying as a loving conversation with God, and silent, receptive contemplation. In contemporary times, many Catholics as well as Protestants practice *Lectio Divina* with a variety of sacred texts and keep journals on their experience. See also Ann and Barry Ulanov, *Primary Speech: A Psychology of Prayer* (Atlanta, GA.: John Knox Press, 1982) for a rich study of prayer that gives the imagination a central role and draws on depth psychology.
44. See Llewellyn Vaughan-Lee, *Catching the Thread: Sufism, Dreamwork, and Jungian Psychology* (Inverness, CA: The Golden Sufi Center, 1998).
45. One intriguing exception to Jung's insistence on remaining within the boundaries of the psyche is to be found in his idea of the "psychoid," which points to a unitary reality embracing both the human psyche and the principles of matter and energy in the physical world. Archetypes are psychoid: they bridge between the psyche and matter. The principle of synchronicity is also an expression of the psychoid, referring to events in the physical world which are connected through meaning (a principle of the psyche) rather than physical causation.
46. John Welwood, *Toward a Psychology of Awakening* (Boston: Shambhala, 2002), 64.
47. Welwood, 66.

## Chapter 6

1. James Fowler, *Stages of Faith* (San Francisco: Harper and Row, 1981), 4.
2. Fowler, *Stages of Faith*, 5.
3. Fowler, *Stages of Faith*, 25.
4. Fowler, *Stages of Faith*, 198.
5. Elizabeth Liebert, *Changing Life Patterns* (St. Louis, MO: Chalice Press, 2000), 35.
6. Robert Kegan, *In Over Our Heads* (Cambridge: Harvard University Press, 1994).
7. Jane Loevinger, *Ego Development: Conceptions and Theories* (San Francisco: Jossey-Bass, 1976), and Ken Wilber, *Integral Psychology* (Boston: Shambhala, 2000).
8. Howard Gardner, *Frames of Mind: The Theory of Multiple Intelligences* (New York: Basic Books, 1983).
9. The nature of consciousness is a mystery that has been discussed from many perspectives. It is held by some to be a by-product or epiphenomenon of the brain. By others, it is experienced as the essential nature of reality. For an introductory exploration from a transpersonal perspective, see Roger Walsh and Francis Vaughan, eds., *Paths Beyond Ego* (New York: Jeremy P. Tarcher/Putnam, 1993), 13–21, and Allan Combs, *Consciousness Explained Better: Towards an Integral Understanding of the Multifaceted Nature of Consciousness* (St. Paul, MN: Paragon House, 2009).

10. For more background, see Walsh and Vaughan, *Paths Beyond Ego*. For a good introduction to transpersonal psychotherapy, I recommend Brant Cortright, *Psychotherapy and Spirit*. Stanislav Grof has written a first-person account of the history of the field: http://www.stanislavgrof.com/wp-content/uploads/pdf/A_Brief_History_of_Transpersonal_Psychology_Grof.pdf.
11. Wilber, *Integral Psychology*, 66–67.
12. See Dustin DiPerna, *Evolution's Ally: Our World's Religious Traditions as Conveyor Belts of Transformation* (San Francisco: Integral Publishing House, 2015). Cindy Wigglesworth makes the case for a spiritual line of intelligence in *SQ21: The 21 Skills of Spiritual Intelligence* (New York: SelectBooks, 2012), but also proposes a web of relevant skills.
13. Jenny Wade takes this approach in *Changes of Mind* (Albany: State University of New York Press, 1996). Her reading of the research points to a divergent developmental path after the conformist stage. Males tend to move toward individual achievement. For females, social connectedness is the emergent structure. In Belenky et al., *Women's Ways of Knowing* (New York: Basic Books, 1986), the authors elaborate on the shift from received knowledge (a conformist position) to subjective knowing, and then to procedural knowing.
14. See Susanne Cook-Greuter, *Postautonomous Ego Development: A Study of Its Nature and Development*, Integral Publishers Dissertation Series (Tucson: Integral Publishers, 2010). She has described her work, based on the Sentence Completion Test, in various volumes. See, for example, Angela Pfaffenberger, Paul Marko, and Allan Combs, eds., *The Postconventional Personality: Assessing, Researching, and Theorizing Higher Development* (Albany: State University of New York Press, 2011), and M. E. Miller and S. R. Cook-Greuter, eds., *Transcendence and Mature Thought in Adulthood: The Farther Reaches of Adult Development* (Lanham, MD: Rowman and Littlefield, 1994), 119–146. Her website provides the best access to her writings: http://cook-greuter.com.
15. Wigglesworth, *SQ 21*.
16. Wigglesworth, *SQ 21*, 8. She intentionally makes room for a variety of spiritual perspectives and terms.
17. Daniel Goleman, *Emotional Intelligence: Why It Can Matter More Than IQ* (New York: Bantam, 1995).
18. Frances Vaughan, "What is Spiritual Intelligence?" *Journal of Humanistic Psychology*, 42: 2 (Spring 2002), 16–33.
19. Mark Forman, *A Guide to Integral Psychotherapy* (Albany: State University of New York Press, 2010). Forman's book offers practical suggestions for working with different developmental levels.
20. See Michael Washburn, *The Ego and the Dynamic Ground* (Albany: State University of New York Press, 1995), and *Embodied Spirituality in a Sacred World*

(Albany: SUNY Press, 2003). Washburn and Wilber disagree about the necessity of this regressive movement into the deep unconscious, which Washburn calls the *dynamic ground*. See the discussion in Donald Rothberg and Sean Kelly, eds., *Ken Wilber in Dialogue* (Wheaton, IL: Theosophical Publishing House, 1998).

21. See Forman, *A Guide to Integral Psychotherapy*, and also Wilber, *Integral Psychology*.

22. See a fuller discussion of this point in Ken Wilber, *Integral Spirituality* (Boston: Integral Books, 2006), 119–141.

23. Sam Harris, *Waking Up: A Guide to Spirituality Without Religion* (New York: Simon and Schuster, 2014). "Atheism" refers to a lack of belief, or disbelief, in a God or gods. Buddhism is one example of a spiritual path that might be described as non-theistic.

24. For a developmental perspective on religion, with consideration of extremist and moderate versions, see Dustin DiPerna, *Evolution's Ally*, where he gives detailed consideration to examples from Christianity, Islam, Hinduism, and Buddhism.

25. See Christopher Bache's (initially skeptical) exploration in *Life Cycles: Reincarnation and the Web of Life* (St. Paul, MN: Paragon House, 1998).

26. This apparent affinity between particular stages and particular Enneagram patterns is an intriguing phenomenon. For instance, do such connections make it more difficult to move out of a certain stage? We can point to the similarity between the Rational, Modern stage and the Five Observer, or between the Perfectionist One and the Conformist stage, where right and wrong are very clearly defined and important.

27. Liebert, *Changing Life Patterns*, 66.

28. From an ultimate perspective, the journey through time, and time itself, are often recognized to be illusory. In relation to the possibility of Awakening/Realization/Enlightenment/Mystic Union occurring early in life, we are likely to stumble over the controversial territory of reincarnation (see note 25, ch. 6). There are stories of those who seem to come into human life already very evolved, and who seem to manifest something close to realization even in childhood.

## Chapter 7

1. A potential point of confusion arises when we talk about an "outside" perspective on individual experience. The "outside view of the inside" is not the same as the "it" point of view. This distinction comes from Wilber, who describes the inside view as zone 1 and the outside view of the inside as zone 2. See Wilber, *Integral Spirituality*.

2. Wilber, *Integral Psychology*. More information is available in *Integral Spirituality*, and for a deeper dive, see *Sex, Ecology, Spirituality* (Boston: Shambhala, 1995).

3. See the work of Harold Koenig, MD, psychiatrist and director of the Center for Spirituality, Theology and Health, as well as professor of psychiatry and behavioral sciences at Duke University Medical Center. One source is *Faith and Mental*

*Health: Religious Resources for Healing* (West Conshohocken, PA: Templeton Press, 2009).

4. I first encountered this phenomenon in my doctoral program, viewing videos of mother-infant interaction. The name of Colwyn Trevarthen stands out as an early researcher in this area, and his articles are cited in numerous books on attachment and interpersonal neurobiology. See Daniel Siegel, *The Developing Mind,* 2nd ed. (New York: Guilford Press, 2015), and David Wallin, *Attachment in Psychotherapy* (New York: Guilford Press, 2007).

5. Elaine Aron, *The Highly Sensitive Person* (New York: Broadway Books, 1997).

6. Here is a suggestive list of other practices which involve behavior/action: movement-based practices, such as ecstatic dance, the dance of the Sufi whirling dervishes, Tai Chi, Qigong, martial arts; dietary practices, including fasting; ritual ablutions, or purification by washing (baptism, washing of feet, Catholics dipping fingers in holy water before entering church, or Hindus bathing in the Ganges); creative expression (music, song, visual art, etc.).

7. Daniel Siegel, *Mindsight: The New Science of Personal Transformation* (New York: Bantam Books, 2010).

8. Wallin, *Attachment in Psychotherapy*, 90–91. This is a valuable source for understanding attachment patterns, the neurobiology of attachment, and working with attachment patterns in therapy. Consideration of cross-cultural variations in attachment dynamics introduces additional factors.

9. Wallin, *Attachment in Psychotherapy*, 61.

10. Wallin, *Attachment in Psychotherapy*, 67.

11. The growing literature on the neurobiology of attachment gives us a fascinating picture of the upper right quadrant's role: brain and body play a crucial role in the development of the self, which is a self-in-relation. See Allan Schore, *Affect Regulation and the Origin of the Self: The Neurobiology of Emotional Development* (New York: Lawrence Erlbaum Associates, 1999).

12. Jenny Wade, *Changes of Mind*, 43.

13. Stanislav Grof has written numerous books over his long career. See *Holotropic Breathwork* (Albany: State University of New York Press, 2010), and *The Adventure of Self-Discovery: Dimensions of Consciousness and New Perspectives in Psychotherapy and Inner Exploration* (Albany: State University of New York Press, 1988).

14. This concept has been popularized by Siegel, *The Developing Mind.* Wallin attributes its origin to Mary Main (Wallin, *Attachment in Psychoherapy*, 87).

15. See https://www.ptsd.va.gov/professional/co-occurring/moral_injury_at_war.asp. The spiritual impact of war trauma is pivotal in the work of Edward Tick, *War and the Soul* (Wheaton, IL: Theosophical Publishing House, 2005).

16. This notion of the "triune brain" comes from Paul Maclean, *The Triune Brain in Evolution* (New York: Springer, 1990). For somatic approaches to trauma work,

see Bessel van der Kolk, *The Body Keeps the Score: Brain, Mind, and Body in the Healing of Trauma* (New York: Penguin, 2014); Peter Levine, *In an Unspoken Voice: How the Body Releases Trauma and Restores Goodness* (Berkeley, CA.: North Atlantic Books, 2012); Pat Ogden, *Trauma and the Body: A Sensorimotor Approach to Psychotherapy* (New York: Norton, 2006); Sharon Stanley, *Relational and Body-Centered Practices for Healing Trauma: Lifting the Burdens of the Past* (New York: Rutledge, 2016).

17. See J. Lebron McBride, *Spiritual Crisis: Surviving Trauma to the Soul* (New York: Haworth Pastoral Press, 1998). This is a valuable exploration in the tradition of Christian pastoral care.

18. See, for instance, Janice Holden, Bruce Greyson, and Debbie James, eds., *The Handbook of Near-Death Experiences: Thirty Years of Investigation* (Santa Barbara, CA: Praeger, 2009), and Jeffrey Long and Paul Perry, *Evidence of the Afterlife: The Science of Near-Death Experiences* (New York: HarperOne, 2010).

19. For example, see "Asian Nation: Asian American History, Demographics, & Issues," http://www.asian-nation.org/religion.shtml.

20. Miriam Greenspan, *Healing Through the Dark Emotions* (Boston: Shambhala, 2003), 117.

21. William Styron, *Darkness Visible: A Memoir of Madness* (New York: Vintage Books, 1990).

22. Greenspan, 157.

23. Thomas Merton, *New Seeds of Contemplation* (New York: New Directions Books, 1962), 221.

24. Greenspan describes this particular form of despair as "despair for the world," which demands a response from us.

25. Grof, *Psychology of the Future* (Albany: State University of New York Press, 2000), 22.

26. Richard Schwartz, *Internal Family Systems Therapy* (New York: Guilford Press, 1997). See also John Rowan, *Subpersonalities: The People Inside Us* (New York: Routledge, 1990); Helen Watkins and John Watkins, *Ego States: Theory and Therapy* (New York: W.W. Norton and Co., 1997); Robin Shapiro, *Easy Ego State Interventions: Strategies for Working with Parts* (New York: W.W. Norton and Co., 2016).

27. Wilber, *Integral Psychology*, 246–7.

28. Hal and Sidra Stone, *Embracing Ourselves: The Voice Dialogue Manual* (Novato, CA: New World Library, 1998). For an explicitly spiritual adaptation of this approach, see *Big Mind, Big Heart: Finding Your Way*, by Zen Master Genpo Dennis Merzel (McLean, VA: Big Mind Publishing, 2007).

29. For an interesting historical account of Western approaches to the "experienced body," see Don Hanlon Johnson, "From Sarx to Soma: Esalen's Role in Recovering the Body for Spiritual Development," in Jeffrey Kripal and Glenn

Shuck, eds., *On the Edge of the Future: Esalen and the Evolution of American Culture* (Bloomington, IN.: Indiana University Press, 2005), 250–267. Johnson founded the first graduate degree program in the field of somatics.

30. Celia Falicov, "Religion and Spiritual Traditions in Immigrant Families," in Froma Walsh, ed., *Spiritual Resources in Family Therapy*, 2nd ed. (New York: Guilford Press, 2009), 156–173.

31. Peter Levine and Maggie Philips, *Freedom from Pain: Discover Your Body's Power to Overcome Physical Pain* (Boulder: Sounds True, 2012), 72.

32. The idea of the "felt sense" comes from the work of humanistic psychologist Eugene Gendlin. A practical self-help introduction is offered by Ann Weiser Cornell in *The Power of Focusing* (Oakland, CA: New Harbinger Publications, 1996). For therapists, there is a more recent volume entitled *Focusing in Clinical Practice* (New York: W. W. Norton, 2013).

33. For a substantial exploration of the chakra system in relation to both psychology and spirituality, see Anodea Judith, *Eastern Body, Western Mind: Psychology and the Chakra System as a Path to the Self*, rev. ed. (Berkeley: Celestial Arts, 2004).

34. *Nous* is related to the term "noetic" and "gnostic," suggesting a "higher" form of reason and understanding.

35. Mimi Guarneri, *The Heart Speaks: A Cardiologist Reveals The Secret Language of Healing* (New York: Touchstone, 2007), 157. See also J. Andrew Armour and Jeffrey Ardell, eds., *Basic and Clinical Neurocardiology* (New York: Oxford University Press, 2004).

36. See "HeartMath Institute's Mission and Vision," HeartMath Institute, https://www.heartmath.org/about-us/hmi-mission/.

37. Llewellyn Vaughan-Lee, *Sufism: The Transformation of the Heart* (Point Reyes, CA: The Golden Sufi Center, 2012).

38. Michael Gershon, *The Second Brain: The Scientific Basis of Gut Instinct and a Groundbreaking New Understanding of Nervous Disorders of the Stomach and Intestines* (New York: Harper, 1998).

39. Malidoma Somé, "African Ritual and Initiation," DVD (Oakland, CA: Thinking Allowed Productions, 1988).

40. Prendergast, *In Touch: How to Tune In to the Inner Guidance of Your Body and Trust Yourself* (Boulder, CO: Sounds True, 2015)

41. See Byron Katie, *Living With What Is: Four Questions That Can Change Your Life* (New York: Crown Archetype, 2002).

42. Prendergast, *In Touch*, 113.

## Chapter 8

1. See Roger Walsh and Frances Vaughan, eds., *Paths Beyond Ego*, 110. They attribute the second quote to Maslow.

2. Wilber, *Sex, Ecology, Spirituality*, 264–8. See also Ken Wilber, Jack Engler, and Daniel Brown, *Transformations of Consciousness: Conventional and Contemplative Perspectives on Development* (Boston: Shambhala, 1986).
3. I am drawing on Wilber's account of the transpersonal stages, finding it to be a concise and useful summary of versions from numerous spiritual traditions.
4. Wilber, *Sex, Ecology, Spirituality*, 284.
5. "Illumined mind" is a term used by Sri Aurobindo (1872–1950), a widely recognized Indian nationalist, philosopher, and guru. See a summary in Combs, *Consciousness Explained Better.*
6. Yvonne Kason, *Farther Shores: Exploring How Near-Death, Kundalini and Mystical Experiences Can Transform Ordinary Lives* (Toronto, Ontario: Harper Collins, 1994), 37.
7. Ken Wilber, "The Spectrum of Transpersonal Development," in Walsh and Vaughan, eds., *Paths Beyond Ego*, 117.
8. Cited in Karen Armstrong, *A History of God: The 4,000-Year Quest of Judaism, Christianity, and Islam* (New York: Ballantine Books, 1993), 232.
9. Cited in Wilber, "The Spectrum of Transpersonal Development," 117.
10. F. C. Happold, *Mysticism: A Study and Anthology*, rev. ed. (London: Penguin Books, 1990), 212. This approach is known as apophatic (or negative) theology, the *via negativa*, which maintains that we can only describe God by means of negation, in terms of what we *cannot* say. In a similar vein, some Hindu scriptures take a meditative approach to Brahman in terms of *neti neti*, "not this, not that." Aspects of the causal stage also appear in the experience of Bernadette Roberts, a former Catholic nun who describes her journey in such books as *The Path to No-Self* (Boston: Shambhala, 1985) and *The Experience of No-Self*, rev. ed. (Albany: State University of New York Press, 1993).
11. Wilber, *Sex, Ecology, Spirituality*, 309–10.
12. For discussion of nonduality in relation to psychotherapy, see John Prendergast, Peter Fenner, and Sheila Krystal, eds., *The Sacred Mirror: Nondual Wisdom and Psychotherapy* (St. Paul: Paragon House, 2003), and John Prendergast, G. Kenneth Bradford, eds., *Listening From the Heart of Silence* (St. Paul: Paragon House, 2007). See also Stephan Bodian, *Wake Up Now* (New York: McGraw Hill, 2008).
13. See Evelyn Underhill, *Mysticism: The Nature and Development of Spiritual Consciousness.* For contemporary Christian perspectives on stage development and nonordinary states, see Cynthia Bourgeault, *The Heart of Centering Prayer: Nondual Christianity in Theory and Practice* (Boston: Shambhala, 2016); Jim Marion, *Putting on the Mind of Christ* (Charlottesville, VA: Hampton Roads Publishing, 2011); Paul Smith, *Integral Christianity: The Spirit's Call to Evolve* (St. Paul: Paragon House, 2011).
14. See an unusual articulation of this both/and perspective in A. H. Almaas, *The Alchemy of Freedom* (Boulder: Shambhala, 2017).

15. For a complex but insightful discussion of this issue, see Dustin DiPerna, *Streams of Wisdom: An Advanced Guide to Integral Spiritual Development* (Occidental, CA: Integral Publishing House, 2014) and *Evolution's Ally* (Occidental: Integral Publishing House, 2015).
16. Wilber, "The Pre/Trans Fallacy," in Roger Walsh and Frances Vaughan, eds., *Paths Beyond Ego,* 124–129.
17. Wade, *Changes of Mind*, 43. She offers a valuable exploration of both the Transcendent and Unity stages.
18. Forman, *A Guide to Integral Psychotherapy*, 220.
19. For Susanne Cook-Greuter, see ch. 6, note 14. The work of Terri O'Fallon is beginning to be publicized after years of research: her STAGES model and assessment tool may be explored at https://www.stagesinternational.com.
20. This broad stage roughly corresponds to Cook-Greuter's unitive stage, Fowler's universal stage, and Wade's transcendent stage, although the latter adds unity consciousness.
21. Forman, *A Guide to Integral Psychotherapy*, 157.
22. See Michael Washburn, *The Ego and Dynamic Ground*, 2nd ed., and *Embodied Spirituality in a Sacred World* (Albany: SUNY Press, 2003).
23. Brant Cortright, *Psychotherapy and Spirit.* Also see Robert Assagioli, *Transpersonal Development: The Dimension Beyond Psychosynthesis* (London: Thorsons, 1991. English tr., Aquarian Press, 1991), 31.
24. For an introduction to the complex territory of Almaas's writing, see John Davis, *The Diamond Approach: An Introduction to the Teaching of A. H. Almaas* (Boston: Shambhala, 1999).
25. Charles Tart, "The Systems Approach to Consciousness," in Walsh and Vaughan, eds., *Paths Beyond Ego*, 34.
26. Wilber, *Integral Spirituality*, 74.
27. Wilber, *Integral Spirituality*, 75–82.
28. See Grof, *Psychology of the Future.*
29. See Dustin DiPerna, *Streams of Wisdom.* DiPerna argues that the structure stages (up through integral) involve increasing degrees of complexity in terms of the *relative* self. These *vantage point* stages are more about the shifts in identity that occur *beyond the personal.* They pinpoint what the basic model of transpersonal stages does not (identification), and at the same time allow for the fluid nature of state experiences (defined in terms of objects of awareness). The development of vantage points adds another dimension to the standard model of state-stages, which does not distinguish between the field of experience and the *source* of awareness or identity.
30. This points to the phenomenon of out-of-body experiences, a subject on which there is considerable literature as well as controversy. See the classic by Robert

Monroe, *Journeys Out of the Body: The Classic Work on Out-of-Body Experience* (New York: Broadway Books, 2001).

31. Aldous Huxley, *The Perennial Philosophy* (New York: Harper Perennial Modern Classics, 2009), vii. For a concise source, see Aldous Huxley, "The Perennial Philosophy," in R. Walsh and F. Vaughan, eds., *Paths Beyond Ego*, 212–213.

32. Wilber, *Integral Spirituality*, 234.

33. See Dean H. Hamer, *The God Gene: How Faith is Hardwired into our Genes* (New York: Anchor Books, 2005), 135–136.

34. See Andrew Newberg and Eugene D'Aquili, *Why God Won't Go Away: Brain Science and the Biology of Belief* (New York: Ballantine Books: 2001). The term *neurotheology* was first used, as far as I can tell, in Aldous Huxley's novel *Island* (New York: Harper & Row, 1962).

35. This is discussed in a more recent volume by Andrew Newberg and Mark Waldman, entitled *How Enlightenment Changes Your Brain* (New York: Avery, 2016). Despite the fascinating research, I find their definition of "enlightenment" to be relatively superficial.

36. Mario Beauregard and Denyse O'Leary, *The Spiritual Brain: A Neuroscientist's Case for the Existence of the Soul* (New York: HarperOne, 2007).

37. See Michel Ferrari, ed., *The Varieties of Religious Experience: Centenary Essays* (Exeter, UK: ImprintAcademic, 2002).

38. For a deeper exploration, see Neal Goldsmith, *Psychedelic Healing: The Promise of Entheogens for Psychotherapy and Spiritual Development* (Rochester, VT: Healing Arts Press, 2010).

39. See, for example, Thomas Keating, *Intimacy with God: An Introduction to Centering Prayer*, 3rd ed. (New York: Crossroad Publishing: 2009), and Martin Laird, *Into the Silent Land: A Guide to the Christian Practice of Contemplation* (Oxford: Oxford University Press, 2006).

40. See Huston Smith, *Cleansing the Door of Perception: The Religious Significance of Entheogenic Plants and Chemicals* (New York: Jeremy P. Tarcher/Putnam, 2000).

41. James Griffith and Melissa Griffith, *Encountering the Sacred in Psychotherapy*, 172.

42. Wilber, *Integral Psychology*, 91.

43. John Welwood, *Toward a Psychology of Awakening*, 36.

44. Welwood, *Toward a Psychology of Awakening*, 36.

45. I am drawing from the work of Charles Tart, *Waking Up: Overcoming the Obstacles to Human Potential* (Boston: Shambhala, 1987), 107–114.

46. See John Engler, "Becoming Somebody and Nobody: Psychoanalysis and Buddhism," in R. Walsh and F. Vaughan, eds., *Paths Beyond Ego*, 118–121.

47. Engler, "Becoming Somebody and Nobody," 120.

48. Engler, "Becoming Somebody and Nobody," 120.

49. See also Mark Epstein, "The Varieties of Egolessness," in Walsh and Vaughan, eds., *Paths Beyond Ego*, 121–123.

## Chapter 9

1. R. Walsh and F. Vaughan, eds., *Paths Beyond Ego,* 133. They cite the work of David Lukoff.
2. Christina and Stanislav Grof, *The Stormy Search for the Self: A Guide to Personal Growth through Transformational Crisis* (New York: Jeremy P. Tarcher/Putnam, 1990), 73. In addition to the categories included here, the Grofs often include the shamanic crisis, communication with spirit guides and channeling, and experiences of close encounters with UFOs.
3. See Lee Sannella, *The Kundalini Experience: Psychosis or Transcendence* (Lower Lake, CA: Integral Publishing, 1987). Sannella discusses some of the salient differences between the classical yogic description of symptoms and his own clinical observations in this brief introduction: Lee Sannella, "Kundalini: Classical and Clinical," in Stanislav and Christina Grof, eds., *Spiritual Emergency: When Personal Transformation Becomes a Crisis* (New York: Jeremy P. Tarcher/Putnam, 1989), 99–108. For a more clinical introduction, see Bruce Scotton, "The Phenomenology and Treatment of Kundalini," in Bruce Scotton, Allan Chinen, and John Battista, eds., *Textbook of Transpersonal Psychiatry and Psychology* (New York: Basic Books, 1996), 261–270. Examples of more in-depth explorations may be found in Gurmukh Kaur Khalsa et al., *Kundalini Rising: Exploring the Energy of Awakening* (Boulder, CO: Sounds True, 2009), and Bonnie Greenwell, *Energies of Transformation: A Guide to the Kundalini Process*, 2nd ed. (Saratoga, CA: Shakti River Press, 1995).
4. Janice M. Holden, Bruce Greyson, and Debbie James, *The Handbook of Near-Death Experiences: Thirty Years of Investigation,* 2nd ed. (Westport, CT: Praeger Publishing, 2009). Other prominent authors in this field include scientists and physicians, among them Kenneth Ring, Melvin Morse, and Jeffrey Long. The International Association for Near-Death Studies has been in existence since 1981.
5. William James wrote in *The Varieties of Religious Experience* (first published in 1902) that the term *noetic* refers to "states of insight into depths of truth unplumbed by the discursive intellect. They are illuminations, revelations, full of significance and importance, all inarticulate though they remain; and as a rule they carry with them a curious sense of authority." (New York: New American Library, 1958), 293.
6. See John Weir Perry, *Trials of the Visionary Mind: Spiritual Emergency and the Renewal Process* (New York: State University of new York Press, 1998).
7. See the chapter entitled "The Challenges of Psychic Opening: A Personal Story," by Anne Armstrong, in Christina Grof and Stanislav Grof, *Spiritual Emergency,* 109–120.

8. See Robert Monroe, *Journeys Out of the Body*. He also wrote subsequent books on the subject.
9. "Three in Four Americans Believe in Paranormal," Gallup, June 16, 2005, http://www.gallup.com/poll/16915/Three-Four-Americans-Believe-Paranormal.aspx. See also "Many Americans Mix Multiple Faiths," Pew Research Center, December 9, 2009, http://www.pewforum.org/2009/12/09/many-americans-mix-multiple-faiths/
10. See Jenny Wade, *Transcendent Sex: When Lovemaking Opens the Veil* (New York: Gallery Books, 2004).
11. Ian Stevenson, a psychiatrist at the University of Virginia, School of Medicine, did years of research with children who claimed to remember past lives. See *Children Who Remember Past Lives: A Question of Reincarnation*, rev. ed. (Jefferson, NC: McFarland, 2000). See also the previously mentioned research of Christopher Bache, professor of religious studies at Youngstown University, entitled *Lifecycles: Reincarnation and the Web of Life.*
12. Jack Kornfield, "Obstacles and Vicissitudes in Spiritual Practice," in Stanislav and Christina Grof, eds., *Spiritual Emergency*, 137–169. Kornfield suggests that these kinds of pitfalls may arise in the course of any "systematic discipline that trains awareness and concentration," 141.
13. Kornfield, "Obstacles and Vicissitudes in Spiritual Practice," 145. He offers a detailed discussion of the Buddhist "hindrances" and suggestions for working with them.
14. Kornfield, "Obstacles and Vicissitudes in Spiritual Practice," 154.
15. Kornfield, "Obstacles and Vicissitudes in Spiritual Practice," 159.
16. A useful discussion of this and other pitfalls is Mariana Caplan, *Eyes Wide Open: Cultivating Discernment on the Spiritual Path* (Boulder: Sounds True, 2009).
17. Caplan, *Eyes Wide Open*, 115.
18. Welwood, *Toward a Psychology of Awakening*, 12.
19. Robert Masters, *Spiritual Bypassing: When Spirituality Disconnects Us from What Really Matters* (Berkeley: North Atlantic Books, 2010), 2. I also recommend the section devoted to spiritual bypassing in Brant Cortright, *Psychotherapy and Spirit*, 209–215.
20. Mark Forman, *A Guide to Integral Psychotherapy*, 214.
21. John Battista, "Offensive Spirituality and Spiritual Defenses," in Bruce Scotton, Allan Chinen, and John Battista, eds., *Textbook of Transpersonal Psychiatry and Psychology*, 250–260.
22. See Forman, *A Guide to Integral Psychotherapy*, 182–183, 218.
23. Forman, *A Guide to Integral Psychotherapy*, 220.
24. James Griffith and Melissa Griffith, *Encountering the Sacred in Psychotherapy*,

219. I also recommend James Griffith, *Religion that Heals, Religion that Harms: A Guide for Clinical Practice* (New York: Guilford Press, 2010).
25. Welwood's perspective grows out of his own observations as well as his participation in a study group on authoritarian patterns in nonmainstream religious movements, sponsored by the Center for the Study on New Religions and funded by the National Endowment for the Humanities. This section draws on Welwood's discussion in *Toward a Psychology of Awakening*, 268–275.
26. Welwood, *Toward a Psychology of Awakening*, 275.
27. For this crucial distinction between moderate and extremist versions of the developmental levels, see Dustin DiPerna, *Evolution's Ally.*
28. Kenneth Pargament, *Spiritually Integrated Psychotherapy*, 136.
29. Kenneth Pargament, *Spiritually Integrated Psychotherapy*, 137.
30. In most Western cultures we also tend to place a high value on the opposite quality: self-esteem. This makes sense in the context of our bias toward individualism, autonomy, and agency, a bias which has been criticized by feminist and relational approaches in psychology. In mainstream American culture, and in the field of psychology which is influenced by that culture, the spectrum from self-deprecation to "healthy" self-esteem has to do with *selfhood.* Ego-inflation and ego-deflation both center on the notion of a separate ego, no matter how vaguely defined. Despite being widely viewed as a therapeutic goal, from a spiritual/religious perspective, self-esteem may be too limited. Moderate self-esteem may be a developmental accomplishment along the way but not the final aspiration. Just as we need a basic functional ego to navigate the world, we may need at least a basic sense of "okayness." With this foundation in place, we then have the *potential* to shift our attention *beyond the self.* If development continues to unfold, concern with a positive or negative self-image is transcended by, or submerged in, a focus on relationship or oneness with God/Goddess/Allah/the Holy/Beloved/Being.
31. Kenneth Pargament, *Spiritually Integrated Psychotherapy*, 136. I find the problem of fit between individual and social context to be a particularly challenging category, since many people find themselves evolving beyond their sociocultural environment. We have briefly addressed the ways in which there may be a cultural center of gravity (lower left quadrant) which tends to hold back individual development. In such cases, collisions with the surrounding social system may be inevitable. Finding a smaller community of support can then be very helpful. On the other hand, we see examples of a "lack of fit" in the lives of Jesus, the Buddha, and Muhammad, who clearly forged their own pathways.
32. Robert Kegan, Harvard developmental psychologist, offers a valuable exploration of the ways in which we often expect others—our teenagers, partners, employees, clients, students—to be capable of more mental complexity than they currently are.

He explores the evolution of consciousness in practical life contexts, as well as the "hidden curriculum" that culture imposes on its participants. See Robert Kegan, *In Over Our Heads: The Mental Demands of Modern Life.*

33. James Griffith and Melissa Griffith, *Encountering the Sacred in Psychotherapy*, 39.

34. *Diagnostic and Statistical Manual of Psychiatric Disorders, Fifth Edition* (Washington DC: American Psychiatric Publishing, 2013), 725.

35. David Lukoff, Francis G. Lu, and Robert Turner, "Diagnosis: A Transpersonal Approach to Religious and Spiritual Problems," in Bruce Scotton, Allan Chinen, and John Battista, eds., *Textbook of Transpersonal Psychiatry and Psychology*, 234. For further discussion of the background, see Robert Turner, David Lukoff, Ruth Barnhouse, and Francis Lu, "Religious or Spiritual Problem: A Culturally Sensitive Diagnostic Category in the DSM-IV," *The Journal of Nervous and Mental Disease*, 1995, 183 (7), 435–444. Lukoff also has a website which offers CEU courses and other useful information: www.spiritualcompetency.com.

36. Kenneth Pargament, Harold G. Koenig, Nalini Tarakeshwar, et al., "Religious Struggle as a Predictor of Mortality Among Medically Ill Elderly Patients: A Two-year Longitudinal Study," in *Arch. Internal Medicine,* 2001, Aug. 13–27; 161 (15): 1881–5. Variables such as patients' health, mental health, and demographic status were taken into consideration.

37. There are support systems available for those who seek to depathologize such experiences, but for obvious reasons they are controversial. For instance, The Icarus Project is a "support network and education project by and for people who experience the world in ways that are often diagnosed as mental illness." (http://theicarusproject.net/)

38. Cited in Stanislav Grof, *Psychology of the Future*, 136. On the same page Grof comments that the mystic's experience may also be "difficult and taxing" and not all a matter of delight. But, he points out, "the mystic is capable of seeing these challenges in the larger context of a spiritual journey that has a deeper purpose and a desirable goal."

39. John Nelson, *Healing the Split: Integrating Spirit into Our Understanding of the Mentally Ill*, rev. ed. (Albany: State University of New York Press, 1994).

40. David Lukoff, Francis Lu, and Robert Turner, "Diagnosis: A Transpersonal Approach to Religious and Spiritual Problems," 244.

41. James Griffith, *Religion that Heals, Religion that Harms: A Guide for Clinical Practice* (New York: Guilford Press, 2010), 181.

42. This invitation to *grow up, wake up, clean up, and show up* comes from the integral theory literature but is now widely used.

# Index

Figures are indicated by italics and *fig* following the *page number*.

## B

## E

## G

## Q



## R

## T

# Acknowledgments

The people who have directly inspired this work are the students and clients who have shared their questions, hopes, and direct experiences over the last decades. In gathering together all these perspectives and resources, I hope I have honored their contributions and their journeys.

Special thanks go to Neville Kelly, who patiently and skillfully listened, read, offered feedback, and encouraged my efforts early in the writing process. I am deeply grateful to my son, Casey Hoffman, for substantial editorial comments and ongoing support. Kema Larsen and Ned Farley gave the manuscript careful reading and their well-informed comments are deeply appreciated. I owe a lot to Brad Reynolds for his skillful support with images and diagrams. To my consultant, Renie Hope, go my thanks for deepening my understanding of the Enneagram and for offering feedback on the Enneagram characters. I am also indebted to numerous other Enneagram teachers, including David Daniels, Russ Hudson, Sandra Maitri, and Beatrice Chestnut.

My editor, Elisabeth Rinaldi, was invaluable, offering her wealth of editing knowledge, keen sense of language, and diligent research to get the project to the place it is today. Lisa Reddick, my friend and colleague, steered me towards She Writes Press and continued to support my publishing journey. To all of those at SWP who made this undertaking possible, my heartfelt thanks. And to Gordon Hallgren, my appreciation for technical help and tremendous patience.

# About the Author

Alexandra Hepburn has a master's degree in special education from Teachers College, Columbia University, and received her PhD in human development from the University of Pennsylvania in 1983. She has been in private practice as a counselor since 1994, focusing on loss and grief, life transitions, and spirituality. Having grown up overseas as the daughter of diplomat, she has a long-standing interest in diverse ways of making meaning. Other contributing influences include her work as a learning disabilities specialist,a massage therapist, the founder of a hospice program, the coordinator of two bereavement programs, and the supervisor of a community college grant program focused on the immigrant experience. In her twenty-six-year faculty role at Antioch University Seattle, she taught in a graduate counseling program and a BA completion program, focusing on loss and grief, personality theory, developmental psychology, and the interplay of psychology and spirituality. She also directed a non-clinical master's degree program in psychology and spirituality. After living on both East and West coasts, she has now settled among cedar trees and near a beach in the Pacific Northwest.

## SELECTED TITLES FROM SHE WRITES PRESS

She Writes Press is an independent publishing company founded to serve women writers everywhere. Visit us at www.shewritespress.com.

*Tell Me Your Story: How Therapy Works to Awaken, Heal, and Set You Free* by Tuya Pearl. $16.95, 978-1-63152-066-2. With the perspective of both client and healer, this book moves you through the stages of therapy, connecting body, mind, and spirit with inner wisdom to reclaim and enjoy your most authentic life.

*Note to Self: A Seven-Step Path to Gratitude and Growth* by Laurie Buchanan. $16.95, 978-1-63152-113-3. Transforming intention into action, *Note to Self* equips you to shed your baggage, bridging the gap between where you are and where you want to be—body, mind, and spirit—and empowering you to step into joy-filled living now!

*Painting Life: My Creative Journey Through Trauma* by Carol K. Walsh. $16.95, 978-1-63152-099-0. Carol Walsh was a psychotherapist working with traumatized clients when she encountered her own traumatic experience; this is the story of how she used creativity and artistic expression to heal, recreate her life, and ultimately thrive.

*The Art of Play: Igniting Your Imagination to Unlock Insight, Healing, and Joy* by Joan Stanford. $19.95, 978-1-63152-030-3. Lifelong "non-artist" Joan Stanford shares the creative process that led her to insight and healing, and shares ways for others to do the same.

*Braided: A Journey of a Thousand Challahs* by Beth Ricanati, MD. $16.95, 978-1-63152-441-7. What if you could bake bread once a week, every week? What if the smell of fresh bread could turn your house into a home? And what if the act of making the bread—mixing and kneading, watching and waiting—could heal your heartache and your emptiness, your sense of being overwhelmed? It can.

**This Trip Will Change Your Life: A Shaman's Story of Spirit Evolution** by Jennifer B. Monahan. $16.95, 978-1-63152-111-9. One woman's inspirational story of finding her life purpose and the messages and training she received from the spirit world as she became a shamanic healer.

Printed in the United States
by Baker & Taylor Publisher Services